FABIAN FEMINIST

FABIAN FEMINIST

Bernard Shaw and Woman

Edited by
Rodelle Weintraub

THE PENNSYLVANIA STATE UNIVERSITY PRESS
University Park and London

Library of Congress Cataloging in Publication Data
Main entry under title:

Fabian feminist.

Bibliography included.
1. Shaw, George Bernard, 1856-1950—Political and
social views. 2. Women in literature. I. Weintraub,
Rodelle.
PR5368.W6F3   822'.9'12   76-41698
ISBN 0-271-01235-8

Printed in the United States of America

To Erica Beth—and her generation—
for whom this Fabian Feminist may
at last become "old-hat"

CONTENTS

INTRODUCTION

Fabian Feminist   1
Rodelle Weintraub

I LITERARY AND MYTHIC INFLUENCES

Shakespeare's *The Taming of the Shrew* vs. Shaw's   14
Pygmalion: Male Chauvinism vs. Women's Lib?
Lisë Pedersen

Kipling on Women: A New Source for Shaw   23
Janie Caves McCauley

The Shavian Sphinx   30
Rhoda B. Nathan

Eliza's Choice: Transformation Myth and the Ending of   39
Pygmalion
Timothy G. Vesonder

Ann and Superman: Type and Archetype   46
Sally Peters Vogt

II POLITICAL AND ECONOMIC INFLUENCES

The Legal Climate of Shaw's Problem Plays   68
Dolores Kester

Press Cuttings: G.B.S. and Women's Suffrage   84
Michael Weimer

Mill, Marx and Bebel: Early Influences on Shaw's   90
Characterizations of Women
Norbert Greiner

The "Unwomanly Woman" in Shaw's Drama   99
Sonja Lorichs

III SEX ROLES OR TRUE VOCATION?

The New Woman and the New Comedy   114
Barbara Bellow Watson

Whatever Happened to Shaw's Mother-Genius Portrait? 130
Susan C. Stone

Mr. Shaw's Many Mothers   143
Andrina Gilmartin

Feminism and Female Stereotypes in Shaw   156
Elsie Adams

A Whore in Every Home   163
Germaine Greer

IV SHAW'S LIBERATED WOMEN

Vivie Warren: A Psychological Study   168
Marlie Parker Wasserman

Shaw and Women's Lib   174
Gladys M. Crane

Shaw's Lady Cicely and Mary Kingsley   185
Stanley Weintraub

V INFLUENCE OF SHAW'S FEMINISM:
THREE GENERATIONS

The Making of a Feminist: Shaw and Florence Farr   194
Josephine Johnson

The Gift of Imagination: An Interview with   206
Clare Boothe Luce
Rodelle Weintraub

The Center of Life: An Interview with Megan Terry   214
Rodelle Weintraub

VI SHAW ON FEMINIST ISSUES

Torture by Forcible Feeding is Illegal   228
Bernard Shaw

G.B.S. and a Suffragist   236
Maud Churton Braby

Sir Almroth Wright's Case Against Woman Suffrage 243
Bernard Shaw

Why All Women Are Peculiarly Fitted to Be Good Voters 248
Bernard Shaw

The Root of the White Slave Traffic 255
Bernard Shaw

VII   BIBLIOGRAPHY

A Bibliographical Checklist 262
Lucile Kelling Henderson

Contributors 273

Credits 275

INTRODUCTION: FABIAN FEMINIST

Rodelle Weintraub

In life and art, Bernard Shaw refused to be bound by conventional approaches to the role of women in society. As early as 1895, he was so identified with feminism that Robert Buchanan in *Diana's Hunting*, a book intended for a conservative popular audience, satirized Shaw as Marcus Aurelius Short, a paradoxical, arrogant champion of women.

"Another of your paradoxes!" said Horsham with a laugh.

"And what are the egotists about now?" continued Short, heedless of the interruption. "Dissecting and vilifying the rational people, and trying to prove that womankind are as ugly and as stupid and as vicious as themselves. Somebody—George Meredith, isn't it?— has told us in one of his books that Woman is the last thing to be civilised by Man. Just the reverse is true! For centuries Woman has been trying in vain to civilise *us*, and she can't do it, because we're beasts *au fond*."

"Now you've mounted your hobby, I'll be off!" said Horsham, making for the door. Pausing at the door with a smile, he delivered this parting shot—"A lot you know about women, living like Diogenes in the tub; and a pretty Realist *you* are, to retain all the old bunkum about the superiority of Womanhood."

To others besides Frank Horsham, Marcus Aurelius Short seemed a savage mass of inconsistencies. Believing in almost nothing, and looking upon sacred things as merely shibboleths, he was an ardent champion of Women, seeing in what Goethe christened *Das Ewig-Weibliche* the promise and potency of our future social life. So far as regarded this phase of his opinions, he was a veritable Don Quixote, supporting the weaker sex in all its struggles toward emancipation, and reserving all his contempt and satire for that sex which is generally considered the stronger.

A vigorous exponent of women's freedom to be themselves, to liberate themselves from their traditional roles and traditional subservience, Shaw argued eloquently in their behalf, as in *The Quintessence of Ibsenism* (1891):

> Now of all the idealist abominations that make society pestiferous, I doubt if there be any so mean as that of forcing self-sacrifice on a woman under pretence that she likes it: and if she ventures to contradict the pretence, declaring her no true woman . . . it is not true. The domestic career is no more natural to all women than the military career is natural to all men; although it may be necessary that every able-bodied woman should be called on to risk her life in childbed just as it may be necessary that every man should be called on to risk his life in the battlefield. It is of course quite true that the majority of women are kind to children and prefer their own to other people's. But exactly the same thing is true of the majority of men, who nevertheless do not consider that their proper sphere is the nursery. . . . If we have come to think that the nursery and the kitchen are the natural sphere of a woman, we have done so exactly as English children come to think that a cage is the natural sphere of a parrot—because they have never seen one anywhere else.

Shaw catalogued the types of "parrots" who could argue in defense of their own imprisonment: the Philistine parrot who agrees with her master that so long as she be well fed, the cage is the proper place and the better place to be; the idealist parrot who believes it is her mission to cater to the whims and happiness of her captors; the altruistic parrot who finds satisfaction in her sacrifice of her liberty; the rationalist parrot who can prove that the dangers outside the cage are too cruel to expose the delicate parrot to, for even if she survived the dangers she would lose her delicacy in the process. He stopped short of the theological parrot who is "convinced that imprisonment is the will of God because it is so unpleasant." For Shaw the only parrot—the only woman—with whom a "free-souled person" could sympathize

> is the one that insists on being let out as the first condition of its making itself agreeable. A selfish bird, you may say: one that puts its own gratification before that of the family which is so fond of it—before even the greatest happiness of the greatest number: one that, in aping the independent spirit of a man, has unparroted itself and become a creature that has neither the homeloving nature of a bird nor the strength and enterprise of a

mastiff. All the same, you respect that parrot in spite of your conclusive reasoning; and if it persists, you will have either to let it out or kill it.

The sum of the matter is that unless Woman repudiates her Womanliness, her duty to her husband, to her children, to society, to the law, and to everyone but herself, she cannot emancipate herself.

In suggesting that women emancipate themselves, Shaw did not, however, reject the traditional domestic role as the road to emancipation, if that were the manner in which a woman chose to fulfill herself. He deplored the lack of respect and self-respect afforded the woman who chose domesticity, and wrote to a young American woman, in response to her praise of the *Quintessence of Ibsenism*:

It may interest you to know that one of my latest works is a play asserting the full strength of the domestic position for women. You call yourself an undomestic woman; but I suggest to you that a lack of aptitude for household management is too negative a qualification to take an effective stand upon. A positive aptitude for something else is better; but such a positive attitude gets recognized nowadays. . . . The really hard position for the moment is that of the domestic woman, whose enormously valuable services, both to society and to her own household are accepted and even exacted as a matter of course, as if they were the least she could do in return for the privilege of being fed and clothed and housed and protected. Except when the death of a man's wife occurs at such a time that he has to pay a stranger to discharge her household and parental duties until he goes back to the cheaper plan by marrying again, it is very hard to convince him that his wife is a productive worker; and the woman, unfortunately, is harder to convince than he is, no doubt because she does so many things, and does them in such an amateur way (not being directly and avowedly paid for them) that she does nothing well, and therefore has no belief in herself.

I therefore am strongly of the opinion that the undomestic woman, when she has secured her position by escaping from domestic servitude as men escape from unskilled labor; that is, by mastering a trade or profession, can maintain her own individuality to the full extent of her own strength (we are none of us very strong in that way, man or woman) with infinitely less difficulty than the domestic woman.

So it is not for your own hand that you will have to fight so much as for that of the domestic woman from whose ill paid, ill organized, ill recognized and consequently ill executed industry, you, as an undomestic woman, will presumably emancipate yourself.[1]

Still Shaw admired emancipated, tough-minded, independent women, like his talented sculptor friend, Lady Scott, who worked for a living, dressed in the mannish attire her craft required, and earned Shaw's praise: "My affection for you is the nearest I ever came to homosexuality."[2] Women who thought and acted for themselves, like his good friend Beatrice Webb, earned more than his approbation, even when he did not agree with them, and were likely to find themselves among his pantheon of character prototypes, Webb becoming the inspiration for the title figure in *The Millionairess*. Others might have recognized themselves in such provocative onstage role-models as cigar-smoking, mannish Vivie Warren; pilot and acrobat Lina Szczepanowska; liberated Lesbia Grantham, who wants children but not the burden of a husband; and outspoken Lysistrata, Powermistress General in the futuristic cabinet of King Magnus.

To effect woman's equality, legally and economically, Shaw felt that Capitalism had to be transformed into Fabianism. It was, he argued, Capitalism that forced women of the lower classes into illicit prostitution, in which the wages and working conditions were frequently far superior to those of the factory worker or laborer's wife, and upper-class women into legal prostitution, i.e., marriage. Shaw (in *The Quintessence*) considered the crime of prostitution to be that of society, not that of the prostitute, for

a child with an interesting face and pretty ways . . . may, by working for the films, earn a hundred times as much as its mother can earn by drudging at an ordinary trade. What is worse, a pretty girl can earn by vice far more than her plain sister can earn as an honest wife and mother. . . . It is easy to ask a woman to be virtuous; but it is not reasonable if the penalty of virtue be starvation, and the reward of vice immediate relief. If you offer a pretty girl twopence half-penny an hour in a match factory, with a chance of contracting necrosis of the jawbone from phosphorus poisoning on the one hand, and on the other a jolly and pampered time under the protection of a wealthy bachelor, which was what the Victorian employers did and what employers do all over the world when they are not stopped by resolutely socialistic laws, you are loading the dice in favor of the devil so monstrously as not only to make it certain that he will win, but raising the question whether the girl does not owe it to her own self-respect and desire for wider knowledge and experience, more cultivated society, and greater grace and eloquence of life, to sell herself to a gentleman for pleasure rather than to an employer for profit. To warn her that her beauty will not last for ever only reminds her that if she takes reasonable care of her beauty, it will last long past the age at which women, "too old at twenty-four," find the factory closed to them, and their places filled by younger girls. . . .

In short, Capitalism acts on women as a continual bribe to enter into sex relations for money, whether in or out of marriage.

For the poor, untrained woman, prostitution often offered a far more satisfactory existence than either menial work or a mean marriage. But it was not to defend prostitution that Shaw argued its economic values. His purpose was to horrify Victorian society and to smite its conscience, as he described to young critic Golding Bright:

> The play [*Mrs Warren's Profession*] is a cold bloodedly appalling one; but not in the least a prurient one. Mrs Warren is much worse than a prostitute. She is an organism of prostitution—a woman who owns and manages brothels in every big city in Europe and is proud of it. With her gains she has had her daughter highly educated and respectably brought up in complete ignorance of the source of her mother's income. The drama, of course, lies in the discovery and its consequences. These consequences, though cruel enough, are all sensible and sober, no suicide nor sentimental tragedy of any sort. Nobody's conscience is smitten except, I hope, the conscience of the audience. My intention is that they shall go home thoroughly uncomfortable. . . . The play has horrified everyone who has heard it, but only as an honest treatment of such a subject ought to horrify them.[3]

Opportunity for economic security, not marriage, was his cure for prostitution. Marriage which was entered into "for the gratification of [the sexual] appetite either in its crudest form or veiled only by those idealistic illusions which the youthful imagination weaves" was only another form of prostitution. Given the opportunity and the education, he felt that women would proclaim, like Lina in *Misalliance*,

> I am an honest woman: I earn my living. I am a free woman: I live in my own house. . . . I am strong: I am skilful: I am brave: I am independent: I am unbought: I am all that a woman ought to be. . . . And this Englishman! this linendraper! he dares to

ask me to come and live in this rrrrrrabbit hutch, and take my bread from his hand, and ask him for pocket money, and wear soft clothes, and be his woman! his wife! Sooner than that I would sink to the lowest depths of my profession . . . I would sink yet lower and be an actress or an opera singer, imperilling my soul by the wicked lie of pretending to be someone else. All this I would do sooner than take my bread from the hand of a man and make him the master of my body and soul. And you may tell your Johnny he shall not buy Lina Szczepanowska; and I will not stay in the house where such dishonor is offered me.

In his own marriage to Charlotte, G.B.S. demonstrated the sincerity of his convictions. Although they shared the same house and she took his name, they did not share each other's bed or—for the most part—income. Shaw had not been celibate prior to his marriage; yet, despite evidence of great affection and physical desire on his part, at Charlotte's request their marriage eschewed sex. Before their marriage, a contract detailing the distribution of their incomes was drawn up. After the marriage, he refused to file a joint income tax return, although British law required married couples to do so, for he felt it was humiliating for wives who had their own incomes to be treated as appendages of their husbands. Protesting to the Commissioners of Income Tax that he could not be responsible for Charlotte's taxes because he could not determine her income and file for her without violating her privacy, he wrote to N.F.W. (later Sir Norman) Fisher in 1910:

Now I have absolutely no means of ascertaining my wife's income except by asking her for the information. Her property is a separate property. She keeps a separate banking account at a separate bank. Her solicitor is not my solicitor. I can make a guess at her means from her style of living, exactly as the Surveyor of Income Tax does when he makes a shot at an assessment in the absence of exact information; but beyond that I have no more knowledge of her income than I have of yours. I have therefore asked her to give me a statement. She refuses, on principle. As far as I know, I have no legal means of compelling her to make any such disclosure; and if I had, it does not follow that I am bound to incur law costs to obtain information which is required not by myself but by the State. Clearly, however, it is in the power of the Commissioners to compel my wife to make a full disclosure of her income for the purposes of taxation; but equally clearly they must not communicate that disclosure to me or to any other person. It seems to me under these circumstances that all I can do for you is to tell you who my wife is and leave it to you to ascertain her income and make me pay the tax on it. Even this you cannot do without a violation of secrecy as it will be possible for me by a simple calculation to ascertain my wife's income from your demand.

Fisher's response that the tax bureau held the husband responsible for any liability for taxes and could furnish information as to how to compute those taxes but had no obligation to advise the husband how he might acquire the necessary information provoked another Shaw letter in which he asked: "The Income Tax Acts give you power to obtain from my wife a return of her income. Do they give me that power? If so, can you refer me to the particular clause?" Eventually, after a meeting between Fisher and Shaw in which Shaw assured Fisher that they "were both up against two obstacles—first, an oversight in the Income Tax Acts; and second, the suffragist movement,"[4] which Shaw fully supported, the government accepted the separate filings but billed *him* for any shortages.

As he did not force marital sex nor assert his husbandly authority upon Charlotte insofar as her income taxes were concerned, he did not foist his idiosyncratic habits, whether dietary or otherwise, upon her. He remained a vegetarian, Charlotte ate meat. He was a teetotaler, she drank whiskey with her dinner. He discussed his philosophy and beliefs with her, but did not impose them upon her nor interfere with her own search for her soul and her very different but equally unconventional faith.

In searching for his god, Shaw not only rejected the idea of an omnipotent one but of a masculine one, recognizing

the absurdity of conceiving of God as a person with sex—the male sex. Nowadays we see that it is ridiculous to keep saying, "Our Father which art in heaven." What about our Mother who art in heaven? The Roman Catholic Church may claim the glory of having seen the need for our Mother who art in heaven, and it is she who has kept it alive. Clearly, if you have a personal God, one of the first difficulties is to determine the sex of that God. The unhesitating way in which people have assumed that there is a personal God and a male God not only shows that they have not seriously tackled the problem, but that, insofar as they have tackled it, they keep up the Oriental idea that women have no souls.[5]

In his novella *The Adventures of the Black Girl in Her Search for God*, Shaw explored his rejection of a masculine, patriarchal god, ending the Black Girl's frustrating search by having her give up the search to find her elusive god within herself. In his plays he never tried personifying God, yet he felt all his plays were religious. When St. John Ervine suggested that Shaw write a play about God, G.B.S. responded, "The suggestion that I write a play about God is one I rather resent, because I have never written a play on any other subject."[6] Perhaps. But while neither his contemporary nor modern audiences readily recognize God as suffusing Shaw's canon, they did and do recognize and respond to his women, women with souls.

In his plays he created perhaps the most fascinating gallery of women in modern drama, female characters who usually prove more interesting and more vital than his male characters. His impatience with female stereotypes, although he used them where dramatically valid—and sometimes subconsciously in spite of himself—is everywhere in his writings. In *The Apple Cart*, Orinthia as royal mistress is no longer a sexual vessel but, in effect, a government employee whose "relationship" to the king satisfies the vestigial and vicarious machismo of the populace. In *Heartbreak House*, the husband, not the wife, is kept. In *Pygmalion*, the cockney flower girl is a human being clever enough to rise by her ability, and, if she chooses, to support a husband rather than fulfill her stereotypic destiny of seeking social and financial security through the prudent bartering of herself in marriage, as her male sponsors Pickering and Higgins recommend. As for romance between Eliza and Higgins, Shaw rejected, from *Pygmalion*'s original performance to its being made into a film, any suggestion that there could be a romantic attachment between the "middle-aged bully" and the now beautiful, young flower girl. In *Getting Married*, "Leo" Hotchkiss is not the victim of a mistress-seeking husband; she herself desires a legal, everyday husband and a "Sunday husband" for variety. (As far as marital relations were concerned, Shaw suggested that the public needed "a dose of castor oil" in the form of his plays, and pointed out that his Orinthia-Magnus relationship—a development of "Leo" Hotchkiss's dreams—is an idea Shakespeare had suggested when Beatrice says, in reply to Don Pedro's proposal, "No, my lord, unless I might have another for workingdays: your grace is too costly to wear every day.")

Other plays evoke even more outrageous reversals of traditional female subservience. In the fantasy *The Simpleton of the Unexpected Isles*, a communal—yet matriarchal—group of six persons of mixed races and sexes produces four futuristic offspring. Earlier Shavian women are less unconventional in their rejection of marriage. Lavinia in *Androcles and the Lion* spurns a husband because she has more important work to do, while the former Major Barbara of the

Salvation Army embraces marriage and a husband because only in marriage can she inherit the power to do her work. Cleopatra in *Caesar and Cleopatra* is no seductive sex-kitten. Rather she is an innocent child whom Caesar regards as a future ruler to be trained in politics and governing. Saint Joan leads an army not because she is a woman, or even in spite of that womanhood, but because she has the instincts and the capacity for leadership.

When Shaw does assign a traditionally female role to a character, she is not symbolic of all womanhood. That Nora Reilly, a primarily weak and passive creature, symbolic of the helpless, still passive Ireland of 1900, is the ironic echo of another, but an emancipated Nora—of Ibsen's *A Doll's House*—is surely intentional. Mrs. Dudgeon in *The Devil's Disciple*, the "good wife" who has sacrificed herself and her happiness for duty, is a bitter, unpleasant shrew for whom neither audience nor fellow characters feel any sympathy or admiration. Few others of Shaw's many women embrace domesticity submissively, and those who do usually turn out to run things better that way. Candida clearly wears the figurative pants in the Morrell household. Both of Shaw's later philosopher-kings, Magnus and Charles II, would be helpless without their consorts, whatever their carefully nurtured public reputations.

As in life, where Shaw had chosen celibacy during his marriage, in the plays physical sex became more and more an inconvenience, less and less of any importance. His women are no longer wily in using their sexuality; and after *Cleopatra*, the last play begun before the playwright's sexless marriage, physical sex fails to dominate the energies of Shaw's female characters. Even if the woman, like Ann Whitefield in *Man and Superman*, is dominated by procreative instincts, her sexuality is overshadowed by goals higher than fleshly ones. Physical sex diminishes in importance, until in *Back to Methuselah* sex has become uncomfortable after one passes one's third birthday. Futuristic children are hatched from eggs, the laying, manufacture and fertilization of which are never described. In A.D. 31,290, only automatons created in the image of twentieth-century man and woman by a new Dr. Frankenstein-like Pygmalion have selfishness and sexuality.

What influenced such female characterization, other than Shaw's own experience, is examined in several of the explorations in this book. Mythic and literary elements are powerful, but they only stimulate the artist if in harmony with his/her own psyche. The writer too is in part the creation of the political and social and economic factors surrounding him/her. Shaw was extraordinarily sensitive to the second-class status of women in his society, more so than most intellectuals, since the Fabian movement attracted bright, middle-class young women who were teachers, librarians, and social workers, and who were otherwise emancipated, in part by the occupational needs they filled, while harassed by centuries of legislation and tradition which denied them due process in marriage and divorce, child custody, vocational opportunities, taxation, representation in government, and the vote. Shaw was an early suffragist, drafting as part of his plank when asked to consider running for office as a Liberal candidate in 1889, "suffrage for woman on exactly the same terms as for men."[7] His playlet *Press Cuttings* is his most obvious and perhaps best-known writing on the movement. (Some of his little known suffrage pieces are included in this book.) But *Press Cuttings* is not his most significant contribution to that movement. He supported the Pankhursts even when, in the beginning years of World War I, Mrs. Pankhurst and Christabel, feeling that the pressures of war could win for women more freedoms in exchange for their labor, attacked him for his pacifism. Later in the war, after their "war fervor" cooled, Mrs. Pankhurst included in her speeches lines Shaw wrote for her.[8] The appreciation of the suffragists for his support outlasted the Pankhursts, even until his death. Only a small group of persons who had been close to Shaw, and a representative of the Public Trustee for his estate, attended Shaw's funeral at Golders Green Crematorium in November 1950. Meanwhile:

> A lone old lady stood outside the building. She had once been a suffragette. She stood there erect, holding high an old ragged flag, the flag of the suffragettes.
>
> As if in a last salute to Shaw, the fierce fighter for all human rights, the wind flapped the faded flag against the gray November sky.[9]

What has been the influence of Shaw's gallery of role-defying women and his own feminist proselytizing? Very likely it has been along the lines of my titular characterization of him as a Fabian Feminist. The Fabian Society preached two methods of attaining its social goals: gradualism and permeation. It advocated gradualism rather than violence, evolution rather than revolution, for one frightened away the electorate with frightening images of sudden revolution. What was needed was a gradual accommodation with an electorate subtly propagandized into thinking it was carrying out its own will. The success of Shaw's plays and their successors in every form of literature contributed to that gradual change in perception. The second contribution of Fabianism was the Webb-coined watchword, *permeation*—the subtle penetration of existing political and social institutions by Fabian-minded operatives, themselves the products of two generations of Shaw's relentless impact upon their minds through his plays and pamphlets and pulpitry. The gradual turnabout in popular thought that has resulted in many people deciding that much of Shaw is now out of date and "old hat" suggests how successful he and his like-minded contemporaries were. Yet much of Shaw is not only still fresh but can be seen in the banners and goals of the contemporary feminist movement: equal opportunity to secure employment and equal pay for equal work; contracts for marriage; marriage free from degrading economic and possessive-sexual factors; dignified divorce; financial independence within or without marriage; ownership of property exclusive of one's husband; the bearing of children outside of marriage and the refusal to bear children; equal opportunity to participate in athletics; legal equality of every variety. There is still a long way to go.

Fabian Feminist is not the first examination of Shaw from a feminist perspective nor should it be the last. It is but a beginning of the exploration of the causes and effects of the special brand of feminism in his work, and as in the beginning of any exploration, there may be false starts and contradictory views expressed. Still, these are dimensions of Shaw which can furnish new insights into his work—and into Woman.

For assistance and encouragement in bringing this volume to fruition, I am indebted to the contributors, to Dan Laurence, to Ronald Heldrum, to T.F. Evans, to my husband, and to Shirley Rader.

Notes

1. Letter to an unidentified young American woman, undated (1895), *Bernard Shaw: Collected Letters 1874-1897*, ed. Dan H. Laurence (1965), pp. 474-75.

2. Lady Scott, *Self-Portrait of an Artist* (1949), diary entry, 19 September 1929.

3. *Bernard Shaw: Collected Letters 1874-1897*, p. 566.

4. *Bernard Shaw: Collected Letters 1898-1910*, ed. Dan H. Laurence (1972), pp. 924-25, 926-27.

5. "Modern Religion I," speech printed as a supplement to the *Christian Commonwealth*, 3 April 1912, as reprinted in *The Religious Speeches of Bernard Shaw*, ed. Warren Smith (1963), pp. 42-43.

6. Quoted from the *Christian Commonwealth* in Stanley Weintraub, *Journey to Heartbreak* (1971), p. 74.

7. J. Percy Smith, *The Unrepentant Pilgrim* (1965), p. 117.
8. Weintraub, *Journey to Heartbreak*, p. 135.
9. Valerie Pascal, *The Disciple and his Devil* (1970), p. 222.

I

LITERARY AND MYTHIC INFLUENCES

SHAKESPEARE'S *THE TAMING OF THE SHREW* VS. SHAW'S *PYGMALION:* MALE CHAUVINISM VS. WOMEN'S LIB?

Lisë Pedersen

Shaw's comparisons of himself to Shakespeare and his frequent, explicit and often extravagant criticisms of Shakespeare are so prominent a part of his critical writings as to be familiar to everyone who knows anything at all about Shaw. Nevertheless, critics have for the most part failed to notice that these same criticisms are often indirectly expressed in Shaw's plays through his handling of characters and situations similar to characters and situations handled in quite different ways by Shakespeare. To be sure, implicit criticisms of *Julius Caesar* and *Antony and Cleopatra* occurring in *Caesar and Cleopatra* have been widely noted and commented upon;[1] indeed, they could hardly have been overlooked since Shaw himself points them out and discusses them under the heading "Better than Shakespeare?" in the preface to his play. In a number of other cases, however, Shaw deals with fictitious characters who, though bearing different names and occurring in different ages, are nevertheless in themselves or in their situations so similar to characters and situations depicted by Shakespeare that it is difficult to believe that Shaw's depiction was not, whether consciously or unconsciously so, suggested by Shakespeare's. In these cases the similarities of depiction establish the relationship between the two plays but the differences in treatment illustrate one or more of the major criticisms which Shaw has elsewhere made of Shakespeare.

Basic to all Shaw's criticisms of Shakespeare is Shaw's belief that the purpose of drama is "to force the public to reconsider its morals" and that Shakespeare, except in the three "problem" comedies and possibly in *Hamlet*, makes no attempt to fulfill this purpose. Quite the contrary, in most of his plays he is content to dramatize a conventional, "reach-me-down," or "readymade" morality instead of working out an original morality as Shaw believed any writer of the "first order in literature" must do.[2] Two plays which illustrate this fundamental difference in the approach of the two playwrights to a similar situation are *The Taming of the Shrew* and *Pygmalion*. Indeed, Shaw's working out of the central situation of the two plays is so diametrically opposed to that of Shakespeare that *Pygmalion* seems deliberately designed to challenge and contradict Shakespeare's handling of this central situation.

The similarities in the two plays are readily apparent. In both plays a man accepts the task of transforming a woman from one kind of person to another, radically different kind. In both plays the man who undertakes this task is an overbearing bully. Petruchio consistently plays the role of a bully in his relationship with Kate, and it is, indeed, the means by which he transforms her from a quarrelsome shrew to a sweet-tempered and obedient wife. Not only does he frustrate her every wish, but he subjects her to mental anguish in the humiliation brought upon her by his attire and behavior at their wedding and to physical abuse in causing her horse to dump her into the mud, in preventing her from sleeping night after night, and in keeping food from her with the declared intention of starving her into submission.

Though Higgins does not resort to physical abuse of Eliza, except for a moment in the last act when he completely loses control of himself as a result of her taunts, he nevertheless does bully Eliza in every other way, ordering her about in a very brusque manner without the slightest concern for her feelings and uttering threats of physical violence which in the early stages of their acquaintance she takes quite seriously. In the Act II interview in his flat, when Eliza has first come to inquire about taking elocution lessons from Higgins, his treatment of her is extremely rude and abusive. He orders her *"peremptorily"* to sit down, and when she does not do so immediately he repeats the order, *"thundering"* it at her. When she interrupts his speculations about the price she has offered for the lessons, he barks out, "Hold your tongue," and when as a consequence of those speculations and of his rudeness, she begins to cry, he threatens, "Somebody is going to touch you, with a broomstick, if you dont stop snivelling." Immediately upon deciding to undertake the challenge to transform her into a duchess, Higgins begins to issue orders to Mrs. Pearce about giving Eliza a bath, disinfecting her, and burning all her clothes, without consulting Eliza at all, just as though she had nothing to say in the matter, and as Eliza begins to protest he tells Mrs. Pearce, "If she gives you any trouble, wallop her." Pickering's objection to Higgins's rudeness—"Does it occur to you, Higgins, that the girl has some feelings?"—elicits the quite serious reply from Higgins, "Oh no, I dont think so. Not any feelings that we need bother about." Subsequently Higgins adds that Pickering ought to realize from his military experience that there is no use trying to explain matters to Eliza, who is too ignorant to understand any such explanation, and that therefore the proper treatment of her is simply to "Give her her orders: thats enough for her." Furthermore, in Act V Higgins calls Eliza, among other things, one of the "squashed cabbage leaves of Covent Garden" and a "damned impudent slut," and instead of inviting her to come back to Wimpole Street he orders her to do so: "Get up and come home; and dont be a fool." Thus he demonstrates that his bullying treatment of her has not changed in the course of the play, though she has in that time changed into an entirely different person from what she was at the beginning of the play.[3]

Petruchio and Higgins are alike, then, in being bullies, though they are different in that Higgins does not resort to physical abuse and in that the motivation behind their bullying tactics is different. Petruchio has deliberately adopted such tactics to order to "tame" Kate in the same way that he would tame a falcon, as he reveals in a soliloquy:

> Thus have I politicly begun my reign,
> And 'tis my hope to end successfully.
> My falcon now is sharp and passing empty,
> And till she stoop, she must not be full gorged,
> For then she never looks upon her lure.
> Another way I have to man my haggard,
> To make her come and know her keeper's call,
> That is, to watch her, as we watch these kites
> That bate, and beat, and will not be obedient.[4]

On the other hand, Higgins's bullying treatment of Eliza is merely his natural way of behaving toward people and is not a special behavior adopted in connection with the task of transforming Eliza. On the contrary, as he insists to her, his behavior toward all people is the same:

The great secret, Eliza, is not having bad manners or good

manners or any other particular sort of manners, but having the same manner for all human souls. . . .

A number of similarities in the development of the basic plot by the two dramatists are easily discernible. In each case a test is set up to determine the success of the transformation of the woman in question: in Shakespeare's play the test compares Kate's response to an order of her husband's with the responses of Bianca and the Widow to similar orders of their husbands, and in Shaw's play the test involves passing Eliza off as a duchess at an ambassador's garden party. In each case there is a wager on the outcome of the test. And in each case the transformation of the woman succeeds beyond anyone's expectations and she passes the test with ease.

There is even a parallel in subordinate figures between Christopher Sly and Alfred Doolittle, both of whom provide an implied commentary on the major plot developments because they undergo transformations of their own in social status and external circumstances, Sly temporarily and Doolittle permanently, but these transformations do not include any real changes in the fundamental character or personality of either. Sly's main concern in life before he comes to think he is a lord has apparently been in sensual indulgence, and this concern continues unabated. Before he becomes convinced that he is a lord, the person who most naturally comes to his mind when he feels the need of someone to substantiate his real identity is "Marian Hacket, the fat ale-wife of Wincot," to whom he owes fourteen pence for sheer ale. After he is convinced that he is a lord, he first calls for "a pot o' th' smallest ale"; then, upon seeing his supposed wife for the first time, he asks her to join him in bed immediately; and when he is denied that request and offered instead the entertainment of a play, he falls asleep during its presentation. Thus, he does not seem to have undergone any fundamental changes in character or personality. Doolittle, too, for all his complaints about the changes his unwelcome prosperity has forced upon him, seems unchanged in manner and speech, and according to Shaw's epilogue "his wit, his dustmanship (which he carried like a banner), and his Nietzschean transcendence of good and evil" continue unchanged. Sly and Doolittle, then, because their transformations are mainly in external circumstances and leave their fundamental characters unchanged, provide contrasting parallels to the leading women of their plays, who do undergo fundamental changes in character and personality.

In examining the differences between Shakespeare's and Shaw's handling of the basic plot of *The Taming of the Shrew* and *Pygmalion*, it is instructive to keep in mind the principal criticisms which Shaw made of *The Taming of the Shrew*. In June 1888, he wrote the *Pall Mall Gazette* a letter signed with a woman's name, Horatia Ribbonson, asking "all men and women who respect one another" to boycott *The Taming of the Shrew*; describing Shakespeare's Petruchio as a "coarse, thick-skinned money hunter, who sets to work to tame his wife exactly as brutal people tame animals or children—that is, by breaking their spirit by domineering cruelty"; and complaining that Katherine's "degrading speech" to Bianca and the Widow to the effect that "thy husband is thy lord, thy life, thy keeper,/ Thy head, thy sovereign . . ." might have been acceptable to "an audience of bullies" in "an age when woman was a mere chattel," but should be intolerable to a modern audience.[5] Nine years later Shaw said virtually the same thing in a *Saturday Review* article. Though he praised the realism of the early acts of the play, particularly in the depiction of Petruchio's selfishness and brutality, he complained that Shakespeare was unable to maintain this realism throughout the play and that the last scene is so "disgusting to modern sensibility" that "no man with any decency of feeling can sit it out in the company of a woman without being extremely ashamed of the lord-of-creation moral implied in the wager and the speech put into the woman's own mouth."[6]

The attitudes toward woman—and toward man, for that matter—implicit in these criticisms are reflected in the differences between Shaw's working out of the *Pygmalion* plot and Shakespeare's working out of the plot of *The Taming of the Shrew*. These differences are principally in the methods by which the woman is transformed and in the final attitudes of the man and the woman toward each other.

At first glance it may seem that a comparison of the methods used to transform the women cannot be valid since the qualities requiring transformation were not of the same kind in both cases, Kate's case involving a change of such psychological qualities as temper and temperament and Eliza's involving changes in qualities which seem much more superficial—speech, dress and awareness of the rules of etiquette. It should be noted, however, that although Eliza was not shrewish at the beginning of her play, she was completely lacking in self-control, very quick to take offense, and very bad-tempered in her reaction to offenses, real or imagined, so that a mere change in speech, dress and superficial manners could not have transformed her into a lady. Like Kate, she too had to learn self-control and consideration for others. Once she has successfully made all the changes necessary to transform her into a woman who can pass for a duchess, Eliza herself recognizes that the acquiring of self-restraint was by far the most important of these changes. She speaks slight-

ingly of Higgins's accomplishment in teaching her to speak correct-
ly, maintaining that "it was just like learning to dance in the
fashionable way: there was nothing more than that in it," and tells
Pickering that her "real education" came from him because he provided her with the example of self-restraint and consideration for
others:

> You see it was so very difficult for me with the example of Pro-
> fessor Higgins always before me. I was brought up to be just
> like him, unable to control myself, and using bad language on
> the slightest provocation. And I should never have known that
> ladies and gentlemen didnt behave like that if you hadnt been
> there.

This speech expresses a direct repudiation of the method by
which Shakespeare allows Petruchio to "tame" Kate, because it asserts that the example of bad-tempered, uncontrolled behavior can
only bring about behavior of the same kind in the learner, not a
change to sweet-tempered reasonableness such as Kate exhibits.
Furthermore, as Eliza continues her indirect attack on Higgins's
methods through her praise of Pickering's treatment of her, she insists to Pickering that the real beginning of her transformation came
with "your calling me Miss Doolittle that day when I first came to
Wimpole Street. That was the beginning of self-respect for me."
This statement is a criticism of Higgins, who calls her "Eliza" from
the first—that is, when he is not calling her "this baggage," "pre-
sumptuous insect" or the like—but it also recalls the fact that Petruchio, on first meeting Kate, calls her "Kate," though, except for
her sister, her family and acquaintances all call her by the more formal "Katherina" or "Katherine." In addition, Kate herself rebukes
Petruchio for calling her "Kate," asserting that "they call me
Katherine that do talk of me," whereupon he replies with a speech
in which he uses the name "Kate" eleven times in six lines:

> You lie, in faith, for you are called plain Kate,
> And bonny Kate, and sometimes Kate the Curst;
> But Kate, the prettiest Kate in Christendom,
> Kate of Kate-Hall, my superdainty Kate,
> For dainties are all Kates—and therefore, Kate,
> Take this of me, Kate of my consolation:

This perverse insistence on using the familiar, informal name which
she has asked him not to use is paralleled by Higgins's reply to
Eliza's request that he call her "Miss Doolittle": "I'll see you damned
first." Thus, again, Eliza's criticism of Higgins's method of dealing

with her is also a criticism of Petruchio's method of dealing with Kate.

Moreover, a repudiation of physical abuse as a means of dominating a woman's spirit is implied by the fact that in *Pygmalion* physical abuse plays no part in transforming Eliza, but instead appears in the play solely as the feeble, ineffectual and unintentional response of Higgins to Eliza's freeing of herself from his domination. When Eliza, realizing that Higgins will never treat her as she wants to be treated and therefore searching desperately for some means by which she can free herself from dependence on him, hits on the idea of becoming an assistant to a teacher of phonetics whom Higgins considers a quack, Higgins lays hands on her to strike her, and is deterred from doing so only by her triumphant non-resistance. Milton Crane construes this loss of self-control on Higgins's part as an indication that "his confusion is complete" and therefore "Galatea has subdued Pygmalion."[7] Thus, instead of being the means to domination, as it is in *The Taming of the Shrew*, in *Pygmalion* the resort to physical abuse is an admission of defeat, a reaction of frustrated rage to the failure to dominate.

In addition to these differences in the method by which the transformation of the woman is achieved, the other major differences in the working out of the plot by the two playwrights are in the final attitudes of the teacher and the learner to one another. Kate's final attitude to Petruchio is shown not only by her instant obedience to him, but also by the speech which Shaw criticized as "degrading," a speech in which she says that in a marriage the husband is the "lord," "king," "governor," "life," "keeper," "head," and "sovereign" of the wife and that the wife owes the husband "such duty as the subject owes the prince," and in which she consequently urges her sisters-in-law to follow her example by placing their hands below their husbands' feet as a token of their willingness to obey their husbands. Eliza's final attitude to Higgins is the direct opposite of Kate's to Petruchio. She exults in having achieved her freedom from his domination:

> Aha! Thats done you, Henry Higgins, it has. Now I dont care that (*snapping her fingers*) for your bullying and your big talk. . . . Oh, when I think of myself crawling under your feet and being trampled on and called names, when all the time I had only to lift up my finger to be as good as you, I could just kick myself.

The reference to her former "crawling" under his feet and "being trampled on" even seems to be a verbal echo of Kate's reference to placing her hand below her husband's foot as a token of her submission to him. Certainly, here, at the conclusion of *Pygmalion*, there is a deliberate repudiation of the idea of male domination of the female which underlies the theme of *The Taming of the Shrew*.

Furthermore, that this repudiation is not simply Eliza's view, but is the view set forth by the play, is suggested by the fact that Higgins shares it. Though he has a habit of expecting that Eliza—and everyone else, for that matter—should automatically fall in with his plans because in his view his plans naturally offer the most proper and sensible course of action open to everyone, Higgins has never consciously desired to make Eliza subservient to him, whereas Petruchio has, of course, expressly declared that the whole purpose of his strange and violent behavior is to make Kate subservient to him. Indeed, Higgins brands the conventionally expected acts of subservience on the part of women toward men as "Commercialism," attempts to buy affection. He tells Eliza:

> I dont and wont trade in affection. You call me a brute because you couldnt buy a claim on me by fetching my slippers and finding my spectacles. You were a fool: I think a woman fetching a man's slippers is a disgusting sight: did I ever fetch your slippers? I think a good deal more of you for throwing them in my face. No use slaving for me and then saying you want to be cared for: who cares for a slave? If you come back, come back for the sake of good fellowship . . . and if you dare to set up your little dog's tricks of fetching and carrying slippers against my creation of a Duchess Eliza, I'll slam the door in your silly face.

And after Eliza has declared her independence of Higgins, he says:

> You damned impudent slut, you! But it's better than snivelling; better than fetching slippers and finding spectacles, isnt it? . . . By George, Eliza, I said I'd make a woman of you; and I have. I like you like this.

At the conclusion of *Pygmalion*, then, both Eliza and Higgins reject the concept of male dominance over women, a concept which is not only supported but actually exalted by the conclusion of *The Taming of the Shrew*.

In supporting this concept in *The Taming of the Shrew* Shakespeare was, of course, supporting the conventional morality of his own day, and in rejecting this concept in *Pygmalion* Shaw was rejecting the conventional morality of his own day and substituting for it an original view of morality. Thus Shaw clearly used his play not only to repudiate the male chauvinism of his day and Shakespeare's and to support women's liberation, a cause for which he was an early pioneer, but also to dramatize a criticism which was fundamental to all Shaw's complaints about Shakespeare and which Shaw had often expressed in very explicit terms in his critical writings—that Shakespeare failed to create and espouse an original morality in opposition to the conventional morality of his time.

Notes

1. See, for example, Gordon W. Couchman, "Comic Catharsis in *Caesar and Cleopatra*," *Shaw Review* 3 (January 1960), 11–13; Daniel I. Leary, "The Moral Dialectic in *Caesar and Cleopatra*," *Shaw Review* 5 (May 1962), 45; and Wilhelm Rehbach, "Shaw's 'Besser als Shakespeare,' " *Shakespeare Johrbuch* 52 (1916), 125–38.

2. Preface to *The Shewing-Up of Blanco Posnet*; postscript to the Preface to *The Irrational Knot*, reprinted in *Shaw on Shakespeare: An Anthology of Bernard Shaw's Writings on the Plays and Production of Shakespeare*, ed. Edwin Wilson (1961), pp. 229–30.

3. All quotations from Shaw's plays, prefaces, appendices and program notes in this volume, unless otherwise noted, are from the seven volume *Definitive Edition Bernard Shaw Collected Plays with their Prefaces* published in the United States by Dodd, Mead (1975) and in England as the *Bodley Head Edition*, Bodley Head (1970–74).

4. All quotations from *The Taming of the Shrew* are from G.B. Harrison's *Shakespeare: The Complete Works* (1968).

5. *Pall Mall Gazette* (8 June 1888), reprinted in *Shaw on Shakespeare*, pp. 186–87.

6. Article dated 6 November 1897 reprinted in *Shaw on Shakespeare*, pp. 187–88.

7. "*Pygmalion*: Bernard Shaw's Dramatic Theory and Practice," *PMLA* 66 (December 1951), 884.

KIPLING ON WOMEN:
A NEW SOURCE FOR SHAW

Janie Caves McCauley

According to their biographers, Rudyard Kipling and G.B. Shaw met only once during their lifetimes, which overlapped by the whole of Kipling's seventy-one years. Although the two marched together as pallbearers at Thomas Hardy's funeral in February 1928, they apparently did not talk to each other, and Shaw is reported to have remarked later that it had been "ludicrous" for the funeral directors to pair one so tall as he with one so small as Kipling.[1] Several years later at Kipling's own death Shaw observed that his contemporary had been outdated throughout his career and, in fact, had never really grown up. Said G.B.S., "I don't think that the reading of Kipling has ever changed anybody's life very much."[2]

That there was no friendship or overt mutual admiration between Shaw and Kipling is, of course, not surprising when one considers their divergent politico-economic views and the varying paths that their literary careers took, not to mention their basic differences in personality. For example, Kipling, whose "vision of life" is defined by Elliot L. Gilbert as belief in "the irrationality of the universe and man's need to find some order in it,"[3] was a technocrat: he advocated rule of the world's economic organization by professional "technicians." He therefore did not appreciate the Fabians, and left-wing pacifists like Shaw and Wells disgusted him. He opposed liberal social betterment schemes, which he described as "robbing selective Peter to pay for collective Paul."[4] And while Shaw achieved notoriety for consciously playing the role of G.B.S., the outspoken idiosyncratic personality who rarely approved of anything or anybody, Kipling evidently was a rather quiet man of action.[5]

A rare direct literary link between Shaw and Kipling appears in *Man and Superman* when Ann Whitefield calls Octavius Robinson, the young romantic poet whom she pampers and manipulates, "Ricky-ticky-tavy," the name of the mongoose that is the title character in a short story from Kipling's *The Jungle Book* collection, published in 1895, some eight years before Shaw's play appeared. On the surface it appears that Shaw is merely having some fun with his unsophisticated literary allusion while perhaps subtly commenting further on the female embodiment of the Life Force who goes around making up such babyish names as "Annie's Granny" for her legal guardian, the stuffy Roebuck Ramsden; "Jack the Giant Killer" for her young revolutionary friend Jack Tanner; and "Ricky-ticky-tavy" for the man who is enamored of her. In addition, these nicknames contribute to Shaw's characterization of the three men to whom they are applied, for they all show themselves martyrs to feminine wiles by permitting Ann to so designate them. When she asks "Must I call you Mr Robinson in the future?" Octavius earnestly replies, "Oh please call me Ricky-ticky-tavy. 'Mr Robinson' would hurt cruelly." Similarly, Ramsden says, "I insist on Granny. I won't answer to any other name than Annie's Granny." It is only Tanner who initially objects to Ann's nonsense. Although he says "I think you ought to call me Mr Tanner," he soon capitulates and allows "Jack" when she threatens to call him "Don Juan" instead. Obviously, then, Kipling's "Rikki-tikki-tavi" provided Shaw with a clever diminutive form of *Octavius* which, because it is childish, emphasizes Ann's tendency to mother every man with whom she comes into contact.[6] But an examination of Kipling's story reveals that Shaw has more in common with this source than a silly nickname.

In the opening paragraph of "Rikki-Tikki-Tavi" Kipling offers the following synopsis of his story:

> This is the story of the great war that Rikki-tikki-tavi fought single-handed, through the bathrooms of the big bungalow in Segowlee cantonment. Darzee, the tailor-bird, helped him, and Chuchundra, the muskrat, who never comes out into the middle of the floor, but always creeps round by the wall, gave him advice; but Rikki-tikki did the real fighting.[7]

We then learn that Rikki-tikki-tavi, a mongoose named for the sound of his "war-cry" as he brushes through the grass, was one day washed from the burrow of his parents and deposited by a summer flood on the garden path of Mr. and Mrs. Bird's bungalow. There he was found in a bedraggled condition and befriended by young Teddy Bird. After eating and becoming revived, Rikki-tikki-tavi decided to remain with the boy, at least until he had thoroughly surveyed the premises. The Birds gave Rikki-tikki the run of the house and even permitted him to sleep with Teddy. One morning while roaming in the garden, Rikki-tikki encountered the tailor-bird, Darzee, and his wife in a state of misery because one of their babies had fallen out of the nest the day before and been eaten by Nag, a big black cobra. The mongoose himself soon came face-to-face with Nag, and while they were talking, the snake's evil wife, Nagaina, crept up behind Rikki-tikki and tried to kill him. But mongooses are faster than snakes, and Rikki-tikki jumped away and managed to wound Nagaina instead. Later in the same day he also killed a dangerous brown snakeling named Karait. Meanwhile, Nagaina had been persistently tormenting her husband about the necessity of his providing a suitable home for their young. She reminded him, "[A]s soon as our eggs in the melon-bed hatch . . ., our children will need room and quiet." Therefore Nagaina wanted to get rid of the Bird family by any means possible so as to have the garden all for herself and her babies. To accomplish her purpose, she persuaded Nag to sneak into the house and try to kill father, mother, and child.

But while Nag slept coiled up in the Birds' bathroom, Rikki-tikki attacked and killed him. Out in the garden Darzee and his wife rejoiced over Nag's death. Darzee naively sang, "He will never eat my babies again." The danger was not over, however, for Nagaina, described by Rikki-tikki as "worse than five Nags," was still alive. Besides, she had a nest of eggs that might hatch any day. At the very moment Darzee was singing, in fact, Nagaina was planning her strategy for murdering little Teddy Bird as revenge. Fortunately Darzee's wife was much more sensible than he, and she worked out a plan for helping Rikki-tikki trap Nagaina. While Darzee's wife flew around in front of the wicked cobra to distract her, Rikki-tikki sneaked around to the snake nest and smashed all the eggs except one. This last cobra egg he then used to ensnare Nagaina herself. Thus Rikki-tikki-tavi had saved the lives of Mr. and Mrs. Bird and Teddy and rendered their bungalow a safe dwelling place. The Birds had been well rewarded for their kindness in taking in the orphaned mongoose. Teddy had a nice, snake-free garden to play in, and Darzee and his wife could rear their young in peace.

While presenting an entertaining and didactic bestial story which can be understood and enjoyed by all children, Kipling also makes some obvious and fairly important points in "Rikki-Tikki-Tavi," and the major issues with which he deals are also of primary concern to Shaw in *Man and Superman*. For example, the story as a whole seems to illustrate Darwin's theory of the survival of the fittest: The snakes kill the birds' young; the mongoose kills the father snake; the mother snake retaliates by trying to kill the human beings' (ironically also named the Birds') young; the mongoose kills the mother snake. Thus the human beings, birds, and mongoose who survive prove themselves better adapted to the particular environment in the story than the snakes, who fail in their attempt to take over the garden and bungalow for themselves and their young. But Kipling attributes a mind and a will to survive to each of these creatures, therefore coming close to the anti-Darwinism propounded by Shaw which sees design and purpose in the universe.[8] Note Kipling's treatment of the evolutionary theme in the story:

> Darzee was a feather-brained little fellow who could never hold more than one idea at a time in his head; and just because he knew that Nagaina's children were born in eggs like his own, he didn't think at first that it was fair to kill them. But his wife was a sensible bird, and she knew that cobra's eggs meant young cobras later on; so she flew off from the nest, and left Darzee to keep the babies warm, and continue his song about the death of Nag. Darzee was very like a man in some ways.

The last sentence quoted brings us to another of Kipling's points in "Rikki-Tikki-Tavi" which Shaw explores in *Man and Superman,* that the male of the species is usually dominated by the female. This theory is illustrated by the relationships of Nag and Nagaina and of Darzee and his wife. Kipling depicts both Nagaina and Darzee's wife as more intelligent and cunning than their mates. Another male animal in the story, Chuchundra the muskrat, is also depicted as a pitifully weak creature who laments the fact that he "never had spirit enough to run out into the middle of the room." Similarly, in *Man and Superman* the male characters are dominated by the females. Ann's authority over Octavius and Ramsden is unquestionable throughout the play, and she uses her feminine powers to gain control over the proud Tanner by the final curtain. Violet Robinson, Tavy's sister and Ann's friend, also dominates the important men in her life.

Unattractive as these domineering females may be, they are not left unmotivated for their crafty means of gaining supremacy over males by either Kipling or Shaw. The female creatures in "Rikki-Tikki-Tavi," like the human Mrs. Bird who is appalled by the idea of her son's sleeping with a mongoose, are driven by a desire to nurture and protect their young. Shaw clearly develops this same idea in *Man and Superman,* where he expounds his philosophy of the Life

Force through the mouth of Jack Tanner. This character, who eventually becomes the comic victim of the play, explains that women "have a purpose which is not their own purpose, but that of the whole universe," man being "nothing to them but an instrument of that purpose." He later identifies this high purpose as "to increase, multiply, and replenish the earth." Like ·Kipling's female cobra Nagaina, Shaw's Ann Whitefield is described as a snake. In the stage directions Shaw emphasizes that she is "a well formed creature . . . with ensnaring eyes and hair," just as Darzee's wife underlines Nagaina's power to charm a bird with her eyes. Before Ann ever enters the play, Tanner likens her to a boa constrictor. Later as she confronts him directly he ironically exclaims, "I feel the coils tightening around my very self, though you are only playing with me." When Tanner finally realizes that he, not Tavy, is the one whom Ann wants to marry, he says, "Then I—*I* am the bee, the spider, the marked down victim, the destined prey."

Kipling alludes to Nag the cobra in one of his later works, a poem entitled "The Female of the Species" which was published in 1911. According to Carrington, the satiric piece was intended as a comment on suffragettes and is not an indication that Kipling scorned female intelligence. Nevertheless, it brought to the poet the negative reaction of many women of his day, and even his own daughter Elsie expressed her disapproval of the poem at first.[9] "The Female of the Species," although it could not have influenced Shaw's *Man and Superman*, strengthens the tie between Shaw and Kipling concerning woman's role in evolution which is suggested in "Rikki-Tikki-Tavi." The piece, key portions of which are quoted below, is a sort of poetic version of Shaw's philosophy in *Man and Superman*. Composed of thirteen quatrains, "The Female of the Species" hypothesizes that "the female of the species is more deadly than the male":

> But the Woman that God gave [man], every fibre of her frame
> Proves her launched for one sole issue, armed and engined
>   for the same;
> And to serve that single issue, lest the generations fail,
> The female of the species must be deadlier than the male.
> . . . .
> She is wedded to convictions—in default of grosser ties;
> Her contentions are her children, Heaven help him
>   who denies!—
> He will meet no suave discussion, but the instant,
>   white-hot, wild,

> Wakened female of the species warring as for spouse
> and child.
> . . . .
> And Man knows it! Knows, moreover, that the Woman that
> God gave him
> Must command but may not govern—shall enthral but not
> enslave him.
> And *She* knows, because She warns him, and Her instincts
> never fail,
> That the Female of Her Species is more deadly
> than the Male.

Other illustrations for the views of Kipling on woman's role in the universe which parallel so closely those of Shaw can be found throughout his works. For example, in the poem "The Vampire" he develops the idea that woman is unconscious of the destructive role that she plays in the male-female relationship. It is man's "natural bent" to fall prey to her, although she does not know nor can she know of her negative effect on him. After his wasted years, tears, and work and all his unrealized plans, the most stinging part of a relationship gone bad is "coming to know that she never knew why/ . . . And never could understand."[10] In the story "The Light that Failed" Kipling demonstrates another favorite Shavian thesis, that woman has a deadly effect upon the artist man.[11] In some of the poems he depicts the responsibilities of marriage as prohibitive to a man's performing his duties in any realm of life. "The Married Man," for example, proposes that a husband cannot be as good a soldier as a bachelor, for the former does all "For 'Im an' 'Er an' It." In " 'Birds of Prey' March," while troops are boarding a ship for foreign service, women follow their husbands on board, faint, and have to be handed off. The married men thus block up the gangway with their farewells and hold up the bachelors who are eager to board. Indeed, in all his works Kipling manifests an unusual attitude toward women, which Gilbert defines in terms strongly reminiscent of Shaw:

> Kipling's attitude toward women is idiosyncratic. Women as individuals may be charming and wholly innocent and yet at the same time may be acting, unconsciously, as the agents of a terrible power totally beyond their understanding or control. And though this power may originally have been generated by some overwhelming creative urge, its random, mindless application can just as easily be deadly and destructive.[12]

Such ideas on the role of women were popular topics in the era in which Kipling and Shaw lived, so popular that many people were talking and writing about them, not just Kipling and Shaw. But while the ideas themselves are not sufficient to link Shaw to Kipling, the playwright's ironic use of the name "Ricky-ticky-tavy" in *Man and Superman* cannot be coincidental. Furthermore, Shaw's play does parallel Kipling's story philosophically in several points. This, of course, does not mean that Shaw's ideology was influenced by Kipling. It does mean, however, that these two literary contemporaries had something in common, although after Kipling's death Shaw refused to own any such affinity, and it would probably have also been denied by Kipling had he been the one who lived longer. In addition, the fact that Kipling served as a minor source for Shaw to at least a small extent invalidates Shaw's dismissing Kipling as "outdated," for Kipling in at least one work voices some of Shaw's major ideas several years before Shaw himself does so. Finally, the parallels between Shaw's and Kipling's depictions of women should partially vindicate Kipling from the critical opprobrium that his reputation has suffered on the basis of the women characters in his stories.

Notes

1. C.E. Carrington, *The Life of Rudyard Kipling* (1955), p. 383.

2. Hilton Brown, *Rudyard Kipling* (1945), pp. 4-5.

3. *The Good Kipling: Studies in the Short Story* (1970), p. 113.

4. Carrington, p. 316.

5. Carrington, p. xx.

6. See also "Ann and Superman: Type and Archetype," Sally Peters Vogt, p. 46.

7. All quotations from the prose works of Rudyard Kipling are taken from *Kipling: A Selection of His Stories and Poems,* ed. John Beecroft, vol. 2 (1956).

8. See Archibald Henderson, *George Bernard Shaw: Man of the Century* (1956), pp. 122, 768, 786-87.

9. Carrington, p. 318.

10. For a full discussion of this poem, see Carrington, pp. 194-96, and Basil M. Bazely, cited by Gilbert, p. 102. All quotations from Kipling's poems are taken from *Rudyard Kipling's Verse: Definitive Edition* (1940).

11. See André Maurois, "A French View of Kipling," in *Kipling: The Critical Heritage,* ed. Roger Lancelyn Green (1971), pp. 380-81.

12. Gilbert, p. 102.

THE SHAVIAN SPHINX

Rhoda B. Nathan

When Ellie Dunn comes to Heartbreak House at Hesione Husha-bye's invitation, she is driven, after a lengthy conversation with Hesione, to ask her why she looks so "enigmatic." In some exasperation, Ellie declares, "You are such a sphinx: I never know what you mean." Hesione, of course, does not choose to enlighten her. In another play, Shaw's turn of the century marriage farce, *You Never Can Tell,* the smitten Valentine complains to the hard-hearted Gloria Clandon that in twelve years he has learned nothing about women. Gloria's mother also accuses her daughter of enigmatic utterances: "Gloria! More engimas!" Gloria responds with equanimity: "Oh no. The same enigma." To the very end of the play, the Gloria of Valentine's imagination remains unreconciled with the real Gloria because he cannot understand her, nor does she wish him to.

The concept of woman as sphinx was neither new nor exclusive to Shaw. It seized the imagination of at least two of his contemporary novelist-dramatists, Oscar Wilde and Henry James, both of whom Shaw knew. Wilde's is the most celebrated of the sphinx allusions, possibly because it was delivered as an epigram by the arch-cynic Lord Henry Wotton in the novel *The Picture of Dorian Gray.* Challenged at a dinner party to characterize women as a sex, Lord Henry devastated his coy interlocutor with the terse and unflattering "sphinxes without secrets." James, a subtler and more sensitive delineator of character, fashioned a "serene, exquisite, but impenetrable sphinx" in the enigmatic May Bartram of *The Beast in the Jungle.* May is the creature who bears the closest resemblance to the mute and mysterious sentinels of the pyramids of the Egyptian desert. She guards her secret to the end of her days, tormenting the poor fatuous Marcher, fated to live out his sterile expectant days without penetrating the mystery of her unrevealed wisdom. His punishment for his audacity in daring to ask his fate is the terrible dawning awareness that she will die without "giving him light," a fate appropriate to the hubris which impels one even to consider unraveling the mystery of the sphinx.

Shaw appeared to combine the two distinct traditions of the sphinx legend—the Greek and the Egyptian—and mix them to suit a particular characterization in any given play. The sphinx of the Hellenic tradition, most clearly delineated in Sophocles's *Oedipus the King*, is a "daimon"[1] of supernatural origin and power. This creature is all-powerful, all-knowing, and malign in nature, traditionally female and endowed with the head of a woman, the body of a lion, the tail of a serpent, and the wings of an eagle. She guarded the unanswerable riddle to the secret of life, and although she would appear to reward the mortal who guessed it, in fact she would punish him severely for his arrogance in solving the divine enigma. The Greek mythic sphinx was thus a monster essentially inimical to man, possessed of secrets too profound and sacred for mortal man.

The sphinx of Egyptian cultural tradition is not a single evocation but rather a religious concept made concrete in many representations. Although many sphinxes fashioned for worship are female by design, the Greek Sphinx of Giza is a male divinity. The sheer size of even the smallest of the sphinxes offers pointed evidence of the gigantic scale of the cultural imagination that translated idea into form. Whereas the mythical Theban sphinx was designed to induce terror and obedience, the colossal Egyptian sphinx was fashioned for awed worship. While the Greek sphinx was winged and malign, the Egyptian models were in the main wingless and benign. They were stationary and passive, whereas the Greek monster gave the impression of being always on the ready to swoop down and attack. The Egyptian sphinxes were conceived to denote superhuman size and potency. Their eyes were heavy-lidded with slumberous unrevealed wisdom, their lips full and benevolent. Their very bulk and passivity suggest dignity and timelessness.

The name "sphinx" means "living image," suggesting religious immortality. The nineteenth-century novelist Harriet Martineau, recording her impressions of the Great Sphinx in 1846, captured the ambience surrounding the divinity in her awed reaction to the "full serene gaze of its round face" and its eyes which "have gazed unwinking into vacancy" while through the unpausing ages men have looked into those eyes, "so full of meaning, though so fixed."[2]

Other sacred or secular interpretations aside, the essence of sphinx worship in both Greek and Egyptian cultures is enigma. To this day sphinx means "puzzle" by virtue of the inexplicable yet fluid union of beast and human. And, setting aside the greater frequency of the male to the female representation in Egyptian culture, it is agreed by all interpreters, including Shaw's misguided Caesar (who was historically wrong but instinctually right) that the underlying principle of the sphinx is primarily and indisputably female. Operating, therefore, on the presupposition of the sphinx's femaleness—as all daimons were female in Greek mythology—Shaw shaped a great many heroines who may properly be called sphinxes.

One must begin with a disclaimer. Not all Shaw heroines are sphinxes. Oddly enough, Cleopatra, the most likely candidate for sphinxhood by virtue of her cultural origin and historical role, has nothing of the sphinx about her. As Shaw conceives of her and dramatizes her behavior, Cleopatra ripens from nursery kitten to full-blown monarch without pausing to acquire the psychic and spiritual trappings of the chief of her country's religious symbols. Shaw himself, in a letter to Ellen Terry, discounts Cleopatra as a person to whom moral superiority was "incomprehensible." He describes her as someone who would "always guess wrong," reducing her irrevocably to mere mortality.[3] If there is a sphinx in Shaw's *Caesar and Cleopatra*, it is not Cleopatra but Caesar, who declares himself as "part brute, part woman and part god—nothing of man in [him] at all." It is Caesar who, in his remarkable homage to the sphinx in the first act, captures the essential mystery and vital force of the sphinx, which he sees as a mirror image of his persona as he declares: "For I am he of whose genius you are the symbol." It is Caesar who is drawn on a colossal scale, brooding, philosophical, far removed from the petty vengeance and retribution of the mortals who surround him. Cleopatra is too much the creature of the moment, too much the sensualist and power-seeker to qualify even as a person of wisdom, let alone enigmatic depth. Though she does gain some stature and does learn how to deal with people, her knowledge is hard-bought and in the main pragmatic.[4] She learns to rule and mediate, but develops no philosophic insight nor fund of intuitive wisdom.

When Shaw's Caesar asks the sphinx, "Have I read your riddle, Sphinx?" it is safe to assume that he is expressing Shaw's own profound curiosity about the enigmatic wisdom of woman in general. The superiority which Shaw's women have over his men is largely a consequence of some immense secret store of unuttered knowledge. In a letter to his French translator, Augustin Hamon, Shaw suggests that Hamon turn to his wife for some help in amending a particular phrase in his translation: "Ask Henriette: les femmes comprennent cela."[5] In the same letter, Shaw expresses the certainty that Henriette would understand the "paralysing Calvinism" which prohibits his becoming an "effective homme de coeur," just as Candida Morell understands everything about her husband, whereas Morell, blindly worshiping her sphinxlike serenity, understands nothing about her. Gifted with supernatural omniscience as well as prescience, Candida knows what has been going on before she has entered a room. "I know what you have done as well as if I had been there all the time," she accuses the unrepentant Eugene Marchbanks. Sensing that the poet is destined to make trouble for her husband, she warns him, "My boy shall not be worried. I will protect him." In her absolute authority and control, she reduces all men to boys and thus renders them helpless. She calls Eugene a "bad boy" and warns him not to bully her "boy," Morell. She reminds the reader of Lady Cicely Waynflete, of *Captain Brassbound's Conversion*, who pronounces with some scorn that "all men are children in the nursery." But more to the point, Candida is a woman of deep intelligence and insight, and possessed of total autonomy. Like the sphinx, she knows and understands everything, while poor Morell understands nothing. She assures him that he may tell her anything, promising that she will not misunderstand. And because she is entirely and effortlessly autonomous, she becomes genuinely and fearsomely angry only when she is told she must choose between her husband and her poet-admirer. Because she is a divinity she belongs to nobody. To the contrary, men belong to her and must placate her with fealty. From the height of her unchallenged power, she can then afford to be magnanimous, but when threatened, she will become dangerous and punitive. Moreover, like a true sphinx, she speaks in riddles. When asked to make a choice between her two adorers, she replies enigmatically, "I give myself to the weaker of the two." The response is sphinx wisdom, truth veiled in irony. Eugene, who has something of the female in his nature by virtue of his artist's temperament, understands immediately, but poor Morell, a mere mortal, is flummoxed and must be enlightened.

In a letter to James Huneker, Shaw explained Candida's character as he conceived it without convention, "free from emotional slop," and therefore "mistress of the situation."[6] He calls her an "immoral female," which is not to say that she is a wicked woman, but that she is far removed from conventional morality because she is above it. She teaches without talking too much. She does not preach her doctrines as does her husband, but imparts her wisdom subtly for the limited few who are worthy of it. Those who flout her authority or deny her allegiance or defy her protection run the risk of exile from her august presence. She is the best synthesis of the two sphinx traditions, an enigma embodying the overlapping and sometimes contradictory powers of magnanimity, protectiveness, ambiguity, omniscience, hypnotic charm, and authority. Other Shaw heroines have some of these sphinx qualities, but few achieve Candida's totality. Hesione Hushabye and Ann Whitefield are more siren than sphinx, because in Shaw's conception they work their particular magic by "ensnaring" men rather than dominating them with unquestionable authority. They are possessed of a "vital genius" and depend on their eyes and hair for the entrapment of their victims, whereas Candida enjoys automatic allegiance and has no need to rely on such devices. Still, Ellie calls Hesione a witch as well as a siren, hinting at magical powers of intuition and control. Specifically, since the Greek sphinx is an emblem of that unconquerable and inscrutable force that lays men low, the ladies may be regarded as sphinxlike. Ellie Dunn is called a "fiend" by Hesione, and Ann is dubbed a cat, a beast of prey, and a lion who eats its victims. She has a "sort of fascination" about her, and she does not permit a man to keep his own soul. Like a divinity, she warns Tanner to take care because he misinterprets her designs to be on Tavy rather than on himself. Tanner does not feel safe with her, both because and in spite of her "devilish charm." In short, she is much like the dangerous Greek sphinx, both more and less than human, a species of monster. Still, Ann is not to be classed with Shaw's relentlessly respectable women, like Violet Robinson, nor with his one-dimensional steamrollers like Lady Britomart Undershaft. She is not cold and rational like Vivie Warren, nor is she a "fried-fish shop" natural woman like Mrs. Warren. Her character is conceived on a larger-than-life scale. It incorporates male and female elements in generous proportions. Ann's vital genius urges her to be progenitor, producer, and nourisher all in one. Shaw describes her as neither a moralist nor a sensualist, but rather as a being "specialized by nature to be a breeder of men and endowed with enormous fascination for it" (p. 475). Like the Theban sphinx, she has laid her trap at the beginning, as Tanner discovers to his mock horror too late to save himself. Shaw claimed that she was his most "gorgeous female creation," and boasted of her colossal drive for power. "The only really simple thing is to go straight for what you want and grab it" (pp. 385, 394). She is both powerful and cunning, but she is forgiven because she serves a force higher than her own. As a guardian of the future she fulfills a benevolent purpose with necessarily ruthless tactics.

Like Ann, Hesione is a guardian, not of the future, but of the domestic establishment. If Ann has a "wicked streak" (p. 528), Hesione is without honor. She and her sister, Lady Ariadne Utterword, known as the two "demon daughters" of the demented old skipper Captain Shotover, are celebrated for weaving spells over hapless men. One victim, Hector Hushabye, advises his sister-in-law's brother-in-law, Randall Utterword, that he is under a spell cast by the "two demon daughters." Ellie calls Hesione a siren and accuses her of leading men about by the nose. Moreover, she charges that Hesione has the "trick of falling in with everyone's mood." Still, Hesione, with her vast store of benevolence, offers indulgence and protection to her philanderer husband, even though she is capable of announcing to him in mid-caress: "Now I am going off to fascinate somebody."

Fascinating and hypnotizing and casting spells are natural to Shaw's sphinxes. Even Ellie Dunn, a species of mini-sphinx, has supernatural power. She throws Boss Mangan into a trance so that he cannot move hand or foot. Her patroness, Hesione, calls her a fiend. She is intuitive and quick to penetrate Captain Shotover's defenses, which all the other members of the household take as extreme eccentricity. "I have found out that trick of yours," she declares boldly, alluding to his habit of running away and hiding from direct confrontation. She appears to share a "sixth sense" with another mini-sphinx, Jennifer Dubedat of *The Doctor's Dilemma*, which faculty Jennifer announces to Dr. Colenso Ridgeon she possesses and he sadly lacks. This sense is an instinctual understanding of people, a dangerous gift because it enables one to control the destiny of others as well as oneself. For instance, Jennifer wins out against seemingly insurmountable odds at the end in an act of unconscious irony. Having loftily discarded an earlier plan to kill Ridgeon, thereby establishing that she had considered taking the law into her own hands without qualm, she nonetheless destroys him effortlessly by marrying immediately after her husband's death. In so doing, she fulfills her own destiny, gratifies her husband's abhorrence of widows, and incidentally robs Ridgeon of the happiness of marrying her. Her victory is more complete because it is the consequence of her natural superiority to the men in the play. She need not resort to bullying as Ann Whitefield often does, because she can "get round" everyone and control the situation. Ridgeon's punishment is almost a by-blow of her primary goal, which is to satisfy her own personal destiny as guardian of her husband's genius and reputation.

Even minor Shavian women have some sphinx attributes, and they are not necessarily limited to the young or the sexually ensnaring female. Henry Higgins's mother, in *Pygmalion*, sees truths that her brilliant and eccentric son is incapable of recognizing. Mrs. Higgins is quick to see that Eliza, even after she is made over into respectability by Henry, is not "presentable." This observation is not owing merely to a more finely developed social sense but to an intuitiveness denied to most men, however clever. Mrs. Higgins calls Henry and Colonel Pickering "two infinitely stupid male creatures," not without cause. They know everything, but understand nothing. They are babies when it comes to human affairs, and like many of Henry James's men, they regard women as commodities. It will be remembered that when James's sphinx, May Bartram, is utilized as a commodity by the weakling John Marcher, she exacts a terrible vengeance through a conscious withdrawal of her commodity into death, taking her secret sphinxlike with her. But Shaw is not James, and his solutions are more often comic than tragic. Besides, Eliza Doolittle is no sphinx. Henry's housekeeper, Mrs. Pierce, is better qualified for her role than is Eliza. In a flash of recognition, she tells her employer, "You dont think, Sir," and of course she is right. Her intuition is shrewd and accurate, establishing that it is not necessary to be clever, or educated, or even well-bred to possess that extra dimension.

In support of the foregoing suspension of criteria for sphinxhood, one draws inevitably on the *echt* sphinx of the Shavian canon, Mrs. George of *Getting Married*. Mrs. George is middle-aged, lower class, uneducated and unpretty. Still, Shaw draws her in bold large strokes, describing her countenance as "an ageless landscape ravaged by long and fierce war," and her face as "a battle-field of the passions." Because of the grand scale in which she is drawn, she suggests immortality. Further, Shaw endows her with mythological qualities reminiscent of the fearsome Sophoclean daimon. The youthful and importunate St. John Hotchkiss refers to her variously as "harpy, siren, mermaid, and vampire." Like little Ellie Dunn, she is a "fiend in human form," causing St. John to feel he must flee from her mesmeric powers because he is bewitched by her. At the height of his frenzy of fascination and fear, he charges her: "Your name is Ashtoreth—Durga—there is no name yet invented malign enough for you." Responding to the same hypnotic force which affected Caesar as he stood beneath the sphinx in the moonlight, and Boss Mangan as he struggled under Ellie's paralyzing spell, Hotchkiss complains: "Something stronger than my reason and common sense is holding my hands and tearing me along. I make no attempt to deny that it can drag me where you please and make me do what you like." Her superior powers exempt her from conventional morality as they do Candida, who would give herself to Eugene as readily as she would give her shawl to a beggar. Having divine virtue and wisdom, Mrs. George, like Caesar, has no need of mere goodness or decorum. Through her supernatural second sight she qualifies as a genuine divinity. In her visionary trance, she utters supernal truth about the female mystique: "When you loved me I gave you the whole sun and the stars to play with. I gave you eternity in a single moment, strength of the mountains in one clasp of your arms, and the volume of all the seas in one impulse of your souls." Mere mortals who surround her and cannot attain her empyrean are puzzled. They speculate that her effusion is variously the "ecstasy of a saint," the "convulsion of the pythoness on the tripod," and "possession by the devil." We know better. Classless, ageless, enigmatic, she incorporates the unuttered accumulated wisdom of female force and experience. Neither a slave to her passions nor a monument to respectability, she transcends the limitations of goals and achievements which are purely human. Along with Candida, Hesione and the Caesar of the female principle, she eschews human happiness as a worthy life goal. She appears to be a fulfillment of Shaw's own philosophical dictum, which he explained in a letter to one of his "disciples," Eva Christy: "Happiness is not the object of life; life has no object: it is an end in itself; and courage consists in the readiness to sacrifice happiness to an intenser quality of life" (p. 203). Mrs. George personifies that intenser quality, and, even more to the point, in Shaw's own words, "the entire female sex crying to the ages from her lips" (p. 786).

There is no precise measure of the influence which Egyptian and Greek mythology and symbolism had upon Shaw's female characterizations. It is true that he visited Egypt, but that was late in his life. It is also true that he had a long friendship and correspondence with Gilbert Murray, the classical scholar, upon whose knowledge of Greek Shaw drew on occasion.[7] How much the Greek "daimon" or Egyptian divinity affected his conscious conception of women's character is not known. It is safe to say, however, that his absorption with the enigmatic personality of the female is reflected in some of his superior women, and reveals at least a coincidence with, if not a pervasive indebtedness to, the sphinx. For the sphinx embodied those qualities which he found most admirable in his most formidable and affectionately drawn women: powerful vitality, freedom from restrictive convention, instinctive guarded intelligence, and unequivocal authority. In lesser or greater degree, these are the components of women such as Candida, Hesione, Mrs. George, and all the other permutations of the Shavian sphinx.

Notes

1. In Greek mythology, the term "daimon" or "daemon" had two significances: (1) a supernatural agent or intelligence, lower in rank than a god, such as the Corybantes, Erinyes, and Satyrs; (2) a ministering spirit, which was generally considered by the Greeks to be a protective agent. The original "daimon" in the Greek *Oedipus* trilogy by Sophocles is variously translated as "sphinx" by some, and, in William Butler Yeats's translation, as "unearthly power." The specific passage in which the word "daimon" appears occurs in the last episode, when the horrified chorus asks the blinded Oedipus: "What daimon (unearthly power) has caused you to put out your eyes?"

2. Harriet Martineau, *Eastern Life, Present and Past* (1846).

3. *Collected Letters 1898-1910*, p. 99.

4. *Vide* the scene in which Cleopatra, having been instructed by Caesar in the handling of underlings, treats her serving women, Iris and Charmian, with some detachment and magnanimity, and thereby earns their scorn.

5. Letter to Augustin Hamon, dated February 1911, from Hofstra University's Special Collection. By special permission.

6. *Collected Letters 1898-1910*, pp. 414-15. Further references to this edition appear within the text in parenthesis.

7. For a detailed analysis of Shaw's indebtedness to Murray, see Sidney P. Albert, "Major Barbara's Debt to Gilbert Murray," *Educational Theatre Journal* 20 (May 1968), 123-40.

ELIZA'S CHOICE:
TRANSFORMATION MYTH AND
THE ENDING OF *PYGMALION*

Timothy G. Vesonder

In writing *Pygmalion*, Shaw borrowed and adapted many myths which led, rather inevitably, to confusion over the last moments of the play. Unable to identify the controlling mythic pattern, actors as well as audiences were unprepared for and unsatisfied with the feminist thrust of Eliza's decision to leave Higgins. The first as well as the most influential of the misled was Beerbohm Tree, the Henry Higgins of the play's London premiere. Tree ignored Shaw's instructions and at the end of every performance threw flowers to Mrs. Patrick Campbell (Eliza Doolittle), suggesting a romantic attachment that would end in marriage. When Shaw complained, the actor wrote to him: "My ending makes money: you ought to be grateful." Shaw countered: "Your ending is damnable: you ought to be shot."[1]

Generally, audiences preferred the more romantic ending of Tree's interpretation; and Shaw could not convert them from this error even with his prose epilogue, which he published in 1915 to prove that Eliza married Freddy and remained only a friend to Higgins. In 1938, ignoring both the epilogue and Shaw's film script, Gabriel Pascal gave movie audiences an ending similar to Tree's, in that a seemingly docile Eliza returned to Higgins.[2] Shaw had died before the production of the musical adaptation of the play, *My Fair Lady*, but even had he been alive, it is unlikely that he could have changed the then familiar romantic finale. Actors, audiences and producers were joined by many critics who also favored the revised ending. In a recent book on Shaw's work, Maurice Valency even argued that Eliza and Higgins would make an ideal couple, and that the Shaw ending is dramatically unsatisfying and unacceptable.[3]

Rarely has an author's intention been so ignored or a classic work so mistreated. However unfortunate, the misinterpretations of *Pygmalion* are understandable when we recognize that the confusion comes largely from the conflicting myths which Shaw used in the play. The most obvious mythic source is underlined by the title. Henry Higgins's re-creation of Eliza Doolittle parallels many details of the Greek myth in which an artist, Pygmalion, disenchanted with the women around him, sculpts a statue of his ideal woman. The artist falls in love with his creation and prays to Aphrodite to give his ivory maiden life. When the lover's plea is answered, Pygmalion marries his creation. Along with the Greek myth, Shaw's *Pygmalion* also contains many elements of the Cinderella folk tale. Just as the poor and mistreated Cinderella becomes a princess through the intervention of her fairy godmother, Shaw's flower girl is elevated briefly into the aristocracy and permanently into the middle class.

A crucial difference between these stories and Shaw's play is that Eliza does not marry Henry Higgins at the end of the play, nor does she continue to live with him as servant, secretary, and protegée, the roles Higgins wants her to play. In the last scene, Eliza announces that she wants more out of life than the companionship Higgins offers her, and she threatens to marry Freddy Hill. Remembering, at least subconsciously, that the Pygmalion myth and the Cinderella folk tale end in the marriage of the principal characters, audiences expect Shaw to end his play similarly.

Despite the expectations of its audiences, Shaw's intention for the ending of *Pygmalion* is quite clear. Historically, Shaw's argument with Tree, his epilogue and his movie script solidly confirm his original ending. Textually, no line or stage direction even remotely suggests that Eliza will choose Higgins over Freddy. Realistically, as Shaw explains in the epilogue, Eliza cannot marry Higgins. True, they are both very charming, very bright and very strong characters who engage our affection and admiration; and the matchmaking part in all of us wants to see these two likeable personalities joined in lasting connubial bliss. But common sense should tell us otherwise. Higgins, after all, is a confirmed bachelor who can love only one woman, his mother; but even mother and son find life under the same roof—if for only a few hours at a time—intolerable. Higgins wants his independence and his work; Eliza wants her independence and affection. A compromise between these strong characters is as unlikely as it is undesirable.

Dramatically, *Pygmalion* repeats patterns and techniques that Shaw used consistently in his earlier plays. He delighted in irony, especially in denying audience expectations by inverting material. A Pygmalion who does not marry his creation is a rather mild departure from the expected, compared to many previous Shavian ironies, such as a hero who retreats, a minister who turns revolutionary, a world conqueror who abhors violence, a Don Juan who is pursued by a woman, and a doctor who kills. Eliza also is typical of many of Shaw's female characters. By leaving Higgins, she joins a long line of Shaw women who reject marriage to likely candidates. As early as 1893 in *The Philanderer*, Grace Cuthbertson refused to marry Leonard Charteris simply because she would not marry a man she loved. In other plays, Candida rejects Marchbanks for the more prosaic Morell, Jennifer Dubedat scorns Dr. Ridgeon, and in perhaps the closest parallel to the Eliza-Freddy-Higgins triangle, Cleopatra chooses a younger Antony to the more heroic Caesar. An audience that remembers these independent women will not be surprised when Eliza leaves Higgins for Freddy. Moreover, the many Shavian women who avoid marriage altogether help to explain Higgins's bachelorhood. Women such as Vivie Warren, Cicely Waynflete, Lina Szczepanowska, Lavinia and the later Joan, like Higgins, have important work that does not permit the luxury of marriage. These dynamic characters could well support their anti-marital stands in the words of Lavinia, who says: "Marriage is the sacrifice of the adventurous attitude towards life: the being settled. Those who are born tired may crave for settlement: but to fresher and stronger spirits it is a form of suicide."

Despite the strength of these arguments, many still wishfully push Higgins and Eliza toward marriage, and in so doing they are imposing the conventions of archetypal comedy on the structure of *Pygmalion*. In the archetypal comic plot, blocking characters and obstacles are overcome by the lovers, whose marriage at the end of the play signals the reconciliation and renewal of their society.[4] Although this comic convention enjoys great popular appeal, it is wrong to apply it to a Shaw play which does not show a man and a woman hurdling obstacle after obstacle to land finally in each other's arms. Such is the case in *Arms and the Man* and *You Never Can Tell*, but in *Pygmalion* the two marriages that do figure in the closing scene are incidental and not important in themselves.

To find the mythic model for *Pygmalion* we must look beyond the conventions of comedy with its devices of trickery, deceit and coincidence to the conventions of archetypal romance. The structure of this archetype is built around the hero, the possessor of great power which he attains from his semidivine birth or from divine favor. With this great power the hero performs wondrous deeds, defeats evil forces and thereby insures the well-being of his society.

Even a superficial examination of *Pygmalion* will show that the main focus of the play is not erotic involvement but the power of language and that Henry Higgins is much more the hero than the lover. Shaw's story, simply stated, portrays an expert linguist who accepts a challenge to re-create a poor, uneducated young woman by teaching her how to speak properly. Linguistic knowledge and skills are the great weapons which Higgins uses to defeat evil and improve society. When he first meets Eliza, he notes that her kerbstone English will keep her in the gutter. She is in the clutches of the monster of poverty, which was to Shaw the greatest modern demon. Higgins cannot kill this monster, but he can use his powers to free Eliza from its grip. Just as the classical hero received help from gods, friends and benevolent spirits, the Shavian hero receives necessary assistance from his mother and from Colonel Pickering. Higgins supplies the technical skill and the discipline, but his assistants give Eliza the necessary qualities of common sense and humanity.

Even if we see *Pygmalion* in the pattern of archetypal romance, the problem with the ending remains, for the hero often receives a woman as the reward of his labors at the culmination of his quest.[5] Just as Perseus has his Andromeda and Sigurd his Brynhild, it is mythically consistent that Higgins should have his Eliza. Their marriage, however, is not a necessity, for in myth celibacy also has its models in many gods, the forerunners of the heroes, who do not take mates. Often those divinities most involved in the lives of men, such as Athena, Artemis, Apollo and Dionysus, avoid marriage to devote themselves to their missions. Recalling the stories of Theseus and Ariadne and of Aeneas and Dido, we can see that even heroes do not always leap into marriage with the first likely candidate.

Apart from these mythic precedents, we can understand and defend the changes Shaw makes in the archetypal romance if we acknowledge the theory of displacement, which holds that a writer will make changes in a myth to make his story more realistic, more credible to his audience.[6] Thus, Higgins does not go on a long and perilous journey looking for monsters to kill; nor does he have a magic sword or shield or a protecting deity hovering over him. As a displaced hero, Higgins is devoted to science, which is a modern quest to improve life, to rid the world of weakness and evil. His powerful weapon is his linguisitic expertise, which he uses in his quest to make earth a little more like heaven, "where there are no third-class carriages, and one soul is as good as another," where all men are treated equally. In his quest the modern hero does not always want or need the fulfillment of marriage, and the modern maiden, more independent than her classical counterparts, may ignore the savior whose ideals she does not share. In the mythic retelling, then, Eliza may leave Higgins and marry Freddy, and Higgins, having freed his Andromeda from a living death, can move on to further adventures.

The most satisfying mythic understanding of the Shaw ending does not come from an examination of Higgins as hero or of *Pygmalion* as romance. Although the play is the story of a modern hero with modern powers, it is likewise the story of the effect of these powers, a story not only of liberation but also of transformation.

Eliza begins the play as a poor flower girl who is ignored by Freddy Hill and family and is easily intimidated by Higgins. With much work and the help of Higgins and company she begins to change. Her success at the Embassy Ball marks one stage in her growth, but it is hardly the climax or the great victory that the film-makers would have us believe. It is after the ball that Eliza shows her new powers: she has charm enough to keep a man, who in Act I never noticed her, at a constant vigil near her doorstep, and she has money enough to secure a cab to drive about in all night, an experience that was impossible for the flower girl. Most importantly, Eliza shows her new strength and independence when she walks out on Higgins, a decision that she confirms in the final scene. Here Eliza explains to Higgins that she doesn't want to live in his house and be treated as a maid or a personal secretary. She doesn't want to be treated as an equal, as "one of the boys," the way Higgins treats everyone he respects. She has no interest in the "higher life." Eliza does want "a little kindness," the simple love and affection that a Freddy Hill can supply. This revelation upsets Higgins, who tries to bully Eliza into submission. At this point, the real climax of the play, Eliza shows that she is no longer the flower girl who was tempted by chocolates or intimidated by threats. Announcing that she is as good as he is, that she has her own dreams and ideals, Eliza firmly establishes her independence. Higgins himself is forced to admit that she can make it without him and that he will miss her. He is forced to admit that she is finally a total person—her transformation is complete.

That the last act of *Pygmalion* does not emphasize marriage is reinforced by the reappearance of Alfred Doolittle. The dustman too has been transformed with the help of Higgins. The poor worker with few obligations has become the middle-class lecturer with many responsibilities. His impending marriage, unimportant in itself, is another indication of the drastic change in his life style. Doolittle himself is basically the same character: his change is largely economic. In contrast, Eliza's change is largely spiritual: she is a new person inside and out.

The transformations we see in the last act of *Pygmalion* are a basic mythic motif. An obvious and predominant pattern in Ovid's *Metamorphoses*, transformations occur so often in myths and in folk tales that they seem to be a basic exercise of man's imaginative powers. In trying to explain this common theme, Northrop Frye suggests that man, by virtue of his imagination, can gain some control over a world which is alien and often hostile.[7] In his imagination man can re-create the world or at least understand its mysteries, which is another form of control. He can change the sun into a god, a god into a man, or a man into a constellation. He can change a statue into a living woman, a poor girl into a princess, and a flower girl into a "consort battleship." The core of the Pygmalion myth and of the Cinderella folk tale is the transformation, not the marriage: while Shaw does not use his sources as a prescription for his plot, he does preserve the fundamental pattern common to both stories. In this sense, he does not invert the myths so much as he retells them.

From this perspective we can understand why Shaw would be so concerned by the productions which hinted at a deeper attachment between Eliza and Higgins. If Eliza remains with Higgins, in mythic terms, the hero would receive his reward, and Eliza would have to submit herself to her savior. This, in fact, was probably the ideal that animated many of those who wanted Eliza to remain with Higgins: the submissive woman, fetching slippers and managing the household, while the eccentric hero tends to higher affairs. What these revisionists failed to see is that in their ending Eliza only would trade masters—poverty and vulgarity for Higgins—and her own transformation would not be as deep or as dramatic.

In effect, the popular interpretation changes the focus of the ending: it elevates Higgins and reduces Eliza; it emphasizes the hero over his work, the transformer over the transformation, one myth over another. On the other hand, when we recognize the play as a retelling of an archetypal transformation, we can see that Shaw gave the first part of the play to Higgins but reserved the last for Eliza. She was not to be a reward for the hero, slipper-fetcher and house manager. The flower girl was changed into a strong and independent woman—a woman equal to the hero. Joining the ranks of the other strong female characters such as Vivie Warren, Candida Morell, Ann

Whitefield, Barbara Undershaft and Lina Szczepanowska, Eliza Doolittle stands up to Higgins and thus takes an active role in deciding her own destiny. Although we may respect and applaud Higgins's powers, in the end the triumph is Eliza's, and the greatest applause should be reserved for the new woman, Shaw's modern Galatea and twentieth-century Cinderella.

Notes

1. Hesketh Pearson, *Beerbohm Tree: His Life and Laughter* (1956), p. 182.

2. Cf. Bernard F. Dukore, "'The Middleaged Bully and the Girl of Eighteen': The Ending They Didn't Film," *Shaw Review* 14 (1971), 102–6.

3. Maurice Valency, *The Cart and the Trumpet: The Plays of George Bernard Shaw* (1973), pp. 316–22. For a brief review of criticism on both sides of the debate over the ending, cf. Charles A. Berst, *Bernard Shaw and the Art of Drama* (1973), pp. 196–97, fn. 1.

4. For a more detailed treatment of archetypal comedy, cf. Northrop Frye, *Anatomy of Criticism: Four Essays* (1957), pp. 163–86.

5. Cf. Frye, *Anatomy of Criticism*, p. 193.

6. Cf. Northrop Frye, "Myth, Fiction, and Displacement," *Daedalus* (Summer 1961), reprinted in *Fables of Identity: Studies in Poetic Mythology* (1963), pp. 21–38.

7. Cf. Northrop Frye, "The Motive For Metaphor," *The Educated Imagination* (1964), pp. 13–33.

ANN AND SUPERMAN: TYPE AND ARCHETYPE

Sally Peters Vogt

Despite the voluminous criticism devoted to *Man and Superman*, Ann Whitefield, Shaw's most persuasively feminine heroine, continues to be an enigma. Most critics would agree with Arthur H. Nethercot that Ann is Shaw's "prototype of predatory females,"[1] but assessments of her specific role vary. Thus Barbara Bellow Watson celebrates Ann's vitality and originality; Margery M. Morgan denounces her calculating conventionality; and Elsie Adams finds that Ann is merely "a composite of traditional types" of heroines.[2] Nor is this surprising, since within the play itself Ann appears in many guises, so that her fellow *dramatis personae* perceive her from their own narrowly circumscribed perspectives. But while the characters' restricted views of Ann provide a major source of the comedy, a coherent assessment of her role requires a broader viewpoint that will discern the genesis of apparent discrepancies in her characterization.

Curiously, the implicitly mythic nature underlying much of the dramatic action has been largely ignored, although a number of studies have focused on the relation between the Don Juan legend and the play.[3] Yet Shaw's use of both the Don Juan legend and his philosophy of Creative Evolution is an ordering of once powerful mythic patterns that, even though now attenuated, continue to survive and function in the modern world. Once the presence and function of these mythic patterns are revealed, Ann's role will be clarified. It will then be possible to assess the ways in which Ann is a typical, and not so typical, Victorian heroine, and the ways in which her role demands archetypal formulation. Since Ann's characterization suspends from mythic elements, this dimension of *Man and Superman* will be explored in an effort to uncover the ultimate face behind Ann's many masks. While all four acts of the play will be considered, it is in the crucial third act that mythic elements are most clearly discernible.

That Shaw was aware of and sympathetic to the possibilities of myth is evident from both his admiration of Wagner and his symbolic reading of *The Ring* in *The Perfect Wagnerite*, a reading that supports Shaw's own evolutionary view.[4] Underlying this affinity to myth is Shaw's essentially religious nature, which manifested itself in his lifelong evangelicalism. Shaw's devotion to his own particular view, however, did not prevent him from recognizing basic similarities between diverse phenomena that function as hierophanies, that is, to reveal what is "sacred" to the believer. In the preface to the *Plays Pleasant* he can thus assert of the times:

> Religion was alive again, coming back upon men, even upon clergymen, with such power that not the Church of England itself could keep it out. Here my activity as a Socialist had placed me on sure and familiar ground. To me the members of the Guild of St Matthew were no more "High Church clergymen," Dr Clifford no more "an eminent Nonconformist divine," than I was to them "an infidel." There is only one religion, though there are a hundred versions of it. We all had the same thing to say; and though some of us cleared our throats to say it by singing revolutionary lyrics and republican hymns, we thought nothing of singing them to the music of Sullivan's Onward Christian Soldiers or Haydn's God Preserve the Emperor.

A hundred versions of one religion—this is the view of the comparative religionist and the cultural anthropologist. Shaw's version emerges in the harmonies of Creative Evolution scored for both virtuoso performance and background music in *Man and Superman*. Inquiry into this implicitly mythic and religious play can be enriched by a widening of critical perspective, so that our range of vision more closely approximates Shaw's. Consequently, in order to reevaluate Ann, the mythic dimension of the play will be explored, using the insights of scholars who approach myth from the viewpoints of the history of religions (Mircea Eliade), anthropology (Joseph Campbell), psychology (Carl G. Jung), symbolism (J.E. Cirlot) and literary criticism (Northrop Frye). In addition, these insights will facilitate a wider frame of reference in describing certain formal properties of the play.

It is noteworthy at the outset that the action of *Man and Superman* is located in two different structures: the immediately apparent dramatic surface reveals the familiar action of comic romance, with its stereotypic pursuing and pursued characters; this in turn derives from a conceptual deep structure, mythic in both content and origin, whose forward thrust directs the surface action. The two structures, therefore, do not merely coexist; they are hierarchically related, with the second grounding the first. But the specific relationships between the two are by no means self-evident. In fact, it is precisely the reduction and deletion of much of the overtly mythic material in three of the four acts that has led to the apparently anomalous surface form of the play. Thus, in Acts I, II and IV, the romantic comedy of Ann's pursuit of John Tanner is so much to the fore that the mythic deep structure appears to be, if not entirely eliminated, then at least largely submerged. Conversely, in the crucial third act, the formerly latent deep structure surfaces with almost startling clarity, while the action of the romantic comedy is held in abeyance. Both these structures must be understood and explicitly correlated, if Ann is to emerge in her totality, and if the pattern behind the woman-dominated, woman-motivated dramatic action is to be clearly perceived.

Before the underlying mythic pattern and Ann's place in this pattern can be revealed, however, we must first examine the familiar surface structure. Female domination of the male is one of the most obvious characteristics of the surface structure,[5] a truly remarkable paradox since the women have no outlet for their energies outside their narrowly and traditionally defined social and biological roles. Biology is indeed destiny in the not always comic world of Ann Whitefield and Violet Robinson. Nevertheless, within the confines of their roles, these women exert a powerful, though always decorous force. The consequence is remarkable: *the men are defined through their relationships with women.* Thus, despite Tanner's protests against marriage and his pretensions to being a utopian philosopher, we view him as a frightened male fleeing from Ann. Similarly, Roebuck Ramsden may be a *"president of highly respectable men,"* as the stage directions inform us, but we see only what Ann calls "Annie's Granny," a pompous and ineffectual man. Just as Ramsden is rendered powerless by his myopic view of Ann, so the aspiring poet Octavius is paralyzed by a romanticized conception of Ann, which pervades all his speeches and actions.

But Ann is not the only strong woman in the play. Both Hector Malone, Sr., and his son are dominated by Violet's desire to have money as well as marriage—Malone Jr. at the outset; Malone Sr. finally. Nor, as we discover in the dream frame, must the women necessarily be present to shape their men's lives. Unrequited love for the absent Louisa has made a mountain brigand out of the urbane waiter Mendoza. Romantic longing impels Mendoza to reveal his love to the supremely rational Henry Straker. As the long arm of comic coincidence would have it, Straker is Louisa's brother, and Mendoza's news strips him of rationality, goading him into an emotional reaction at odds with his scientific outlook. In hell, of course, what we already know of Don Juan, and what we will know, centers on his former susceptibility to and present disdain of feminine charms.

Since women exercise such powerful role-defining influence, it is perfectly consistent that the surface structure of the comedy charts Tanner's reactions to women in great detail. In one sense, woman-initiated thought or action is responsible for all the actions, physical and discursive, of Tanner and Don Juan. Thus the entire first act shows Tanner in a series of reactions, first to Ann's insistence on retaining him as her guardian, second in his embarrassing defense of Violet, and finally in his confession to Ann of "the birth in [him] of moral passion." Tanner, in his reactive role, has much in common with the passive hero of melodrama. The stupid conventionalism of the melodramatic hero becomes, paradoxically, converted in Tanner into the opaque brilliance of a would-be revolutionist uttering panegyrics on the Life Force.

Act II shows Ann adroitly manipulating Tanner, who, in response, leaps into *"a sociological rage,"* only to be neatly deflated. Not yet daunted, Tanner replies with the outrageous challenge that Ann race across Europe with him; she stuns him by accepting. Once he learns from Straker of Ann's matrimonial inclinations, Tanner is forced into a frantic dash from her in hopes of preserving his single state. But Ann successfully pursues him into the Sierra Nevadas; even while yelling "Caught!" he continues to react against the idea of marriage, not verbally acquiescing until the very end of Act IV. Still he valiantly tries to persuade himself and his auditors that he is in command of the hour, precisely, though fruitlessly, outlining his spartan terms for the marriage ceremony and its accoutrements. Unruffled, Ann assures him that he should "go on talking," to which Tanner can only indignantly sputter "Talking!"—his final reaction to Ann and, fittingly, the final speech of *Man and Superman.*

It is obvious, therefore, that in the surface structure of the romantic comedy, women not only influence but actually control the action. Though stoutly fending off marriage until the very end of the play, Tanner speaks of the inevitability of his reaction by alluding, in Schopenhauerian terms, to the intangible force that directs men's lives: "We do the world's will, not our own." Thus Tanner's reactions culminate in his engagement to Ann because, as he so deterministically puts it, "It is the world's will that [Ann] should have a husband."

Just as the surface structure of the romantic comedy is a comic inversion of the pursuit of the heroine by the hero, so the dramatically slender surface of the dream symposium revolves around the comic inversion of the Don Juan theme. Don Juan, the arch libertine, becomes the pursued prey who seeks only a meditative respite from the rigors of ever-pursuing, ever-amorous women. Because of a duel over a woman Don Juan is in hell, and even there Woman continues to direct his destiny, a result of having on earth "interpreted all the other teaching" for him, consequently revealing the extent of his susceptibility to irrational life. Thus, in a perverse parody of Descartes's *cogito ergo sum*, he confesses, "It was Woman who taught me to say 'I am; therefore I think.' And also 'I would think more; therefore I must be more.' "

On one level, then, the play seems to exist merely to dramatize Shaw's joke about women who pursue. Much of the humor of the joke lies in Shaw's manipulation of conventional melodramatic roles. As an example of type, Ann resembles the heroine less than she does the siren of melodrama, but high passion has been channeled into its single respectable course, which leads—however lively the wooing—to marriage. Part of the waywardness Ann radiates can therefore be attributed to the tension resulting from the intertwining of two radically different melodramatic types: the intriguing siren and the forever chaste heroine. Consequently, Ann appears fascinating to those who admire energetic clever women, or hypocritical to those who are shocked by the covert operation of the marriage trap.

An analysis of the deep structure of the play, however, eliminates the need for such either/or judgments, since it becomes apparent that the complexities engendered by Ann's multiple guises are grounded in her universal-mythic role. This role may at first be difficult to discern, for the play's cosmic focus has been blurred by the use of the traditional, albeit inverted, romantic comedy. The action of the romantic comedy stems, nevertheless, from a mythic base. Ironically, the dialectical structure of the dream symposium (heaven versus hell, reality versus illusion, optimism versus pessimism) has had a similar obscurantist function: first because of its ambiguous relationship to the rest of the play; second because its brilliant rhetoric attracts attention to *lexis*, not *praxis*, verbal meaning seemingly overwhelming any function as action this rhetoric might serve. Shaw's brilliant display in the dream symposium is not mere pyrotechnics, however, but is rooted in a fundamental mythic rhythm. The organizing rhythm of dialectic is, as Frye has shown, as basic a unifying pattern as the cyclical rhythm customarily encountered in mythic works.[6] Thus the major phases of human experience revealed by the action—birth and death, initiation and marriage—are set against the moral dialectic which pits the affirmative Life Force against the negating ignorance and vice of the world. And since unending dialectic is but another name for process, and since process is the essence of Creative Evolution, Shaw constantly suggests his theory through his method.

But even though the third act is dialectically structured, the cyclical nature of the whole of human history is explicitly suggested by the Devil and assented to by Don Juan: "An epoch is but a swing of the pendulum; and each generation thinks the world is progressing because it is always moving." And in Tanner's view, what has so far been applauded in history is just "goose-cackle about Progress." This tendency toward cyclical rhythm is evident in the play as a whole, but it is strongly counterbalanced by dialectical rhythm, especially in the dream symposium, which reveals the mythic deep structure most forcefully. In contrast, the surface realism of the other three acts—where the action is more cyclically oriented—conceals the play's mythic nature through the addition of specific incidents, psychologically plausible motivations and a setting in the very mundane world of Victorian England. Shaw's real joke, therefore, is that he has indeed given the world a Don Juan *play*, not merely a Don Juan *scene*.

In the dream symposium in hell, Shaw presents a void peopled with incorporeal characters. This conscious movement away from the particulars of a given scene is a method of universalizing, since the action is abstracted from concrete time and place, thereby creating a zone in which action becomes ceremony, and actors, archetypes. Instead of Tanner, Ann, Mendoza and Ramsden, Ann's guardian, we find hero, goddess, the Devil and Holdfast, the guardian of the status quo. Hell, with its ease of access to both heaven and earth, becomes, in effect, Shaw's satiric version of a sacred center of the universe. Using ritual techniques, Shaw expresses the philosophy of Creative Evolution, which becomes inclusive in that the major planes of experience are accounted for—the biological, the spiritual and the psychological. The hope for a superman is but another of the messianic visions that characterize many religions and which, like Creative Evolution, look forward to future generations. This belief in a messiah can also be correlated with Shaw's socialistic fervor since, as Eliade points out, "at the end of the Marxist philosophy of history lies the age of gold of the archaic eschatologies."[7]

The age of gold Shaw envisions is possible only through evolution in a future time suggested by the play but not encompassed by the action. Thus, in order to make Creative Evolution dramatically viable, Shaw uses the Don Juan legend as his pre-eminent vehicle. Frequently occurring in musical and literary treatment, the legend has been raised to the level of myth through its reappearance apart from any historical context. Though our popular culture bears witness to the degeneration of many mythic patterns, these same patterns may revivify and function creatively for man. The changing character of Don Juan in treatments subsequent to Tirso de Molina's *El Burlador de Seville* attests to the vigor of this myth. The reason for this vigor is clear, for the myth expresses man's perennial longing for an earthly paradise. But the mundane form of the Don Juan myth does not disguise its similarity to Shaw's myth of Creative Evolution, which also has an earthly paradise as goal. Both Creative Evolution and the Don Juan myth express the same basic human desires, differ though they may in form and level of spirituality. In addition, the appropriateness of the Don Juan myth to Shaw's dramatic needs lies in its protean nature, evidenced in the multiple transformations undergone by the Don Juan figure in succeeding works of art. More important than the specific transformations the unfolding legend provides is the very fact of change itself. Thematically, the fluid Don Juan myth becomes a favorable milieu for Creative Evolution: the evolving form of the sexually based Don Juan myth becomes intimately associated with Shaw's evolutionary myth, which depends on the power of sexual energy for its ultimate triumph. Consequently, the legend—which Shaw alluded to in his first novel through the hero Don Juan Lothario Smith, and later in the short story "Don Giovanni Explains" through the ghost of Don Juan—becomes in *Man and Superman* the vehicle through which Shaw communicates his cosmic philosophy. And the Don Juan character, which has evolved and will evolve in yet uncreated works of art, becomes the logical complement to the elusive and variable Ann.

Against this mythic background, the woman-dominated action becomes at once more comic and also more necessary. It is more comic because, though the frivolity masks the profundity, the cosmic nature of Ann's very mortal quest calls forth the indulgent laughter of the kind that concludes the play. We look at the surface structure and witness, amused, a moral, unmarried woman, afraid to flout convention openly, yet determined to usurp the male prerogatives of choice, chase and capture. Ann's far from original actions place her in a long line of heroines from Shakespeare's Rosalind, as Shaw acknowledges in the Epistle Dedicatory, to Tennessee Williams's Maggie the Cat—women who *will* have their way. Ann's typicality, however, in no way supplants her archetypicality, which is based on the structural simplicity and range of her universal role. But the typicality of her modern role suggests that the role has undergone degeneration, thereby setting up an unrelieved comic tension in the play. Oblivious to this incongruity, Ann plays out her attenuated modern role against the awesome background her mythic precursors have erected.

The mythic background also makes the woman-dominated action more necessary, because the movement of the Life Force toward a more highly evolved human being requires the active participation of the female in capturing the male. If it is to serve Shaw's philosophical purpose, the Don Juan myth *must* be inverted. Of course, the inversion is apparent in both the romantic comedy and the dream symposium. Tanner's participation in a pattern that exactly imitates the acts of his ancestor thus endows with a ritualistic character his simultaneous fascination with and flight from Ann, while the act of repetition makes Tanner a contemporary of Don Juan in mythic terms.

Given this need for active women and, as a consequence, relatively passive men, Shaw's strict observance of the traditional man-woman/mind-body dichotomy is itself an inversion, since that dichotomy assumes the passivity of women and their corresponding domination by men. In examining this traditional phenomenon, J.C. Flugel observes that "there exists a very general association between the notion of mind, spirit or soul, and the idea of the father or of masculinity; and on the other hand between the notion of body or of matter (materia—that which belongs to the mother) and the idea of the mother or of the feminine principle."[8] In general, the Victorians believed that women were passive. Faith in Woman's essential passivity encouraged Victorian men to relegate spiritual and moral concerns to her, thereby freeing the men to assume their aggressive and superior roles as captains of industry.

Shaw ignores this contemporary division in male-female roles in favor of the ahistorical view so vehemently asserted by Nietzsche. Nietzsche's simplistic avowal that "everything in woman hath a solution—it is called pregnancy,"[9] however, is modified by Shaw's Schopenhauerian belief in will. Ann, heir to this will, is consequently endowed with certain aggressive tendencies popularly thought to be masculine. But, psychologically, this is not necessarily so, according to the twentieth-century symbolist J.E. Cirlot, who believes that Western man is currently "dominated by the feminine principle."[10] Thus, in her unrelenting desire to have her way, Ann, the representative of the feminine principle, is the antithesis of the fondly held Victorian view of Woman martyred upon the wishes and demands of others. Yet Ann's willingness to sacrifice her life for her maternal duty delineates ultimately an emotional similarity to the most docile Victorian wife. The means may differ; the end is the same. And what we see is Ann's manipulation of the means available to her, a trait that marks her as an unmistakably Shavian character. Through this manipulation Ann emerges supreme in a way Tanner does not even approximate, since her instincts transcend her limited awareness, while Tanner's intellect is by definition inferior to that of the evolving superman and by nature less forceful than Ann's will.

Although she lacks the higher intellect the superman will supposedly possess, Ann is more than an instrument of the Life Force, for she becomes identified with the essence of Creative Evolution itself. Her elusive nature, ever-changing, ever-various, is symbolic of the unending process involved in Creative Evolution. Such a process defies easy definition. Therefore the characters around her are able to discriminate only those qualities they most desire in a woman or expect to see. To Ramsden she is an inexperienced young woman; to Tanner she is a predatory animal; to Octavius she is a romanticized Earth Mother. These views of Ann all rely on the conception of Woman implicit in the mythic deep structure, making increasingly apparent the truth of Shaw's seeming jest in the Epistle Dedicatory: "every woman is not Ann; but Ann is Everywoman."

Ironically, it is Octavius's view of Ann that synthesizes these qualities and most directly refers to a mythic origin: "*To Octavius* [the stage directions assert] *she is an enchantingly beautiful woman in whose presence the world becomes transfigured, and the puny limits of individual consciousness are suddenly made infinite by the mystic memory of the whole life of the race to its beginning in the east, or even back to the paradise from which it fell.*" The effete Octavius, because of his excessively romantic disposition an object of Shaw's satire and Tanner's pity, becomes a vehicle through which Shaw playfully incorporates mythic motifs; simultaneously, Shaw delights in Tanner's own romantically charged view of himself as *raisonneur* and Life Force advocate. The real humor is that Tanner, who warns Octavius of Ann, is ultimately vanquished by his own romantic temperament. When he recognizes imminent defeat, Tanner characteristically rationalizes his predicament by attributing to the Life Force his personal desires, and "renounc[ing] the romantic possibilities of an unknown future."

Plagued as he is by chronic pragmatic astigmatism, Tanner's perception of Ann can only be partial, and therefore distorted. Octavius's view is also distorted, as long as it is limited to the transfiguring enchantment of a beautiful woman, but the implications of his view are far richer. Paradoxically, the illusion-blinded Octavius sees more of the total configurative pattern surrounding Ann than Tanner, who prides himself on his perception of the order of things. This pattern, which is not perceived in its totality by any single character, subsumes a startling array of roles: daughter, sister, virgin, temptress, bride and mother—all within the mythological role of Queen Goddess of the World, the archetypal goddess who consumes as well as nourishes.[11] Ascribing this role to Ann implies both the humor inherent in all myth, as it perpetually renews itself in strange and marvelous forms, and Shaw's very special sense of the absurd. That the decorous Ann Whitefield, whose name suggests commonplace innocence and nubility, should rise, by means of her vitality, to genius and hence to godhead, is, of course, comically incongruous. But this very incongruity affirms the inexhaustible nature of the mythological experience, which is never naturalistic, but is rendered in fantastic and exaggerated shapes. From the broad comic viewpoint of joy in exuberant life, Ann as a large figure representing such life is eminently plausible. She is archetypal Woman, carrier of the Life Force, Shaw's embodiment of the Blakean credo of celebration: "Energy is eternal delight."

With Ann as goddess, and therefore lure and guide to the hero Tanner, comedy erupts as she tries to lead Tanner from *dianoia* to *nous*, from merely rational knowledge to the unifying wisdom possible only through determined will and faith.[12] But Tanner, like many a mythic hero, does not know a goddess when he sees one. Consequently, he responds to Ann in a classic way, recognizing in her only the temptress, a role he disdains on intellectual grounds. Though Tanner is wonderfully unsuccessful in convincing Ann of anything, his limited view of her role has largely prevailed with the critics. What is amazing is the extent to which Ann's actions are defined through Tanner's labeling. It is the age-old power ploy of manipulation through categorization. Not content to compare Ann to one or two familiar predatory animals, Tanner refers to her variously, but not necessarily imaginatively, as "cat," "boa constrictor," "lioness," "tiger," "bear," "spider," "bee," and "elephant." Ann, however, is merely amused as she becomes a veritable one-woman zoo. And we may wonder if Shaw has not *for once* overdone a good thing.

Yet Shaw has not arbitrarily chosen these unlikely animals only to allude outrageously to Ann's hunting instinct, as has been commonly assumed: These comic epithets playfully underscore a wide range of Ann's attributes. In mythic lore, the lioness is held to be a symbol of the *Magna Mater*,[13] while the queen bee is associated with both the mother goddess and the Virgin Mary. These three roles represent the extreme of views held by Tanner, Octavius and Ramsden, respectively. Similarly, the creativity, aggressiveness and illusion associated with the spider are traits that Ann exhibits as she pursues and persuades, as much as she exhibits the strength and powerful libido which tradition accords the elephant.

But it is the snake epithet that occurs most often, at least four times. In addition, there is the stage business of the feather boa coiled around Tanner's neck. Inextricably identified with Eve—with whom Ann is linked in the stage directions—the snake more than any other creature symbolizes the feminine principle. With its sensuous movements, tenacious strength and glittering coloration, the snake is closely allied to the alluring, vividly garbed Ann, whose power lies in her insinuating charm, which Tanner suggests when he labels her "my dear Lady Mephistopheles." Even Ann's facile movement from young innocent to chaste seductress to unscrupulous huntress is reflected in the snake image, bringing to mind the periodic shedding of skin that gives the snake the appearance of becoming a new and different creature. Once again the evolutionary process, with which Ann is clearly associated, is suggested. Moreover, the snake is regarded as a symbol of energy, thereby epitomizing one of Ann's essential qualities.

The importance of the animal imagery extends beyond these affinities to Ann's portraiture. In the symbolic interpretation that makes the play's deep structure meaningful, the majority of the animals are considered lunar animals. The significance of the lunar relationship increases when we note that the cat (sacred to the Egyptian goddess of marriage), the bear (companion to Diana) and the tiger (symbolic of darkness and Dionysus) all have specific associations with the moon in various mythologies. In addition, there is an implied connection between these animals and basic instincts which preclude spirituality. Ann's powerful instincts and indifference to certain intellectual and spiritual qualities should therefore be viewed within the implied metaphorical framework of the moon, perennially evocative of desire.

The aptness of the lunar metaphor is readily apparent. Thought to be passive because it reflects the sun's light, the moon is traditionally associated with the feminine principle.[14] Indeed, the physiological functioning of the female is viewed as in some way dependent on the fertility-controlling lunar cycle. Consequently, the additional feminine qualities of maternal love and protection are attributed to the moon, even while its half light creates an aura suggestive of danger and the unconscious. These lunar qualities surface in Ann's inability to explain her motives consciously. Nevertheless, she risks all to be wife and mother, even "perhaps death." More pointedly, Shaw's portrait of Ann is directly consistent with the major characteristic imputed to the moon, a felicitous ability to appear as both the chaste Diana and the sorceress Hecate. And the incessant modifications in its apparent shape that the moon undergoes are reflected in Ann's constant role-changing.

Ann's characterization, which is immediately exhibited in the play's surface structure and greatly affects the progress of the action, is, therefore, actually dependent on the mythic substructure. The entire surface structure itself is in fact regulated by the deep structure, which determines Ann's centrality and her metaphorical identification with the moon. For this identification to be in any way conclusive, the body of lunar myths must be taken into account, and they must effectively increase our understanding of the play.

Eliade has shown "the importance of lunar myths in the organization of the first coherent theories concerning death and resurrection, fertility and regeneration, [and] initiation."[15] This is especially significant for *Man and Superman*, since the play's structure expresses Shaw's satiric view of societal interpretations of a number of rites of passage—birth, death, marriage and initiation. The opening of Act I is actually a mock celebration of death, as family and friends manipulate the legal will of the deceased Mr. Whitefield so they can assert their own personal wills. Octavius and Ramsden luxuriate in their sorrow, trade sentimental clichés and gravely discuss Ann's future. The bereaved daughter, beautifully dressed in black and violet silk, *"which does honor to her late father,"* and expressing all the proper sentiments, uses the occasion to begin to have her way. This terrestrial view of death is reflected in Dona Ana's conventional views in the opening scene in hell, integrating the surface structure of the dream symposium with the romantic comedy. Don Juan, believing all such conventions to be masks of reality, disdains the code of conduct, just as Tanner ignores it. But both Ann and Doña Ana instinctively eschew death, being supremely concerned with life.

Dialectically balancing this mock celebration of death is the comic mourning of birth. The disclosure that the supposedly unmarried Violet Robinson is pregnant initiates the parody. In defending Violet, Tanner preaches the triumphant language of the Scriptures, strengthening the scene's ritualistic ties: " 'Unto us a child is born; unto us a son is given.' " This passage is paralleled by the segment in hell in which the superman subject is constantly implied as Don Juan speaks "of helping Life in its struggle upward." The possibility of change, which is evidenced in the restlessness of the characters, becomes all-important in hell's changeless environment. Don Juan wants to exchange his infernal residence for a heavenly one; the Statue wants to trade the tedium of heaven for the illusion of romance that hell provides; and the Devil claims to move back and forth between the two realms, citing the Book of Job as evidence. Implied in the desire for change are natural and supernatural birth, which are alluded to or examined in both structures of the play. Thus, in the romantic comedy, Tanner confesses to the birth of moral passion within him. Thematically, this description of the origin of Tanner's moral consciousness prefigures the discussion in hell, which posits the need for the advent of an intellectually superior being, by drawing attention away from the merely biological aspect of birth.

Having inverted the conventional rituals surrounding death and birth, Shaw inverts the rituals of wooing, with Ann pursuing Tanner on earth and Doña Ana pursuing a father for the superman: "For though by her death she is done with the bearing of men to mortal fathers, she may yet, as Woman Immortal, bear the Superman to the Eternal Father." Shaw thus reinterprets, for the purposes of his myth, essential parts of the cycle of human experience, which satirically illuminate the community he is portraying.

But beneath the surface structure, Tanner moves through a series of adventures, which form a necessary prelude to his marriage to Ann. These adventures, though comic, are akin to the journey of the mythic hero as he is initiated into the mysteries of life. As hero, Tanner implicitly embodies those qualities complementary to Ann's lunar nature. Because of his courageous and vigorous renewal of the world order, the hero has frequently been considered a human analogue of the sun, the sun itself being allied with the masculine principle. In addition, the sun early was identified with the rational intelligence and, hence, with the philosopher. Tanner's characterization, of course, relies on his philosophical aspirations and his faith in the rational intelligence. The single god, however, that is most closely associated with the virtue of judgment is not Apollo, as might be expected. Rather it is Jupiter. The stage directions introducing Tanner are explicit. Not only is he *"prodigiously fluent of speech, restless, excitable"* with *"snorting nostril and . . . restless blue eye,"* but he also has an *"Olympian majesty,"* suggesting *"Jupiter rather than Apollo."* Tanner's belief that strength of judgment should forge destinies is immediately suggested by the analogy, since tradition grants Jupiter this mythical power. Despite such power, it was his union with the Great Goddess that made Jupiter sacred, although—unlike many sky gods—marriage did not diminish his ability to guarantee universal order.[16] Tanner's view of marriage as a muffin-like affair may not be the *only* possibility.

These implicit mythic ascriptions to Tanner prepare us for his nightlong journey into hell, a journey, according to mythic lore, the sun makes each night. Tanner's metaphorical descent into his unconscious is a journey through the labyrinth of his own disordered thoughts and emotions, as he seeks through his pilgrimage an initiation into "absolute reality," what can be called the mystic center of his spirit.[17] This journey takes place largely within the third act. The call to adventure is instigated by Ann's insistence, shocking to the blustering Tanner, that they motor across Europe together. *"Wildly appealing to the heavens,"* Tanner heeds the call, which indicates that he is on the threshold of new experience. Just as Goethe's Mephistopheles guides Don Juan's "cousin Faust," Tanner's supernatural guide is the Devil himself, who will attempt to win over the life-worshiping Tanner-Don Juan.

The Devil is first encountered as the bandit leader, Mendoza. His band of brigands, living in the seclusion of the Sierra Nevadas, is a transmutation of the dangerous creatures of mythology found in isolated places. Whether generally described as dragons, ogres or monsters, or specifically defined like Pan and his satyrs or like the enticing Sirens—all these creatures represent tests for the hero who enters their domain. The kind of geographical isolation in which such creatures are found is fertile ground for the unconscious to project its fantasies, so that frequently in mythology the hero crosses the first threshold into a mysterious zone through a dream.

Tanner's dream—framed by Mendoza's suggestion that "this is a strange country for dreams," and his later question, "Did you dream?"—follows an ancient pattern. As the dream begins, the scene fades into the extraordinary world of hell, which functions as a sphere of rebirth attainable only after self-annihilation and hence metamorphosis have occurred. During the course of the dream, Tanner moves back in time to become his ancestor Don Juan, who, paradoxically, is more advanced spiritually than he. Don Juan's commentary, largely a response to Doña Ana, externalizes the long woman-dependent educational process he has undergone. As a result of this commentary, we glimpse his unrevealed soul, which, in the fashion of a medieval morality play, becomes the prize multiple adversaries vie for. Viewed from the standpoint of the play as a whole, Tanner articulates through his dream those psychological

and intellectual obstacles which impede his struggle toward enlightenment. His reincarnation as Don Juan leads to his subsequent
rebirth as a more mature individual, one better able to assume the
responsibilities of fatherhood and the vagaries of life with Ann.

That this assumption of parental obligation is a *raison d'être* for the
dream symposium is evident from the commentary in hell. There
such subjects as civilization, morality and progress appear to be
disparate. But actually all of the subjects are related to those posited
in the romantic comedy—love, marriage, sex and Woman—since all
contribute to an understanding of Creative Evolution, through
which fathers are fashioned and, ultimately, supermen ascend. The
theme of Creative Evolution is further reinforced by the physical and
spiritual metamorphoses the characters undergo in hell, where the
setting transforms earthly time and space. In the process of
metamorphosis, the characters lose extraneous personal traits exhibited in the romantic comedy, leaving only the quintessential
qualities necessary for the creation of the superman, fertility and
energy in Doña Ana, and intellectual and spiritual striving in Don
Juan. Doña Ana and Don Juan typify these qualities—or type them
in the nineteenth-century vitalist sense—placing them in the line of
inheritance. The entire play moves toward this evolutionary change
that is at once supremely symbolized by Ann in her many guises
and championed by Tanner-Don Juan, for the mythological hero
heralds the Life to Come.

Theme, philosophy, action and psychology intersect, all levels of
dramatic action indicating that the flux of life can be integrated, as-
similated and regenerated through the union of the world-
embracing goddess-mother and the world-renouncing hero-saint.
This union can occur only after Tanner, as hero, has traveled to the
underworld and brought back the boon of his life-restoring private
insight to the waiting community. Very often in myth, because the
hero fails to return unaided or refuses to abandon the joy he has
found, the society which he has left must seek him, as is true in
Tanner's case. He cannot, as Don Juan, be allowed to find his con-
templative bliss in heaven; he must be brought back to the earthly
world of practical reality and coerced by Ann into enriching the social community.

To the mythic journey of the hero, the presentation of rites of
passage and the identification of the characters with archetypal figures must be added a fourth element of the mythic deep
structure—setting. The first two acts are set in the present of Victorian England, suggesting the beginning of a pattern of growth,
whose mature fruit will be evident in the Spanish Sierras of Act IV.

But before that happens, Act III moves toward spatial freedom, opening in the uncertain light of evening and therefore signaling uncertain space amid the inhospitable arid landscape of the Sierra Nevadas. Scattered patches of olive trees, Jupiter's sacred tree, impart an ancient and religious aura. The mountains dominate the action; Tanner refers to the "august hills," and much stage movement involves climbing or sitting on rock formations. The symbolism of the mountains foreshadows the movement into the void of hell, for "the Sacred Mountain—where heaven and earth meet—is situated at the center of the world."[18]

It is not only in Act III, though, that the center of the world is suggested. Again in Act IV, the mountains overshadow the action. The universality of the action to ensue is indicated by the opening description of the setting which could *"fit Surrey as well as Spain,"* except for the *"Alhambra, the begging, and the color of the roads."* But the little drama that Tanner and Ann could act out on English soil is elevated and made more inclusive by the presence of the Alhambra in the background. Taking its name from the red of its clay bricks, the Alhambra, by means of its color, symbolizes passion, blood, fire and sublimation. The dualism suggested by the opposition of passion and sublimation is specifically supported by the history of the Alhambra. This fortress palace was originally constructed in the thirteenth century by Moorish monarchs, who were expelled some two and a half centuries later. Soon after, the already damaged structure was partially demolished by the Spanish Charles V to make room for a Renaissance palace of Italian style. Ravaged in the early nineteenth century by Napoleon's army and then an earthquake, the building remained standing. Man's blood lust and his spiritual ascendancy through created art fuse in the history of the Alhambra, just as ages and cultures fuse in its design. These evidences of the best and worst of man's intentions, which are set against the expansive background of centuries, underscore the Alhambra's symbolic meaning and relate it to the "architectonic symbolism of the Center." Eliade observes that "every temple or palace—and, by extension, every sacred city or royal residence—is a Sacred Mountain, thus becoming a Center. Being an *axis mundi,* the sacred city or temple is regarded as the meeting place of heaven, earth, and hell."[19]

As a center, the Alhambra reflects cosmic images, but it illuminates Tanner's earthly struggle as well. The building is dominated by the famed Fountain of the Lions, and it is the lion that is the animal most closely associated mythologically with the sun and the masculine principle, and therefore with Tanner. Also striking is the unusual architectural design, which includes the ubiquitous use of water in both static and dynamic forms, signifying death and re-birth. This strongly suggests that Tanner's encounter in hell has re-vitalized him in the manner of a religious discipline; his former self is annihilated as the result of the psychological rigor he has under-gone, and a new life awaits him.

At the same time that the action moves toward new life, it ex-pands outward into atemporality. Act I is set indoors, closed within Ramsden's study, which is itself a symbol of outmoded liberalism and narrow perspective. Act II moves outdoors to *"the park of a coun-try house."* In Act III the cultivated regions give way to an unknown mountainous zone, and finally to the timeless eternity of hell. The force of the atemporality of Act III carries over into the fourth act, partially through the symbolism of the Alhambra and partially through the hilly garden landscape. The setting stresses *"a circular basin and fountain in the centre, surrounded by geometrical flower beds, gravel paths, and clipped yew trees in the genteelest order,"* from which steps lead to *"a flagged platform on the edge of infinite space at the top of the hill."* This extremely ordered landscape signals the return to the rational, conscious world, while the steps symbolize the spiritual evolution Tanner has achieved. The flagged stone platform func-tions as an *omphalos,* a ritualistic center, uniting heaven and earth and signifying the presence of the superhuman. Often the *omphalos* bears witness to a covenant—even such as will be made between Ann and Tanner.[20] The fountain, imitative of the Alhambra's foun-tain, suggests the omnipresence of the Life Force and is situated at the absolute center of the sacred zone. Reinforcing the symbolism of the center of the world is the presence of the yew trees, since these trees are considered a particular symbol of immortality and regen-eration. And the implicit greenness of vegetation and water sup-ports the suggestion of fertility and the life process.

This movement into atemporality and regeneration, which the set-ting traces, crucially depends on the existence of the dream sym-posium, the movement corresponding to Jung's hypothesis on dreams. Summarizing Jung's concept, Campbell states that ar-chetypal themes appearing in dreams "are best interpreted . . . by comparison with the analogous mythic forms. . . . Dreams, in Jung's view, are the natural reaction of the self-regulating psychic system and, as such, point forward to a higher, potential health, not simply backward to past crises."[21] Thus Tanner's dream, which transposes a personal relationship into a universal fable of evolution and cre-ation, powerfully affirms the possibilities for a regenerated society, even while it satirizes vice and folly. And Tanner, by means of the labyrinthine dream that has unfolded his hopes and beliefs, has simultaneously attained the center and knowledge of himself. Having journeyed successfully from hell, he has traveled the route Eliade shows the hero eternally traversing, "from death to life, from man to divinity."[22] He has completed his initiation, becoming a worthy mate for Ann. Tanner may pun on being "sacrifice[d] . . . at the altar," still believing he is "scapegoat" and sacrificial lamb, as Ann works her "magic" with "siren tones," but the humor really lies in his wry realization that the Life Force is triumphant. Tanner cries out: "The Life Force. I am in the grip of the Life Force." Soon after, *"the echo from the past,"* based on dialogue from the dream symposium, like the "echo from a former existence" which Ann earlier experienced, brings the dream of the third act directly into the romantic comedy: "When did all this happen to me before? Are we two dreaming?"

In terms of the play's deep structure, the promised marriage becomes a mystical marriage, which unites the contrary qualities of heaven and earth, sun and moon, representing Tanner's apprehension of life through Ann, who *is* life. This unique personal action of Ann and Tanner is so intimately connected with the community at large that only the sudden arrival of family and friends accomplishes the betrothal. The reluctant Tanner is finally brought into the social unit, the anticipated marriage ceremony serving to keep the community intact, thereby ostensibly reinforcing the status quo; however, the hoped-for birth of the superman, issuing from the union of Ann and Tanner, promises a new society rising above the morally archaic, absurdly flawed, human institutions of the present. The chorus of universal laughter attests to the transcendent nature with which life itself is endowed in vitalist philosophies. While Tanner protests that he is not a happy man, and Mendoza claims that life is a tragedy whether or not one gets one's heart's desire, the myth of Creative Evolution overcomes these petty tribulations, clothing Ann's uncertain fate as mother, and Tanner's pretensions, with the dark glory of a modern Divine Comedy.

And undoubtedly the quality of a Divine Comedy so permeates Ann's characterization that to perceive her in any shallow or less complex way is really not to perceive her at all. Once the essential relationship of the mythic deep structure to the surface comedy is revealed, many of the apparent problems and discrepancies in Ann's characterization fall away; indeed her portrait achieves a startling clarity of focus. Far more than merely a strong-willed young woman who overpowers a somewhat foolish bachelor, Ann, as Woman Incarnate in Shaw's dramatic version of evolutionary myth, becomes nothing less than the hope of the race in the movement toward a superman. Certainly Shaw's Everywoman is no less than the complete woman, the perfect realization of womanhood, what Kenneth Burke, after Aristotle, would call the *entelechialization* of woman. For there is that about Ann which can only be termed perfection—perfection of charm, of fascination, of endless complexity married to single-minded drive. Embodying all female biological drives in a plenary way, she is not merely the average woman with average instincts. Nor is she the stereotypical woman who is reduced to caricatured simplicity as mere predator or abortive mother-woman. She is archetypal Woman, whose role subsumes all roles. Biologically she may serve the species and socially she may seem to serve men, but psychologically she is free to woo and win as she chooses. And instead of Octavius, who plays at love and life and poetry, she chooses Tanner, who, infused with moral passion, can tell her he adores creation "in tree and flower, in bird and beast, even in you." Just as she rescues Tanner from his private inferno of self-doubt, thus enabling him to function unseparated from society, so she urges the passions in his soul and psyche to be expressed within the societal framework as he seeks order and renewal. Paradoxically identified with both the origin of life and the end toward which life aspires, Ann is a culminant figure, epitomizing an entire spectrum of related qualities and exemplifying Shaw's art of dramatic imitation in all the richness of its symbolizing and universalizing aspects.

Notes

1. Arthur H. Nethercot, *Men and Supermen: The Shavian Portrait Gallery*, 2d ed., corrected (1966), p. 90.

2. Barbara Bellow Watson, *A Shavian Guide to the Intelligent Woman* (1964), pp. 59-64; Margery M. Morgan, *The Shavian Playground: An Exploration of the Art of George Bernard Shaw* (1972), p. 112; Elsie Adams, "Feminism and Female Stereotypes in Shaw," *Shaw Review* 17 (January 1974), 21. See also p. 156.

3. On the Don Juan legend, see, for example, Carl Henry Mills, "*Man and Superman* and the Don Juan Legend," *Comparative Literature* 19 (Summer 1967), 215-25. For a discussion of mythic overtones, see *Bernard Shaw and the Art of Drama*, pp. 123-27; see also, *The Shavian Playground*, pp. 107-8, on the relationship between Ann and the Lilith Legend; Margaret Schlauch in "Symbolic Figures and the Symbolic Technique of George Bernard Shaw," *Science and Society*, 21 (Summer, 1957), 218, sees Doña Ana as a goddess figure.

4. Alfred Turco, Jr., in "Ibsen, Wagner, and Shaw's Changing View of

'Idealism,' " *Shaw Review* 17 (May 1974), 80, asserts that " 'the Hero' (Siegfried) . . . is nothing more than the former 'realist' placed in a more elaborate scheme of evolutionary eschatology."

5. Don Austin notes that women "dominate the action"; see "The Structural Meaning of 'Man and Superman,' " *Shavian* 4 (Spring 1971), 129. Barbara Bellow Watson recognizes that the women "secure all the desired outcomes through their wit and daring"; see "The New Woman and the New Comedy," *Shaw Review* 17 (January 1974), 8. See also p. 144. J.L. Wisenthal states that "as the play advances Ann comes to dominate Tanner more and more"; see *The Marriage of Contraries: Bernard Shaw's Middle Plays* (1974), p. 37.

6. Frye, *Anatomy of Criticism*, p. 106.

7. Mircea Eliade, *The Myth of the Eternal Return*, trans. Willard R. Trask (1954), p. 149.

8. Quoted in Joseph Campbell, *The Hero with a Thousand Faces* (1949; rpt. 1967), p. 113.

9. Friedrich Nietzsche, *Thus Spake Zarathustra*, trans. Thomas Common (n.d.), p. 18.

10. J.E. Cirlot, *A Dictionary of Symbols*, trans. Jack Sage (1962), p. 208.

11. See Campbell, pp. 109-20.

12. For a full treatment of this Platonic distinction, see Northrop Frye, "Criticism, Visible and Invisible," *The Stubborn Structure: Essays on Criticism and Society* (1970), pp. 74-89.

13. I am indebted to Cirlot's wide-ranging study for many of the details on animals.

14. See Cirlot, pp. 204-7.

15. Eliade, p. 86.

16. For a discussion of Jupiter as sky god, see Mircea Eliade, *Patterns in Comparative Religion*, trans. Rosemary Sheed (1965), pp. 77-94.

17. Eliade discusses "absolute reality" in *Patterns in Comparative Religion*, p. 381.

18. Eliade, *The Myth of the Eternal Return*, p. 12.

19. Ibid.

20. Eliade, *Patterns in Comparative Religion*, pp. 231-34.

21. Joseph Campbell, ed., *The Portable Jung* (1971), p. xxii.

22. Eliade, *The Myth of the Eternal Return*, p. 18.

II

POLITICAL AND ECONOMIC
INFLUENCES

THE LEGAL CLIMATE OF SHAW'S PROBLEM PLAYS

Dolores Kester

It is well known that Shaw's advocacy of so-called women's issues was not limited to the theatre. Thus he was present, with the Webbs, at a Congress of the Second International held in the public galleries of the Queen's Hall in London during the last week of July 1896. The English delegation had come to discuss, among other issues, universal suffrage and the emancipation of women—though the colorful behavior of some Continental Anarchists, shouting and stamping in the halls, made reasoned discussion impracticable. Shaw's observation is salient: "An International Socialist Congress that everybody laughs at and nobody fears is a gratifying step in advance."[1] This sequence illuminates a feature of Shaw's art which has not, I think, been fully appreciated. This is his capacity to make comedy out of material forthrightly political, in the same way that W.S. Gilbert's *Princess Ida* burlesqued Tennyson's poem. Accordingly, many of Shaw's most flamboyant heroines are endowed with beliefs or rhetoric which are so calculatedly anachronistic as to leave to other characters, or to the audience, the search for more appropriate ways of dealing with the issues, through a process of perpetual regeneration. For a similar purpose of showing historical contrast, Shaw also devised calculated elements of anachronism in aspects of language, setting, and theme—particularly in plays where women's issues were prominent.

In *The Quintessence of Ibsenism*, Shaw refers to the "crablike progress of social evolution, in which the individual advances by seeming to go backward." Why did he perceive a need to approach the future through the past, by parading out antique furniture and issues? Objectively, contemporary political forces and the consequent legal climate shed some light on this question. Four distinct waves of historical legal development can be recognized, each correlating with distinguishable patterns of literary emphasis: (1) the *prestatutory*, to 1854, when Parliament first took official notice of women's political claims in an otherwise unimportant statute acknowledging the deed of a married woman;[2] (2) the *statutory*, from 1854 to 1882–83, when the bulk of statutes affecting married women's property interests came in force; (3) the *revisionist*, from 1882–83 to 1919, limited to the interpretation of earlier statutes by the courts, and to parliamentary glosses on them in the form of a couple of minor statutes related more or less directly; and (4) what may generally be termed the *modern*, ushered in after the Great War by the Sex Disqualification (Removal) Act, 1919,[3] which specified removal of disabilities in the "exercise of any public function," in "entering or assuming or carrying on any civil profession or vocation," and in serving as juror.

In this paper there is no need to consider in detail the significance of any but the third of these waves, but I may make the general preliminary observation that pressures generated by literary professionals were noteworthy forces in the passage of such statutes. Moreover, much if not all of the woman-directed literature in nineteenth-century England relied explicitly on the thoroughly mid-Victorian presupposition (for which Jeremy Bentham has been given most of the credit) that whatever social and economic ills were to be cured could be cured through the agency of the reformed, post-1832 Parliament. As a practical matter, however, most of this legislation achieved less than had been supposed—for reasons analogous to those to which Shaw attributed the failure of Wagner's political allegory in *Götterdämmerung*: because Wagner was, like Marx, "too inexperienced in technical government and administration and too melodramatic in his hero-contra-villain conception of the class struggle, to foresee the actual process by which his generalization would work out, or the part to be played in it by the classes involved."[4]

The most pivotal legislation was the Married Women's Property Act of 1882,[5] which came into operation 1 January 1883. Most legal authorities describe it as "revolutionary," nostalgically bemoaning its relegation to the civil jurisdiction matters which, traditionally, since the Civil War, had been the more or less exclusive preserve of the equity courts—Chancery—itself fused administratively with the so-called common law courts in the Supreme Court of Judicature created by the Judicature Acts 1873–75. This 1882 Act practically reenacted the provisions of the Married Women's Property Acts of 1870 and 1874, which it explicitly repealed. The Act of 1870[6] specified, probably in excessive detail, certain limited classes of property which married women were now declared capable of possessing at law. In other words, it created a statutory separate estate for married women on the pattern of the equitable conception of the separate estate which had originated after the Restoration. This meant that all married women on statutory rather than decisional authority could now hold and dispose of the specified classes of property without the need for an equitable settlement—the means by which the daughters of the wealthier classes had evaded the rigors of the property law since the Civil War. Apart from technicalities, the 1870 Act affected only earnings and savings. These conservative aspects of the statute made it more agreeable to those Members of Parliament, elected under the then-recent franchise reforms, who dreaded a revolution in the law regarding family life.[7] At the same time, they were reluctant to forgo the defenses which Chancery had developed to protect married women's separate property, such as the "restraint on alienation," which made it possible to bar access to the wife's separate property against claims by husband or creditors. The Act of 1874[8] was little more than a footnote on the 1870 Act, correcting the deficiency whereby the husband had been entirely freed from liability on his wife's prenuptial debts, even though by marriage he obtained the greater part of her property. Thus the husband in 1874 was made liable for such debts to the extent that he received his wife's assets.

The 1882 Act confirmed but extended these earlier acts by conferring a legal right to possess and to contract *sui iuris* regarding virtually all classes of property (accordingly rendering married women independently liable on tort claims), effectively completing the transfer of a main branch of equity to a rival jurisdiction. In addition, however, the 1882 Act was "revolutionary" in that, unlike comparable American statutes, it was principally conceived and executed not in the name of creditor satisfaction but rather as an official recognition of the redistribution of socioeconomic forces which had been effected by industrialization. It is clear that these married women's acts were not designed for creditor relief. Despite the claims made about them, they left untouched a married woman's practical immunity from bankruptcy as well as the longstanding availability to her of the "restraint on alienation." (The 39th section of the Conveyancing and Law of Property Act, 1881, enabled a sympathetic judge to relieve her of this restraint if it should prove irksome or contrary to her best interests.) Possibly because of these implicit limitations, possibly because it was only a consolidating statute, the "revolutionary" 1882 Act, "like many statutes of importance, did not attract one quarter the interest evoked by a burials bill or a verminous persons bill or other measure interfering but little with the people's everyday life."[9]

Shaw alone among prominent literary professionals of the day took notice of this parliamentary activity. Some of the dialogue in *The Irrational Knot* (written in 1880) alludes directly to the parliamentary debates which were then in process of generating the 1882 Act, in the last major reforming Parliament of the nineteenth century, during Gladstone's second ministry. The novel's most overt commentary on these and related issues is expressed through Nelly McQuinch, a budding novelist marginal to the plot, cousin and confidante to Marian Lind. For example, Nelly penetrates Marian's sentimental view of the marriage relationship by emphasizing its economic dimension. Heterodoxically, Nelly equates the "respectable" marriage with a personal services contract, equivalent to prostitution:

> It is all very well for us fortunate good-for-nothings to resort to prostitution—[Marian is indignant and shocked, but Nelly talks her down]—I say, to prostitution, to secure ourselves a home and an income. Somebody said openly in Parliament the other day that marriage was the true profession of women. So it is a profession; and except that it is a harder bargain for both parties, and that society countenances it, I dont see how it differs from what we—bless our virtuous indignations!—stigmatize as prostitution. *I* dont mean ever to be married, I can tell you, Marian. I would rather die than sell myself forever to a man.

Susanna Conolly, actress and sister of Marian's intended, had by a comparable logic elected natural marriage:

> *I* snap my fingers at society, and care as little about it as it cares about me; and I have no doubts [Marian] would be glad to do the same if she had the pluck. I confess I shouldnt like to make a regular legal bargain of going to live with a man. I dont care to make love a matter of money; it gives it a taste of the harem, or even worse. Poor Bob, meaning to be honorable, offered to buy me in the regular way at St. George's, Hanover Square, before we came to live here; but, of course, I refused, as any decent woman in my circumstances would.

With characteristic flamboyance, Shaw costumes Susanna here in harem dress, because she is studying the part of Zobeida for a harem play; and the room is described as "luxuriously decorated in sham Persian." Despite these fine touches, resonant with midcentury overtones, the solid core of the novel's argument is directed generally toward women's loss of economic independence upon marriage—a condition which the 1882 Act to some degree modified.

The closely related issue of divorce is addressed by Marian Lind much later in the novel, after she runs away to America, breaking free of class rituals along with her marriage. Marian writes back to Nelly from New York: "There is one unspeakable blessing in American law. It is quite easy to obtain a divorce. One can get free without sacrificing everything except bare existence. I do not care what anybody may argue to the contrary, our marriage laws are shameful." It is noteworthy that parliamentary reconsiderations of divorce had developed side by side with statutes in the specific area of women's issues. Indeed, the monumental 1857 Act to amend the law relating to Divorce and Matrimonial Causes in England,[10] usually cited simply as the "Divorce Act," had actually absorbed the first significant draft bill devoted to women's interests, as is made clear in Mr. Shaw-Lefevre's speech in introducing the 1870 Married Women's Property Act.[11] Details of the parliamentary activity in the area of divorce are beyond the scope of this paper, but I may briefly note that the issue had remained alive through the Matrimonial Causes Act of 1878 (which gave women a right to custody of their children up to sixteen years of age), and was again pending in the early eighties concurrent with the married women's property issue. (The statute forthcoming was the Matrimonial Causes Act of 1884.[12]) But even from this general outline it should be apparent that Shaw was actively aware of parliamentary developments then pending. *The Irrational Knot* reflected such developments for the very practical purpose of influencing their directions, although it must be conceded that the novel's delayed publication diluted its political impact considerably.

By the following year, however, even Shaw in *Love Among the Artists* had deserted this narrow emphasis on issues of domestic politics, transforming Ned Conolly (who appears in both novels) from self-sufficient lover-husband—progenitor of Charteris, Sergius, and maybe even James Morell—into Conolly the industrialist, progenitor of the Crofts-Mangan-Undershaft lineage, an emphasis no doubt in part attributable to the growing probability that Gladstone would be obliged to occupy Egypt in order to protect commercial stakes in India and the East. In short, after 1880 and until 1890, Shaw's writing explored themes not directly related to women's issues, possibly from the changed emphasis in national priorities, possibly from a perception that the 1882 Act must have laid these at least temporarily to rest.

It is principally in this sense that Shaw's later return to such issues—directly in *The Philanderer, Mrs Warren's Profession*, and various prefaces and treatises; less directly in *Arms and the Man, Candida* and *You Never Can Tell*—constituted a revival. Parliament too revived these issues in the early nineties by a couple of related statutes. Politically, the need for such a revival is illuminated by the progress of the 1882 Act through the courts.

The purported independent responsibility conferred by the Act of 1882 was undercut implicitly by married women's continuing practical exemption from the bankruptcy laws, and by their "protection" from husband or creditors via the restraint on alienation; hence the statute's failure to afford adequate creditor satisfaction. Further, some difficulties arose after 1883, when the Act came into effect, in litigation to ascertain what it meant in fact for a wife to acquire, hold or dispose—in life, or upon death—of any property belonging to her separately, without the intervention of any trustee, as the statute had directed. As a practical matter, the political climate had changed after Gladstone's second ministry (1880–85), effectively concluding the longstanding Liberal dominance in Parliament. Moreover, this conservative reaction extended not merely to Parliament but also to the courts. There thus arose a doctrine of strictly construing statutes in derogation of the common law, with a result of strained interpretations in the direction of holding new legislation to be merely declaratory of traditional rules.[13] There arose, in short, a general spirit of anachronism which diluted much of the progressive force of prior innovative social legislation. No one is quite certain why this came about—perhaps on the influence of the 1867 Reform Bill, perhaps from the needs of extraterritorial politics, perhaps as a general reaction against oversanguine social legislation. But the net effect was a wavering faith in the power of the state generally to intervene in and direct socioeconomic forces, a kind of Diogenes' answer to the question whether legislated law could actually control the directions and pace of progress. Thus two cases brought under the 1882 Act, adjudicated in 1887, held unenforceable married women's contracts on after-acquired property, irrespective of specific governing provisions in the act.[14] Accordingly, the Married Women's Property Act of 1893[15] was passed during Gladstone's brief, final ministry (1892–94) to resolve just such difficulties, stipulating that property acquired after the husband's death was liable along with the after-acquired property specified by the 1882 Act. This 1893 Act also preserved the immunity from creditors of any property subject to a restraint on alienation, so that the limitations imposed on the 1882 Act by narrow constructions in the courts, though largely removed, were not removed entirely.

Complementing this conservative judicial context after 1885, a parliamentary committee met in late June and early July of 1890—while Shaw was giving that series of summer Fabian lectures better known as *The Quintessence of Ibsenism*—to consider final amendments to a succinct and now obscure bill titled the Slander of Women Act, 1891.[16] This bill was passed 5 August 1891, on the eve of Gladstone's last ministry. It had originated to compensate the hypothetical deficiency created by the Ecclesiastical Courts Act of 1855.[17] This had expressly removed suits for defamation from the ecclesiastical jurisdiction, where there was no requirement to plead or prove "special" or financial loss—thus leaving women virtually without a remedy for slander unless they could show "special" loss in the civil courts. (A man had never had an action for slander; thus a parson in 1681 had no remedy at common law against those who spread a rumor that he had slept with all the women between his parish and the next.[18]) This 1891 statute was anomalous in that suits for slander, though always more numerous in the country districts than in London, had never been common.[19] I know of only two cases in the nineteenth century—one in 1846, and the other in 1861, the latter holding "special" loss a prerequisite for civil recovery.[20]

Notwithstanding this infrequency of slander litigation and thus the difficulty of demonstrating any need for such a bill, the Act of 1891 effectively reinstated a woman's remedy for spoken or published words imputing unchastity or adultery without proving "special" damages, i.e., it made slander (unlike libel) actionable *per se*, creating a remedy at law to replace the ecclesiastical remedy abolished thirty-six years earlier. The Memorandum attached to the bill as printed suggested an exaggerated and sweeping reversionary concern: "The law upon the point dealt with in this Bill has long been the subject of unfavourable observation from the Bench, from the time of Lord Chief Justice Holt in 1704 to the present time."[21] It is noteworthy, however, that debate in committee did not regress this far back in time, inasmuch as Mr. Gully of Carlisle in delineating the need for such a bill referred only to the "great hardship and injustice" (summarized here above) which had been strongly denounced by Lord Campbell and Lord Brougham in the House of Lords thirty years before as "unsatisfactory and barbarous."[22]

Members of the committee were substantially in agreement as to the need for the bill, apart from a few extremely interesting reservations. For example, Captain Verney proposed substituting "person" for "woman or girl" on grounds that it would be "a very dangerous thing" to have "on the Statute Book anything which recognises that that should be lawful which is said of one sex, while it is not if said of the other sex." The bill's sponsor, Mr. Gully, could not agree with this amendment, since the bill's very rationale had been that women might suffer in their characters though not suffering sufficient pecuniary loss to give a cause of action: ". . . men do not suffer under the imputation to the same extent that women do." Mr. Kelly also disagreed, expressing the belief that "to impute unchastity in the case of a woman really means ruin to her; but in the case of a man the imputation is generally a trifling matter, . . . and indeed may be sometimes regarded as a compliment." With the issues thus delineated, this amendment failed.

The plain-speaking Mr. Kelly then put forward another amendment, under the umbrella of a proviso designed to prevent trivial, frivolous or vexatious actions which might arise under the bill for words merely indiscreet and unintentional, spoken rashly and hastily. What Mr. Kelly proposed, in simple outline, was that a wife bringing a slander action should have to join her husband as co-plaintiff, so that in case of a frivolous suit wherein the defendant proved innocent, he would then have a remedy against the husband at least for costs even if the wife had no separate property.

Sir C. Russell's strenuous objections to the form and rationale of the Kelly amendment shed interesting light on developments discussed here earlier:

> Sir C. RUSSELL: The hon. and learned Member has shown no reason why in this Bill, of which he prefesses [*sic*] himself to be in favour, we should make an exception to the general law. I cannot but think he has forgotten the "Married Women's Property Law," which provides that a married woman can sue and be sued without joining her husband in an action of contract or tort. I do not find any reason why this particular form of action and means of redress should be taken out of the general rule. It seems to me that there is strong reason in the other direction. Cases may possibly arise in which a woman is anxious to vindicate her character, but for reasons not creditable to himself, her husband is not willing to join in an action for the purpose; he may be a party even to the very offence.

This Kelly amendment failed too, although the proviso stood in the bill passed the following summer, stipulating only that "a plaintiff shall not recover more costs than damages, unless the judge shall certify that there was reasonable ground for bringing the action."

It was in this general and specific context that Shaw directed the bulk of his attention from criticism to theatre, a turn he ascribes explicitly to the Ibsen revival at the Independent Theatre.[23] Clearly, conservative political forces were in the ascendancy, in Parliament as in the courts, as discussed earlier. Too, there seems to have been a wider spirit of anachronism prevailing, of which an Ibsen revival was itself one kind of symptom. This may aptly be characterized as Shaw's most active "blue book" or parliamentary phase. Most of the plays have an explicit purpose of pressure or leverage on Parliament. Moreover, the prefaces copiously annotate various House of Commons committee reports—though none relating directly to the statutes and cases mentioned here earlier.

This silence is not surprising. Nor can we conclude from it that Shaw was not actively aware of such developments, even if the evidence that he *was* so aware is largely circumstantial. First, there are few references anywhere in Shaw to actual statutes and cases, although he does mention parliamentary debates and blue books. In Shaw's prose of the early nineties, I have been able to find only one reference to actual and immediate parliamentary and judicial reconsiderations of women's issues, namely his note in *Quintessence* on what he called the Clitheroe case,[24] the actual case of *Regina* v. *Jackson*, 60 L.J. 346, an action brought under the Matrimonial Causes Act of 1884.[25] Second, despite the legal terminology with which his prose is salted, despite the legal themes in the plays, Shaw—unlike Dickens, Thackeray, Gilbert, Pinero—never read law. Accordingly, he chose to approach the general issues delineated here by indirect avenues, preserving the spirit rather than the letter or the technicalities of the legal developments. Thus, for the property issue, he persisted in emphasizing—as he had in *The Irrational Knot*—that so long as women's employment opportunities were limited, and so long as their financial independence in marriage was therefore less than complete, marriage would be at best prostitution and at worst slavery. This emphasis was itself anachronistic to the degree that the hard-core issues had already been fully articulated at midcentury by such writers as Mill. But insofar as the progressive parliamentary revisions did not materially advance in terms of substantive issues between 1870 and 1893, it could hardly be said that the issues, though anachronistic, were out of date.

Widowers' Houses, begun in 1885, has little relevance to women's interests or to the statutes considered here, although it may have been suggested in part by Part II of the Criminal Law Amendment of 1885,[26] which for the purpose of suppressing brothels subjected not merely the managers but also the landlords to criminal liability. This is relevant here to the limited degree that a related theme recurs in *Mrs Warren's Profession,* as discussed later. *The Philanderer,* however, is very much in point with legal developments in the area of women's property. It is noteworthy that Parliament had the married women's property amendment under consideration during 1893 when this "topical comedy" was written and produced. Possibly for this reason, the play does not argue directly to the property issue, but is limited to a general display of the extremism compelled by unsatisfactory "marriage laws," as Shaw refers to the matter in the preface to the 1898 printed volume. *The Philanderer* is straightforwardly "advanced" in theme, with patches of dialogue devoted to "the revolt of daughters" and to the Womanly versus the New Woman, as exemplified in Julia Craven and Grace Tranfield. Yet in a play devoted overtly to "Ibsenist" themes, even including an "Ibsen Club," and carried forward by a vehicle of almost unadulterated "discussion," the one moment of genuine spontaneity and animal vitality is Julia's voluble chagrin when she learns she has been tricked—not by fate, not by circumstances, but only by Charteris as classical Intriguer. This surprising displacement suggests that it is not Julia alone whose ardor is "valueless and abhorrent, like the caresses of a maniac"—as Shaw had discussed the question under the head "The Womanly Woman" in *Quintessence*—but that, similarly, Grace and Charteris, by converting Ibsen into dogma, create a "compulsion" not far distinct from that of "custom and law." The play shows, as did *The Irrational Knot,* that "new" or "advanced" views and fashions can themselves become so fashionable and conventional as to be conspicuous anachronisms—despite, or maybe because of, their own professed novelty.

In any case, the 1930 prefatory note makes clear that Shaw designed the play to remedy "anachronisms," presumably legal ones to judge only by the bare reference to unsatisfactory "marriage laws" in the 1898 preface. At the same time, the extremism which makes us smile in *The Philanderer* is arguably an anachronism, a throwback to palmier midcentury days, albeit more sophisticated and less solemn than some of the women's literature earlier in vogue, e.g., Tennyson's *The Princess* and Gaskell's *North and South.* If we can assume that Shaw's pragmatic aim in writing *The Philanderer* was to add force to the tide of opinion which would carry the 1893 amendment, then the characters' jejune political views as exaggerated by the high-comedy mode are quite in keeping with Shaw's doctrine whereby "the individual advances by seeming to go backward," much as Gilbert's *Princess Ida,* burlesquing Tennyson's earlier poem, was produced in the same year that Parliament passed the 1870 Act. Since Parliament in 1893 was acting to remedy the conservative judicial constructions placed on the 1882 Act, the extremism which *The Philanderer* exhibits may reasonably have been construed as unnecessary, if not imprudent.

Mrs Warren's Profession followed the 1893 amendment. With respect to the historical development of the married women's property issue, the play's implicit legal argument may be briefly summarized as follows: even if the 1893 Act has now confirmed the validity of the 1882 Act as to married women's capacity to contract *sui iuris* on their own separate property, whether in the form of wages or an inheritance, what is the practical effect for unpropertied women if they cannot find economic security except by marrying, by such entrepreneurial ventures as result in the network of prostitution, or by the systematic lack of feeling which characterizes Vivie's pursuit of a paralegal career? This argument is a considerable advance over that in *The Irrational Knot*. In view of the intervening parliamentary developments in the property area, Shaw directs his polemic less toward women's loss of independence upon marriage than toward their lack of employments as alternatives to marriage. Collaterally, *Mrs Warren's Profession* argues for wages and hours legislation to regulate the foreseeable widening of employment opportunities, as seems plain from the blue book citations in the preface. The play so argues by flatly declaring the absence of such statutes criminal insofar as this absence creates the "villainous abuses" which the play depicts, on the general theory that bad law is a crime of society against the individual. But there is another basis for the play's criminal metaphor. On the one hand, Mrs. Warren's unmentionable "profession" only makes literal Nelly McQuinch's metaphor in *The Irrational Knot*. On the other, there is the fact that, among other offenses, procurement or use of any premises for prostitution had been made a criminal offense by the Criminal Law Amendment Act of 1885, mentioned above. Although procurement subjected the defendant to up to two years of imprisonment, "with or without hard labour," the sanctions provided in the Act for managers of brothels and for landlords of any premises used as a brothel were negligible.[27] Under §13 of the Act, punishment for these offenses was limited on the first conviction to a fine not exceeding twenty pounds or to imprisonment not exceeding three months; on the second conviction to a fine not exceeding forty pounds or to imprisonment not exceeding four months; and even on the third conviction to imprisonment "for any period not exceeding three months, in addition to any such term of imprisonment as aforesaid"—all of these provisions for imprisonment to be either "with or without hard labour."

In view of these limited sanctions, further parliamentary intervention to control and prevent Mrs. Warren's profession was certainly
in order.

As for the play's argument for wider employment opportunities
and for more effective wages and hours legislation, it has not often
been sufficiently emphasized that Mrs. Warren speaks for an aspect
of women's experience which is calculatedly outdated. In the scene
with Vivie which concludes Act II, the narrative of her history and
range of choices unfolds remarkably like a midcentury novel such as
Gaskell's *North and South,* down to the detail of the "respectable"
half-sister who went to work in a white lead factory and died of lead
poisoning as the Higgins girl in Gaskell's novel died of cotton lung.
Mrs. Warren's lament that there are insufficient employments for
women as alternatives to marriage is the same lament made by Harriet Taylor in "The Enfranchisement of Women" and by Caroline
Helstone in Charlotte Brontë's *Shirley,* both of venerable vintage,
though appropriate to Mrs. Warren's girlhood. Yet, surprisingly,
Shaw has converted all this material incorporating solemn midcentury polemics into the conventional, romantic, sentimental nonsense
against which Vivie bolts. Compounding the difficulty, the play
makes clear that Vivie, whose commitment to money excludes such
other basic human considerations as genuine emotion, is no more
admirable than her mother, for Vivie is limited and flawed, as irra-
tionally rational as Ned Conolly of Shaw's second and third novels.
Accordingly, the play implicitly relies on parliamentary intervention
to remedy the dual evils exemplified by Vivie and her mother.

As should be apparent, it is difficult to distinguish the
components of *Mrs Warren*'s legal arguments because the play is a
conflation of several distinct lines of legal development. This habit of
fusing legal and social issues in one vast, undifferentiated composite
of religion, morals and law was not peculiar to Shaw but had
analogues in the historical-political school of jurisprudence as characterized by such earlier writers as Sir Henry Maine.[28] This tendency in jurisprudence had been reflected in the parliamentary
record of the seventies and early eighties, to the degree that
Parliament effected major and overlapping changes almost
simultaneously in such important areas as court reorganization,
labor, civil and criminal procedure, public health and married
women's property. But it may in fact have been the very diffuseness
and extensiveness of this legislation which led to the juristic
pessimism after 1885. One concrete manifestation of this retreat was
the conservative reception of the 1882 Act in the courts. In short,
Mrs Warren's Profession endeavored to revive a juristic tradition

which had expired some ten years earlier, and thus was fated at the outset to meet with little practical success in the form of remedial statutes.

Notwithstanding the play's implicit reliance on parliamentary intervention to eliminate the conditions which had bred both Mrs. Warren's profession and Vivie's systematic lack of feeling, it is difficult to see that *Mrs Warren* had any practical impact on the desired fronts. The long line of statutory regulation of industrial conditions had commenced in the forties in such limited (but controversial) reforms as the Ten Hours Bill and Lord Campbell's Fatal Accidents Act of 1846.[29] The judicial interpretations of this latter statute concerning the computation of benefits for the deceased worker's survivors are echoed in the actuarial calculations in which Vivie is involved as the curtain drops. Parliament had acted steadily and resolutely in regulating labor not only at midcentury but also through the Trades Unions Act of 1871,[30] the Employers' Liability Act of 1880,[31] and the Principal Factory and Workshops Act of 1878,[32] as amended in 1883, 1889, 1891, 1895 and 1897. The year 1897 also witnessed the passage of the first Workmen's Compensation Act,[33] modeled on the German compensation insurance laws enacted under the sponsorship of Bismarck in 1884. Given the strong independent momentum of Parliament in this area of legislation, it would be implausible to regard the impact of *Mrs Warren's Profession* as anything but negligible. As for its plea for wider employment opportunities, Parliament had resolutely ignored this issue since Harriet Taylor raised the issue in the fifties; and it continued to be ignored until the Sex Disqualification (Removal) Act of 1919,[34] mentioned previously. In the 1933 postscript to the play, Shaw himself refers to the insignificant and belated parliamentary action concerning prostitution as so meager and partial as to be hardly worth mentioning. Thus, for example, the Children Act of 1908[35] made it a misdemeanor to allow a child aged four to sixteen to reside in or frequent a brothel, an offense punishable by fine up to twenty-five pounds or by imprisonment up to two years "with or without hard labour." The Children Act was a supplement to the Criminal Law Amendment Act of 1885, mentioned above, and it was repealed in part and superseded by the Criminal Justice Act of 1925.[36] There was no further modification of the law regarding married women's property until well into the twentieth century.

Later, in the letter to Walkley prefacing *Man and Superman,* Shaw confessed dissatisfaction with the "purely judicial" formula by which much of the theatre of the nineties had proceeded:

Now the conflicts of individuals with law and convention can be
dramatized like all other conflicts; but they are purely judicial;
and the fact that we are much more curious about the
suppressed relations between the man and the woman than
about the relations between both and our courts of law and private juries of matrons, produces that sensation of evasion, of
dissatisfaction, of fundamental irrelevance, of shallowness, of
useless disagreeableness, of total failure to edify and partial
failure to interest. . . . The successes such plays sometimes obtain are due to the incidental conventional melodrama with
which the experienced popular author instinctively saves
himself from failure.

Many of Shaw's plays in the nineties, and particularly the "unpleasant" ones, had an explicit political purpose: to awaken citizen
indignation, and therefore citizen receptiveness, to reform via legislation. Shaw's reliance on the agency of Parliament was itself
anachronistic, however, a reversion to the post-Bentham wave of
parliamentary paramountcy which had begun in the thirties but
which terminated after 1885 as the courts in practice put brakes on
most of the forward momentum of the progressive statutes on the
books. Meanwhile Parliament was incorporating far fewer of the
committee or blue book suggestions within the statutes passed than
it had done in its Benthamistic heyday following Bentham's
suggestion that Parliament actually take some action on committee
reports instead of only taking notice. Too, the conservative
Parliament was creating statutes such as the Slander of Women Act,
which, in the process of nominally remedying a trivial "deficiency"
in justice, narrowly missed diluting so much force as the Married
Women's Act of 1882 had—not by anything so overt as repeal or
amendment (not until 1893), but rather by legislative "intent," to the
degree that this murky issue can be brought to bear subsequently to
contravene a statute's plain and express terms.

I suspect, but cannot verify, that it was Shaw's bout with the
censor over the performance of *Mrs Warren's Profession* which
convinced him of the desirability of moderating his righteous
indignation about pressing issues of the day. In any case, he limited
his consideration of heavy themes thereafter to the occasional
burlesques and verbal anachronisms included within the "pleasant"
plays. After the conservatives returned to power in 1894, it must
have been plain that such retrogressions as the Slander Act were to
become the prevailing pattern rather than a mere temporary interlude. Accordingly this statute is less important as expressing a

controvertible statutory policy than as an indication of the conservative climate in which Shaw wrote *The Philanderer* and *Mrs Warren's
Profession*, leading him in turn to the less polemical mode which
characterizes the "pleasant" plays. Shaw did return to women's
issues again later, in the "discussion" trilogy including *Getting
Married* (1908), *Misalliance* (1910) and *Heartbreak House* (1913-16). For
the nineties, however, he renounced them in *You Never Can Tell*
(1896), an illuminating parable of the limitations of polemic in an
adverse political climate.

In *You Never Can Tell*, heavy, earnest themes—the double standard, the duel of sex, the importance of feeling, inversions of status,
the "old" and the "new"—suffer from levitation, are dissipated by
laughing gas. The judicial branch is itself comical, limited to
adjudicating extremely trivial domestic issues. Indeed, when Bohun,
the learned advocate, takes time before the closing masquerade to
arbitrate the parties' family dispute, he presides in dominoes and a
false nose—insisting, overbearingly, that it is always the trivial
which is the vitally important. Thus Bohun, speaking for The Law,
illuminates not merely why Shaw had returned to women's issues
in the nineties, but also why he temporarily gave them up again.
The two statutes directed toward women's issues in the nineties had
been directed toward minor issues and made little substantive
progress. The 1893 Act resolved some difficulties but preserved the
immunity from bankruptcy and the restraint on alienation.
Moreover, since the widened post-1867 electorate had unexpectedly
returned the Conservatives to power (excepting the Liberal
interludes 1880-85 and 1892-94), and since extraterritorial issues
achieved increasing prominence in the late nineties, it became clear
that there would be little major domestic progress on "sanitary"
issues apart from such limited housecleaning as the Slander Act.
Accordingly, there was little point in pursuing the "purely judicial"
formula with which Shaw's letter to Walkley expressed dissatisfaction, for there was no point in a patently anachronistic reliance on
the agency of Parliament. It is for these reasons that Bohun's
comment sheds light on the complex network of political climates
and legal developments in Victorian England, which *You Never Can
Tell* burlesques. "There will be no difficulty about the important
questions," he insists. "There never is. It is the trifles that will wreck
you at the harbor mouth."

Notes

1. J. Joll, *The Second International* (1966), pp. 74-76.
2. 17, 18 *Vict.*, c. 75.
3. 9, 10 *Geo.* 5, c. 71.
4. *Major Critical Essays* (1932), p. 190.
5. 45, 46 *Vict.*, c. 75.
6. 33, 34 *Vict.*, c. 93.
7. A.V. Dicey, *Law and Public Opinion* (1924), pp. 383-98.
8. 37, 38 *Vict.*, c. 50.
9. *A Century of Law Reform* (1901) pp. 298-99.
10. 20, 21 *Vict.*, c. 85.
11. 191 PARL. DEB. (3d ser.) 1015-25 [25 March to 8 May 1868].
12. 47, 48 *Vict.*, c. 68.
13. R. Pound, *Interpretations of Legal History* (1923), p. 65.
14. *In re Tidswell; ex parte Tidswell*, 56 L.J. 548—bankruptcy; *Paliser* v. *Gurney*, 56 L.J. 546—future property.
15. 56, 57 *Vict.*, c. 63.
16. 54, 55 *Vict.*, c. 51.
17. 18, 19 *Vict.*, c. 41.
18. *Yates* v. *Lodge*, 3 Lev. 18, cited in J.H. Baker, *An Introduction to English Legal History* (1971), p. 252.
19. E. Jenks, *A Short History of English Law* (1922), p. 311n.
20. *Collis* v. *Bate*, 4 Thornton, *Notes of Cases*, 540; *Lynch* v. *Knight*, 9 H.L. Cas. 577.
21. *Great Britain House of Commons, Sessional Papers*, 1890-91 (150) IX 207.
22. 346 PARL. DEB. (3d ser.) 1227-33 [26 June to 16 July 1890]. Subsequent citations to debate in the committee are to this source.
23. Preface to *Plays Unpleasant*.
24. *Major Critical Essays*, p. 35n.
25. 47, 48 *Vict.*, c. 68.
26. 48, 49 *Vict.*, c. 69.
27. See also Lorichs, "The 'Unwomanly Woman' in Bernard Shaw's Drama," p. 99.
28. *Ancient Laws*, 1861.
29. 9, 10 *Vict.*, c. 93.
30. 34, 35 *Vict.*, c. 31.
31. 43, 44 *Vict.*, c. 42.
32. 41 *Vict.*, c. 16.
33. 60, 61 *Vict.*, c. 37.
34. 9, 10 *Geo.* 5, c. 71.
35. 9 *Edw.* 7, c. 67 § 16-18.
36. 15, 16 *Geo.* 5, c. 86.

PRESS CUTTINGS:
G.B.S. AND WOMEN'S SUFFRAGE

Michael Weimer

In 1909, during the long interval between the composition of *Getting Married* and *Misalliance,* Shaw wrote four short plays, three of which he published seventeen years later as *Trifles and Tomfooleries.* One of the so-called tomfooleries, *Press Cuttings,* has attracted almost no critical attention. This neglect is due partly to the author's devaluation of its merit ("a ghastly absurdity," he once called it) and partly to the obscure conditions of its initial production. The Lord Chamberlain refused to license the play in June 1909, and it had to be produced privately in July by an ad hoc committee of the Civic and Dramatic Guild.

Subtitled "A TOPICAL SKETCH COMPILED FROM THE EDITORIAL AND CORRESPONDENCE COLUMNS OF THE DAILY PAPERS DURING THE WOMAN'S WAR IN 1909," *Press Cuttings* was most likely the piece that Shaw had in mind in the second paragraph of his preface to the *Tomfooleries* volume: "On their topical side they are more or less out of date; but as the world continues to excite itself over the same sort of scandal they can always be adapted to the cries of the moment." The moment of this advertisement was July 1926. Less than a year later, in delivering a speech entitled "Woman—Man in Petticoats" (20 May 1927), Shaw was to adapt the materials of the sketch he had resurrected and published. This speech was really an elaboration of the idea behind the character of Rosa Carmina Banger, who is described by Lady Corinthia Fanshawe as "a man in petticoats." Shaw's reuse of the phrase suggests that *Press Cuttings* was less out of date than the other tomfooleries, even though the cause of the suffragettes (whom Shaw allows to be upstaged by the anti-suffragettes in his play) had succeeded by 1919.

The historical significance of *Press Cuttings* emerges most conspicuously when we view it in its original milieu. Shaw, along with eight other noted dramatists and critics, had signed a petition in favor of women's suffrage. The petition was published by the *London Times* on 23 March 1909, and Shaw must have begun writing *Press Cuttings* about that date. On 30 March the National Women's Social and Political Union reacted directly to Prime Minister Asquith's refusal to consider their case when they convened a mock parliament chaired by Emmeline Pankhurst. They assembled first at Caxton Hall and adjourned only to reassemble as a public demonstration outside Westminster Hall. The leaders of this deputation were wearing the Union's sash with the familiar slogan "Votes for Women." Police arrests were made, and the incident was described by the *Times* as a "raid" on Parliament. Further disorders were reported on 1 April. Any intelligent observer might have foreseen an intensified women's war, for April 1909 would bring to London, to cite only two of many scheduled events, a seven-day meeting of the International Suffrage Alliance and the production of a topical melodrama (*How the Vote was Won*, by Cicely Hamilton and Christopher St. John) at the Women's Freedom League Bazaar.

The suffragettes' movement provides the background for several Shaw plays, most notably *Fanny's First Play*. But nowhere is the movement as pervasive as in *Press Cuttings*, which projects it three years into the future and imagines a critical stage of its acceleration. The play belongs to a dramatic genre that Shaw had been developing for some thirteen years since he first dramatized ideological conversion in *The Devil's Disciple* (1896-97). To my mind, *Press Cuttings* is a more interesting conversion play than *Disciple*, which relies on melodramatic conventions at too many crucial points (e.g., when Richard and Anderson exchange coats in Act II). *Cuttings*, a tactical surveillance of the 1909 "woman's war," is a discussion play in which Shaw displays his dexterity in using dramatic confrontation and verbal argument as the agents of conversion.

Elizabeth Robins had already melodramatized the suffragettes in *Votes for Women!*—a London theatrical sensation in 1907. Samuel Hynes provides a good account of this piece's content and reception in his useful study of the Edwardians.[1] Shaw had been in touch with Miss Robins eight years before she wrote her propaganda play, and he seems to have regarded her as an American George Eliot. He advised her against yielding to her "talent for sensationalism" in literature.[2] She was too angry to remember his warning when she wrote *Votes for Women!* Ironically, it was Shaw's less sensational play that was censored, merely because the characters Mitchener and

Balsquith (a well-known cartoon name lifted out of *Punch*) suggested three eminent Englishmen. Shaw attached a satirical note to *Press Cuttings* in order to comply with the Lord Chamberlain's prohibition against irreverent allusions to great men living or dead.

Shaw imagined the action of his 1909 sketch to be taking place in the British War Office on All Fools' Day 1912. The direction of the argument is to demonstrate that women are their own worst enemies in their methods of seeking the just goals of their cause. General Mitchener takes the tough line of maintaining the status quo by force: "Dont be weak-kneed, Balsquith. You know perfectly well that the real government of this country is and always must be the government of the masses by the classes." The cynical Balsquith would just like to prevent a row and contributes this bit of Hegelian wisdom: "We learn from history that men never learn anything from history." The following discussion is more hopeful and suggests that these two men may be capable of learning.

The two women who intrude to dominate the last half of the play call themselves antisuffragettes. They are parodies of the re-actionaries who joined Mrs. Humphrey Ward's Women's National Anti-Suffrage League. It is impossible to say whether Shaw had definite models for Lady Corinthia and Mrs. Banger, but their types could have been extracted from the columns of the *Times* as indicated in the play's elaborate subtitle. Below is a sample of a domestic homily that particularly pleased the East Berkshire branch of the antisuffragettes in early March of 1909. A Lady Haversham presided over the meeting, which resolved to submit an antisuffrage petition supporting the testimony of Mrs. Walter: "From her own personal experience and observation of other women's conduct, those who were best and most successful were those who minded their own business, kept their husband and children in order, and had no parliamentary aspirations."[3] Shaw knew that real power was implicit in the phrase "their own business" and sketched his antisuffragettes in order to expose the dominance of certain women with strong families and positions in English society.

Lady Corinthia is a romantic aristocrat and Mrs. Banger a frustrated Jeanne D'Arc with Bismarckian overtones. They believe that women have been controlling history through their men all along, and they resent any step toward democratizing the process: "The Suffragets would degrade women from being rulers to being voters, mere politicians, the drudges of the caucus and the polling booth. We should lose our influence completely under such a state of affairs." This speech of Lady Corinthia's goes on to mention New Zealand as an open society where politicized women lack the power that Englishwomen of her class exercise secretly. As a topical dramatist Shaw merely elucidated the rationale underlying the antisuffragettes' reaction as it was reflected in the most reliable newspaper reports.

Such bitterness of established women (the wives of the so-called Establishment, commonly thought of as a male domain) against their own sex would eventually backfire, according to the dialectic that Shaw dramatized in *Press Cuttings*. We should not forget the prominent men who were strong advocates of women's suffrage. A highly supportive letter by George Meredith appeared beside the report on the antisuffragettes quoted above. It had been read at a meeting at Mickleham on 3 March:

> I hold that, in spite of much to be said in opposition, the exercise of the vote will gradually enlarge the scope of women's minds. Men who would confine them to the domestic circle are constantly complaining of their narrowness. Women have to contend with illogical creatures. The vote will come in time, and for a time there is likely to be a swamping of Liberalism and a strengthening of ecclesiastical pretensions that will pass with the enlargement of women's minds in a new atmosphere.[4]

Although his arguments would more likely stress the perversities of some women than the illogicalities of men, we can easily imagine General Mitchener writing a similar prosuffrage pronouncement after his exposure to antisuffragism. The General's conversion is the core of Shaw's play. Of course, the P.M. makes several attitudinal turns; but he habitually behaves as a barometer of the political atmosphere. Only the General undergoes a fundamental change of belief.

To be fair to Balsquith, he does exhibit traits of enlightenment when he discusses political tactics with General Mitchener, whose military paranoia reaches as far as the moon: "Can you, as an Englishman, tamely contemplate the possibility of having to live under a German moon? The British flag must be planted there at all hazards." This daydream is provoked by Balsquith's acquiescence to the insecurities of a modern state: "Theres no such thing as security in the world; and there never can be as long as men are mortal." At such points, Shaw's Prime Minister reminds one of former Senator Fulbright arguing the case against the generals before his Foreign Relations Committee. But Balsquith is not without his illusions, Shavian ideals that obstruct progress. Before meeting the antisuffragettes, he idealizes their nature: "I feel extraordinarily grateful to these women for standing by us and facing the Suffragets, especially as they are naturally the gentler and timider sort of women." The twofold fact that he arranges a romantic flirtation with Lady Corinthia as the play concludes and that Mitchener moralizes about this bachelor's chauvinistic tendency to treat women like angels demonstrates that Balsquith has not changed much during the course of the action, despite his political versatility. The P.M.'s first appearance in woman's clothing presages the superficiality of his political transvestitism.

General Mitchener, on the other hand, does undergo a psychological development that we can only call a conversion experience. What makes such a dogmatic person change his convictions? The argument of Shaw's play has it that an intense exposure to the realities of sexual politics would do the trick. Mrs. Banger's female chauvinism—her belief that all strong men are really disguised women—nearly persuades him to campaign against the anti-suffragettes. Lady Corinthia's elaboration of the woman-behind-every-great-man theory makes the General see the grave social harm in the Cleopatras of history.

Thus we observe the first two stages of the General's conversion. We must not assume that the process is altogether rational, for Shaw was a confirmed irrationalist in interpreting such sudden turns of mind. Mitchener is a fundamentally reactionary man, and his change of belief is to be seen as emerging from his exasperation with Lady Corinthia's flagitiously female thinking. Her pun on the word "combinations" has elicited his invitation, only half in jest, that she shoot him in the head: "I should prefer it to any other effort to follow the gyrations of the weathercock you no doubt call your mind." Mitchener's exposure to antisuffragism has provoked him to a vertiginous state of mind which will allow the suffragist opposition to prevail by hook or by crook, probably both. Shaw has adopted here the contraposition of a Blakean proverb in order to show that Progression is Contraries. The dramatic realist has attempted to document history, not to mock any special faction.

The third and most efficient deciding factor is the lady's total lack of sympathy for the unenlightened "average Englishwoman," whom the concerned officer readily perceives as a threat to political order as long as she lacks education and the opportunity for responsible participation in the national life:

> MITCHENER. How do you know where the shoe pinches your washerwoman? you and your high F in alt! How are you to know when you havnt made her comfortable unless she has a vote? Do you want her to come and break your windows?

LADY CORINTHIA. Am I to understand that General Mitchener is a Democrat and a Suffraget?
MITCHENER. Yes: you have converted me—you and Mrs Banger.

Logically enough, Mitchener decides that the best way to understand the problems of a washerwoman is to marry one. He eventually proposes marriage to Mrs. Farrell, one of Shaw's most colorful minor characters and the "only really sympathetic woman in it," as the playwright informed Bertha Newcombe, who had pursued Shaw before his marriage and was arranging the production of his satirical sketch in May 1909.[5]

Sandstone's proposal of marriage to the intimidating Mrs. Banger proves Lady Corinthia's point that women really rule the establishment. Mitchener's disclosure of this new turn of events precipitates his about-face as regards the status of British soldiers: "The horrors of martial law administered by Mrs Banger are too terrible to be faced. I demand civil rights for the army." Reports on a case of insubordination and a lengthy interview with The Orderly, who exposes widespread incompetence among commissioned officers, failed earlier to change Mitchener's mind. The excesses of antisuffragism convince him, then, after indirect evidence has not succeeded as an agent of conversion.

Press Cuttings emerges as an adroit example of Shaw's conversion plays and a spirited discussion of two of the burning issues of the Edwardian period, women's suffrage and the military. I have chosen here to emphasize women's suffrage, for military matters are dramatized as being ultimately dependent upon sexual warfare in the Shavian scheme of things. That the drama's topicality has not gone completely stale three generations later is attributable to Shaw's having brought more than a cartoonist's talent to the task of writing political satire.

Notes

1. Samuel Hynes, *The Edwardian Turn of Mind* (1968), pp. 201-4. Professor Hynes's account of *Press Cuttings* is included in his chapter on theatrical censorship (p. 233).
2. *Collected Letters, 1898-1910*, p. 78.
3. Anonymous, "Woman Suffrage," *The Times*, 4 March 1909, p. 8.
4. *Times*, 4 March 1909.
5. *Collected Letters, 1898-1910*, p. 843.

MILL, MARX AND BEBEL: EARLY INFLUENCES ON SHAW'S CHARACTERIZATION OF WOMEN

Norbert Greiner

Just as Shaw's *Quintessence* essay has been read too much as a dramaturgical rather than a political essay—although the genesis of this essay and the importance Shaw himself attributed to it stress its political character—so the importance of woman's status in society as one of the central problems of nineteenth-century socialist theory, and of Shaw's, too, has not been perceived. It is therefore useful— as it is with all the themes dramatized in his plays—to examine this problem in his essays, and to identify the intellectual tradition, the influence on Shaw's thought.

Even before Shaw began his political career by joining the Fabian Society, he had been confronted with this problem. Shaw had read Mill's *The Subjection of Women* when attending the meetings of the Zetetical Society, a "junior copy" of the Dialectical Society, whose main purpose was the discussion of Mill's radical works.[1] And Frank Harris accordingly tells us about Shaw's reading Mill.[2] Here Shaw had already found a major thesis he would propagate—that "woman's nature," a principle on which capitalist society based its prevailing morality and corresponding modes of behavior, was merely an artificial construction:

> All women are brought up from the very earliest years in the belief that their ideal of character is the very opposite to that of man; not self-will, and government by self-control, but submission, and yielding to the control of others. All the moralities tell them that it is the duty of women, and all the current sentimentalities that it is their nature, to live for others; to make complete

abnegations of themselves, and to have no life but in their affections.[3]

Just take the central terms of this passage: "ideal of character," "no self-will," "submission," "duty," "sentimentalities," "abnegations of themselves," and one has the whole framework of the third chapter of the *Quintessence*, "The Womanly Woman." The man who in 1878 had advised a five-year-old girl, "Let your rule of conduct always be to do whatever is best for yourself. Be as selfish as you can,"[4] would doubtless have found a kindred spirit in Mill.

Mill's moral abhorrence is combined with an economic component in the theories of Marx and Engels. Their influence on Shaw has been acknowledged by himself and has been sufficiently discussed elsewhere. For our present purpose it is of no importance that Shaw as theoretician of the Fabian Society polemicized against Marx's English Social Democratic followers. Shaw had developed his profound intellectual and moral synthesis, the basis of his economic thought, by reading Marx; and this remained his intellectual perspective throughout his life—though in an unorthodox form.

The definition of *family* in *The Communist Manifesto* may be assumed to be valid for Shaw as well.

On what foundation is the present family, the bourgeois family based? On capital, on private gain. In its completely developed form this family exists only among the bourgeoisie. But this state of things finds its complement in the enforced absence of the family among the proletariat, and in public prostitution.[5]

The interpretation of marriage as an artificial institution, constructed by a momentarily ruling ideology and being a mere equivalent to the capitalist rules of production and property, is completed by an unmasking of this "holy picture," which had to be propagated for the purpose of keeping the institution alive. "Marriage itself remained, as before, the legally recognized form, the official cloak of prostitution, and moreover, was supplemented by rich crops of adultery."[6] And Engels's formula that the degree of female emancipation is the natural measure of general emancipation reflects the basic relationship between woman's situation and that of the proletariat, and furthermore demonstrates how central a position woman's emancipation occupied within the theories of the grand masters of Socialism.

August Bebel's *Die Frau und der Sozialismus* (*Woman in the Past, Present, and Future*), written in 1879, also deserves particular consideration, because it may have served as a direct source for Shaw's writings and has not hitherto been regarded as such. Shaw himself does not mention Bebel very often; when he does, it is only with negative connotations regarding the orthodoxy of German Social Democracy.[7] Yet there are so many striking parallels between Bebel's thoughts concerning woman's position in nineteenth-century society and Shaw's *Quintessence* that there must be more than general affinities such as would be found among socialists. Fabian Tract No. 4, *What Socialism Is* (1886), gives the only, though interesting, hint concerning this relation. The chapter on "Collectivism" is subtitled "summarized from Bebel's *Woman in the Past, Present, and Future*."[8] Whether Shaw participated in the preparation of the tract is not known, since the second page merely names "certain members of the Fabian Society" as its authors. Shaw's lecture on "The New Politics: From Lassalle to the Fabians," delivered on 20 December 1889, reveals, however, that the chapter on anarchism was written by Mrs. Wilson, the section on collectivism by F. Keddell. There remains the four-page introduction to this tract, which gives an account of the historical development of the economic system as well as an attempt at defining socialism.[9] Shaw's comment, "We at last resolved to issue a tract entitled 'What Socialism Is,' "[10] need not necessarily be a hint for his participation, but could be a mere confirmation that he too thought such a tract necessary. Nevertheless, his remark about Keddell's section, "mainly borrowed from Bebel's book on 'Woman,' "[11] confirms his intimate knowledge of this book.

Yet even if Shaw did not participate, this book, serving as a basis for the early Fabian interpretation of socialism, may be regarded as one of the standard works on socialism, one which was accepted by the Fabians as an authoritative text. English translations of this book were available at the British Museum, Shaw's "second home."[12] The central place which this book occupied within the socialist theory of the time may be documented by its reissue in the "Bellamy Library" in 1893, a series on socialist literature published by William Reeves. There is no doubt, then, that Shaw the encyclopedist knew its main arguments.

While Engels only indicated the substantial relation between woman and proletariat, Bebel takes it as a basic argument on which he founds his analysis: "Woman and worker have in common that they are suppressed."[13] In analogy to *The Communist Manifesto* he proceeds by stressing the artificial and hypocritical character of marriage, and accordingly sees in it the direct product of the bourgeois organization of labor and property; and consequently questions its naturalness and reasonableness. In this institution—according to him—a specific role, which might be described in terms of dependence and submission, is ascribed to woman. "In the propertied classes woman is very often degraded to a mere birthmachine for legitimate children, a housekeeper, or a nurse for her husband, ruined in debauchery."[14] In analogy to Mill he defines the so-called natural characteristics as a product of processes of education to which woman had been subjected for generations, and in analogy to Marx the practice of marriage is for Bebel just a legal form of prostitution.

Yet Bebel takes on even more significance as far as the affinities to Shaw are concerned, when he analyzes the prostitute's economic situation: "Occasionally the prostitute, being forced into this profession by misery, is a specimen of decency and virtue in comparison with those who are searching for a husband."[15] This might unreservedly be regarded as the thesis for *Mrs Warren*. Equally interesting is the description Bebel gives of the attitude toward marriage of those concerned: "The participants strive to make marriage appear better than it actually is. We here have a degree of hypocrisy not to be found in any other period of society."[16] Read "fancy picture" or "idealism" for "hypocrisy" and you have Shaw's analysis of the ideal of marriage in the *Quintessence*.

These appear to be the three main influences on Shaw as far as this problem is concerned. It is not our purpose to document nineteenth-century influences as such, as J.B. Kaye has done in detail, nor to question Shaw's originality; only the general tradition of these particular thoughts is interesting, and then only insofar as women's emancipation was placed and discussed within a certain context, a context which may also be accepted as Shaw's. Thus, whenever Shaw discusses woman's situation, we should note that he discusses it on this political-economic level, and that the "New Woman" phenomenon—insofar as it is a rebellious attitude toward certain cultural and intellectual fashions—is merely an accompaniment of this more substantial problem.

Shaw himself makes this explicit combination of economics and morals in few instances, possibly because he simply presupposed it. The formula he gave in the Preface to *The Irrational Knot*, "Money controls morality,"[17] may serve for all the other similar remarks scattered in his later writings. The importance of the question of woman's role in society and its relation to general social problems may be seen in the fact that for Shaw a person's attitude toward this particular problem was symptomatic of that person's general political and social opinions. The creation of women characters served as a measure for the respective author's moral and political realism, the most important criterion of Shaw's literary criticism, as is well known. This Shavian critical measure, of course, was confirmed by his analysis of Ibsen's dramatic works. "Until his warfare against vulgar idealism is accomplished and a new phase entered upon in The Master Builder, all his really vivid and solar figures are women."[18]

The explanation for this Shaw repeats long after his fascination for Ibsen had lost its hold. "Ibsen's women are all in revolt against Capitalist morality."[19] This same background serves for his criticism of nineteenth-century theatre, which in its "construction" of idealized women characters veiled the misery of woman's actual situation. His collected dramatic criticism gives an exhaustive account of the contempt he felt for this concept.[20] The same is true for his criticism of Victorian novelists. He rejected "romantic" fiction for its treatment of passionate love and female submission, as well as "women's lib" novels for melodramatic, i.e., oversimplified treatment of revolt.[21] The only exception is Sarah Grand's novel *The Heavenly Twins,* because in it he found a suitable and reasonable representation of woman's situation and her effective revolt.[22] Therefore it is not astonishing that Shaw's analysis of woman's situation and of marriage in nineteenth-century society corresponds to the previously quoted passages in all essential respects.

The starting point for all three was the unmasking of marriage as a product of capitalist society. In his *Quintessence* Shaw repeats this analysis with his questioning of the naturalness of this phenomenon and his definition of it as an artificial arrangement that serves definite aims. "The family as it really is is a conventional arrangement, legally enforced." More clearly, he combines marriage with the capitalist concept of property in his preface to *Getting Married:*

> What it [marriage law] is really founded on is the morality of the tenth commandment, which English women will one day succeed in obliterating from the walls of our churches by refusing to enter any building where they are publicly classed with a man's house, his ox, and his ass, as his purchased chattels.

The analysis of woman's position in society may be derived from such an interpretation. In harmony with Mill and Bebel Shaw sees in the so-called natural characteristics the demands of a morality based on capitalist ideology to conform to this preconceived picture. "Hence arises the idealist illusion that a vocation for domestic management and the care of children is natural to women. . . . The domestic career is no more natural to all women than the military career is natural to all men."

To the inferior status of womankind is added her function as a mere machine of the man's household. With regard to her function of increasing the population and saving man's property (principle of inheritance) woman's usefulness is undeniable; as for the rest, the "birthmachine" is treated like all other objects in the household as man's property. Mill speaks of slaves and submission, Bebel of "machine." Shaw takes over both images:

> Our society . . . comes to regard Woman, not as an end in herself like man, but solely as a means of ministering to his appetite. The ideal wife is one who does everything that the ideal husband likes, and nothing else. Now to treat a person as a means instead as an end is to deny that person's right to live.

Shaw's criticism of liberalism culminates in this statement. Here the theory which claims to have as its highest aim the absolute freedom of individuals is unmasked as an ideology, which not only denies this principle to fifty percent of mankind, but even applies its definition of mankind to only the male half. Bebel, by the way, occasionally points out that the English and French languages have only one term for both "male person" (*man*) and "people in general" (*man*)—which does not mean that those languages that have two terms, e.g., the German *Mann, Mensch,* refer to a different concept of womankind.

Logically Shaw develops the same opinion as to the problem of prostitution. Regarding *Mrs Warren's Profession* there is no need to give evidence of his analysis of prostitution as caused by poverty and misery. This play almost seems to be a dramatization of Bebel's statement that in comparison to the respectable Victorian "ladies," prostitutes are specimens of virtue and decency. But Shaw even follows Engels in his analysis of marriage as the legalized form of prostitution. We find this in his preface to *Plays Unpleasant,* and in Mrs. Warren's defense of her career, as well as in his fine aphorism that "the difference between marriage and prostitution [is] the difference between Trade Unionism and unorganized casual labor."

That Shaw discussed the whole problem within a broader context, that of his criticism of idealism, does not contradict the political-economic context of his socialism. His criticism of idealism is part of his socialist theory insofar as morals and ethics are aspects of socialism. This becomes especially evident in Sydney Olivier's essay on "The Moral Basis of Socialism," which Shaw edited in *Fabian Essays in Socialism.* The same is true for Shaw's development of the principle of self-will, a seemingly total egoism as the basis for woman's behavior, which seems to be a product of his Life Force philosophy rather than his socialism. Yet to the same degree that Creative Evolution and socialism are not contradictory, but logically combined with regard to the anti-tragical, optimistic-utopian element common to both theories, so this principle of self-will is common to both theories. Mill had omitted self-will and government by self-control in the woman's situation. Bebel—who definitely cannot be suspected of any irrational theories—stressed the lack of self-control in her position, and in analogy the only duty Shaw accepts is woman's duty to herself. Thus the repudiation of duty ("Progress must involve the repudiation of an established duty at every step") is nothing less than the negative formulation of Shaw's definition of freedom. "Therefore woman has to repudiate duty altogether. In that repudiation lies her freedom." And thus the term *will*, which is discussed in his Life Force philosophy at length, has become an eminently important term in his politics as well.

The large number of women characters in Shaw's work should be seen against this background. Bebel's thesis that those who solve the problem of women have to cooperate with those to whom the solution of the general social problem appears to be the key problem of man's destiny, may be inverted for Shaw: those who want to represent general social problems on the stage may do so by dramatizing woman's situation.

It is Barbara Watson's thesis that women characters offer themselves as mouthpieces for Shaw's ideas because they are outside the idealist world of male society.[23] Shaw frequently showed that the opposite is true: that it is woman who, because of the educational processes that she was subject to, adopts and realizes man's ideals. It is not her position outside male society, but the fact that her position is a product of male society and its underlying ideology, that makes her interesting. Her position as well as that of the proletariat is a mirror of the nineteenth-century social situation in general. But whoever knows Shaw's attitude toward the proletariat will understand why he chose women, and not proletarians, for the main characters in his plays.[24]

We have seen how Shaw was fascinated by Ibsen's female characters, and it has been shown that the "woman problem" was a central theme in his political theory. One need not necessarily recall his autobiographical statement in *Sixteen Self Sketches*, "For every play I have written I have made hundreds of [political] speeches," to conclude that Shaw's characterization of women owes much to this theoretical background. For example, note his characterization of a poor woman's situation in his "Socialism and Human Nature":

> We then offer a pretty woman a position either behind the refreshment bar at a railway station for fourteen hours a day, or in some other place where her good looks will attract custom and make profit for us, assuring her at the same time that it

would be the lowest infamy for her to use her good looks to make profits for herself.[25]

This was taken over almost word by word into Mrs. Warren's justification of herself, as much as Vivie's attitude toward her mother and life in general shows strong parallels to the advice he gave his "dear Dorothea." To the same extent, *The Philanderer* offers incarnations of the different roles women could play in late Victorian society. This is true for all the women characters in his early plays, who are either in rebellion against their official status (emancipated realists) or affirm it (conformist dolls). A close and more differentiated interpretation of Shaw's female characters against this theoretical background would be valuable especially if accompanied by an analysis of how long these theories maintained their influence on Shaw's dramatic practice. As this is not the purpose of this exposition, we leave it open for further consideration.

Notes

1. Cf. Warren S. Smith, "Bernard Shaw and the London Heretics," in *Shaw: Seven Critical Essays*, N. Rosenblood, ed. (1971), pp. 51-69. According to Shaw himself he had read Mill in "his boyhood." Cf. "How I Became a Public Speaker," *Sixteen Self Sketches*, p. 57.

2. Frank Harris, *Bernard Shaw, An Unauthorized Biography Based on Firsthand Information* (1931), p. 87.

3. John Stuart Mill, "The Subjection of Women," in his *Liberty* (1966), p. 444.

4. Shaw, *My Dear Dorothea*, ed. S. Winsten (1956), p. 25.

5. Karl Marx and Friedrich Engels, *The Communist Manifesto*, Centenary Edition, (1948), pp. 30-31.

6. Friedrich Engels, *Socialism, Utopian and Scientific*, trans. E. Aveling (1892), p. 9.

7. Cf. "Ruskin's Politics," in *Bernard Shaw's Nondramatic Criticism*, ed. S. Weintraub (1972), p. 200.

8. Fabian Tract No. 4, p. 7. Actually it is a summary of the fourth chapter of this book only.

9. It should be mentioned that Shaw's Fabian Tract No. 13 of the same title ("What Socialism Is") is not identical with this introduction, as might have been expected.

10. "The New Politics: From Lassalle to the Fabians," in Shaw, *The Road to Equality*, ed. L. Crompton (1971), p. 87.

11. "The New Politics", p. 88.

12. *Woman in the Past, Present, and Future*, trans. H.B.A. Walther (1885).

13. "Frau und Arbeiter haben gemein, Unterdrückte zu sein." A. Bebel, *Die Frau und der Sozialismus* (1909, 1918), p. 9. As I was not able to find a

copy of the English translation, translations of the passages quoted are my own.

14. "In den besitzenden Klassen sinkt die Frau nicht selten . . . zum blossen Gebärapparat für legitime Kinder herab, zur Hüterin des Hauses oder zur Pflegerin des in der Debauche ruinierten Gatten." Bebel, op. cit., p. 124.

15. "Die Strassendirne, die aus bitterer Not ihr Gewerbe betreibt, ist zuweilen ein Ausbund an Anständigkeit und Tugend gegen diese Ehesucher." Op. cit., p. 115.

16. "Die Beteiligten sind interessiert, ihre Ehe vor aller Welt anders erscheinen zu lassen, als sie in Wirklichkeit ist. Es besteht hier ein Zustand der Heuchelei, wie ihn keine frühere Gesellschaftsperiode in aehnlichem Masse kannte." Op. cit., p. 105.

17. Page x. Cf. as further instances his letters, where he repeatedly affirms this concept, e.g., letter to the editor of *The Star*, 20 September 1888: "There are as many creeds as there are classes"; or letter to E.D. Girdlestone, 26 September 1890: "Virtue, morals, ethics, are all a noxious product of private property." *Collected Letters 1874-1897*, pp. 197-98, 266.

18. *The Quintessence of Ibsenism.* All quotations are from the Constable edition.

19. *The Intelligent Woman's Guide . . .*, p. 503.

20. Lenyth Spenker argues that the creation of idealistic women in a play automatically led to Shaw's rejection of it, thus stressing "woman" as the chief criterion of evaluation. Cf. his "The Dramatic Criticism of George Bernard Shaw," *Speech Monographs* 17 (1950), 28.

21. Cf. *Bernard Shaw's Nondramatic Criticism,* pp. 30-39; also his criticism of G. Allen's *The Woman Who Did* as "amusingly boyish"; *Collected Letters, 1874-1897,* p. 493.

22. Cf. e.g., *Our Theatre in the Nineties,* 2, 170. For Shaw's discussion of Grand and her influence on him see S. Weintraub, "G.B.S. Borrows From Sarah Grand: *The Heavenly Twins* And *You Never Can Tell,*" *Modern Drama* 14 No. 3, (December 1971), 288-97.

23. *A Shavian Guide to the Intelligent Woman* p. 54.

24. He rejected the notion of the proletariat as an "angelic choir" being opposed to "scoundrels" and "exploiters" (cf. Chappelow, *Shaw—The Chucker-Out,*" p. 220), as well as the ". . . melodramatic formula in which the villain shall be a bad employer and the hero a Socialist". (*OTN* 2, 192.)

25. *The Road to Equality,* p. 98.

THE "UNWOMANLY WOMAN" IN SHAW'S DRAMA

Sonja Lorichs

Woman's status in Victorian and Edwardian society before World War I differed considerably from that of the decades following her enfranchisement. During the latter part of the nineteenth century industrialism had changed the social and economic conditions for poor women by engaging increasing numbers of them in factory and office work. Women of the middle class, however, were prevented by class distinctions from earning a livelihood except as governesses, authors or artists. Being insufficiently educated or trained for professions, as there existed practically no such training for women, they were forced to lead lives of idleness until they found husbands who could offer economic security and social position. No wonder clear-sighted and intelligent men and women realized the necessity of achieving parliamentary franchise and of improving education for women. One of their spokesmen was Bernard Shaw.

One of Shaw's attractive traits was his sympathy for and interest in women, his sensitivity toward discrimination against them, and his never-failing readiness to be their advocate. He propagandized for equality between men and women through most of his major plays and some of his minor ones—plays in which the contemporary theatregoer and reader encountered female characters of a new kind. Shaw's New Woman, contrasted to the "womanly woman" who had been the ideal, he labeled the *Unwomanly Woman*. To examine how he depicted this woman in relation to her actual situation in the society he wanted to reform necessitates an investigation of her social and political background, as well as a study of the many problems that had to be solved and whose solution Shaw, indirectly or directly, suggested by creating a new heroine for the English stage.

The first full-length portrait of an Unwomanly Woman is found in 1894 in *Mrs Warren's Profession*: Vivie Warren. Beatrice Webb had suggested that Shaw write a play with "a real, modern, unromantic, hard-working woman" in it.[1] In a stage direction Shaw describes Vivie as "an attractive specimen of the sensible, able, highly-educated young middle-class English woman. Age 22. Prompt, strong, confident, self-possessed. Plain business-like dress but not dowdy." She has passed her examinations at Cambridge and is ready for an independent life as a career woman. It is conceivable that Vivie should have appeared even more unwomanly and unattractive to contemporary critics and playgoers than to modern audiences; her attitude toward her mother, the procuress, is rebellious and contemptuous. Ervine found her "unpleasing" but "undoubtedly, a sign and a portent to those who had discerning eyes in 1893."[2] In creating this stage character, Shaw, with his usual foresight, anticipated the development of women into something quite different from the Victorian "womanly woman," and in several of his plays insists that this development must be through education. As Louis Simon puts it: "Several of Shaw's plays reveal that in many of his characterizations of women there lurks an implicit criticism of the kind of education they have been subjected to."[3]

To some extent Vivie may have been modeled on Ibsen's Nora in *A Doll's House*, who made a strong impression on Shaw, but Vivie is "strong" from the beginning. There are other differences too, since Shaw, no doubt unconsciously, used his sister Lucy for a model.[4] Her brusque treatment of her brother reminds us of Vivie's attitude toward her mother.

Mrs. Warren is described as "rather spoilt and domineering, and decidedly vulgar," but Shaw stresses her vitality, thrift, energy and outspokenness. She has made her way from the slums and prostitution to wealth, independence and an exciting life as the manager of a chain of brothels in Brussels and other towns; and even if it is dirty work, it is stimulating and gives her satisfaction. She is indeed a modern career woman, though her work is suspect. As Mrs. Warren confesses, "I must have work and excitement, or I shall go melancholy mad. . . . The life suits me: I'm fit for it and not for anything else. . . . I cant give it up—not for anybody." The playgoers may have found Mrs. Warren even more interesting than Vivie, the heroine of the play, and that may be due partly to her career from the miserable background of the slums, partly to her emotionality, her hasty changes of temper, her whims and her sex appeal. Assuredly, there had never been such a personality as Mrs. Warren on the English stage.

In *Mrs Warren's Profession* Shaw attacked one of the most revolting abuses of contemporary society: prostitution. A.W. Acton, a physician and now-discredited scientist in sex research, venereal diseases and prostitution, believed that "prostitution was an inevitable, almost organic part of society. Efforts to repress or extirpate it have always ended in failure."[5] Prostitution was the reverse of the Victorian medal. F.N. Charrington, in his article "The Battle of the Music Halls," of which Shaw must have been aware, gives many instances of the life young girls serving as prostitutes were leading in such places in 1862. The halls were licensed by the authorities even though protests were made by the Bishop of Bedford as well as thousands of citizens, both men and women. Life behind the scenes at the halls was often exceedingly crude and licentious, and destructive to both young girls and young men. These conditions still existed when Shaw wrote *Mrs Warren's Profession*; much later he used a music hall as the scene for the riot in *Fanny's First Play*.

The ramifications of prostitution also included white slave traffic. Young girls were decoyed to Paris, Brussels and Ostend by means of tempting advertisements, and kept against their will in brothels. It was evidently not merely a coincidence that Shaw used Brussels as Mrs. Warren's operating base. In the eighties, reports from a special committee, evidence by young girls who had been kept as prostitutes against their will, and William T. Stead's sensational exposé of child prostitution at last brought about an amendment of the English law.[6] Still, as a vestryman of St. Pancras Vestry, Shaw could state that "there were long sections of main streets in which almost every house was a brothel."[7]

Mrs. Warren's career was predestined, as in reality were those of thousands of poor, good-looking girls, unscrupulously exploited and underpaid; the choice was either to starve or to eke out their income by prostitution, and there were thousands of them in London alone. The traffic in girls was an urgent problem as late as 1910, as Kerchener-Knight states: "It has proved the great stumbling block to the free discussion of the abominable traffic in womanhood . . . it has become impossible to ventilate the grievance through the medium of the press."[8] Shaw's criticism of prostitution had not been particularly effective.

Another important theme of the play is the education of a girl who can afford higher education. There were many private and public schools for girls founded in the late nineteenth century. Admission to universities and degrees was not generally granted, though London University opened its doors to women as early as 1878 and was also the first to appoint a woman to a chair in 1913. At the exclusively male Oxford and Cambridge universities, colleges were opened for women students about 1880, but full membership or degrees were not granted until about the middle of the twentieth century and even later.[9] Thus, in Shaw's play, Vivie was permitted to pass the examination for the mathematical tripos, but as a female she did not have the right to a degree at Cambridge University.

Major Barbara (1905), Shaw's next play about a rebellious young woman who has enough courage and self-assurance to break away from conventional life, was also exceptional in presenting a drama with a Salvationist woman as the heroine. The English stage had not seen before a heroine who rejected the conventional life of the daughter of an upper-class family and worked in the slums as a Salvationist. Lady Britomart, Barbara's mother, a very domineering person who bullies the whole family, gives the clue to Barbara's personality, for she bullies the people at the Salvation shelter where she works and is "full of life and vigor and unconsciously very imperious," as Shaw puts it.[10] Unlike her weak brother, Barbara rebels against the family tyrant and chooses her own career. When her mother nags her, Barbara is self-confident enough not to mind. Her affection for her mother seems to have changed into indifference. Two strong wills do not generally get on very well, and Barbara's mind is now occupied with a much more impressive and complicated personality who has come into her life—her father. She is a born leader, a clever organizer, able to handle such difficult brutes as Bill Walker or a ruthless industrial manager like her father, Andrew Undershaft, as the psychologically admirable scene in the second act illustrates. It reveals Shaw's sure intuition when penetrating a new complex of problems: the Salvationist conception of sin, repentance and salvation versus ruthless egoism and crass materialism. Barbara has piety and moral superiority. Her simplicity and innocence are brought out in great contrast to the experienced and cunning Undershaft; she is the idealist who fights in vain to win the soul of the materialist. After his offer of £5,000 has been received by the Army, "tainted money" earned on the production of deadly weapons, Barbara breaks down. Her faith in Army work and in God is shaken, for all that she believed in and all that she tried to achieve through her work in the Army has been in vain. She used to be happy saving souls by bread, prayer and the promise of happiness in the life to come, but now her enthusiasm is gone; the hospitals, the churches and the Salvation Army exist thanks to the antisocial profits of donors like Bodger, the whiskey distiller, and Undershaft, the munitions factory owner. The latter's doctrine voices Shaw's own conviction that poverty is "the worst of crimes," "the vilest sin of man and society." Undershaft is a capitalist; yet in practice he is a Marxist, his doctrine as an industrial manager being that the only remedy for poverty, underpayment, alcoholism and criminality is a well-organized industrial community where the laborers get reasonable wages, good food and housing. The Salvation Army cannot abolish poverty with bread and treacle. Thus Undershaft makes Barbara retest her situation and faith, and when he suggests to her to come and preach to his people, for their souls are empty, she regains her equanimity, finding a new field for her work as a soul-saver. She is the personification of her creator's idea of a New Woman embodied in an ideal Salvationist.

Major Barbara is one of Shaw's most religious plays, in which the problem of poverty is once more introduced and its solution presented in the description of Undershaft's utopian industrial community. Shaw had often listened to Salvation Army meetings and had been struck by the dramatic and inspiring preaching and singing of the "Lasses" in the streets. He united his original idea of writing a religious play with his impressions of the Salvation Army. That he was well aware of its work and the atmosphere of its meetings is evidenced through the whole play. The fourfold scheme of General Booth's Army is also manifested in the play: the "going to the people with the message of salvation," exemplified by Barbara's preaching (her sermon is added in the screen version); the "attracting the people" by the drumming and singing; the "saving the people" by Barbara's efforts to save Bill Walker and Undershaft; and the "employing the people" by her promise to procure some work for Price.[11] General Booth had wanted his officers to be in close contact with the poor and miserable. The work in the slums was not always without risks, as Herman Lagercrantz, the Swedish officer and Salvationist, has described. Some districts were said to be shunned even by the police, but the Salvationists were courageous people, and particularly the "Lasses" merited admiration for their work under the most revolting conditions among ill, destitute and alcoholic men and women.[12] That work demanded courage, patience and optimism; it also called for the ability to handle such downtrodden people. The demands on the "soldiers" and "officers" were exacting; they had to labor hard among the poor and miserable, among prostitutes and criminals. In the Army, women not only devoted themselves to social service, but they were also allowed, even as young girls, to preach, to officiate at the marriage ceremony, and to commit the dead to their last resting place. It has also been possible for women as well as for men to attain all ranks of the Army: Captains, Majors, Commissioners, even Generals, and thus command both male and female Salvationists and the Army of a whole country. The equality between men and women was achieved thanks to Catherine Booth, the General's wife, reverently called "the Army Mother," who was the first woman to preach in the Salvation Army. Thus in the Army equality between men and women was a fact at least half a century before it was in the secular world.

It was not exceptional, however, for young women of the upper classes in England to try to alleviate the misery among the poor in the slums, whether as Salvationists or on their own initiative. In his preface to Bernard Watson's work on the Army, F. Coutts, the Army General, declares that "laymen and women" were "drawn from all levels of society" in later years, which General Booth "could hardly have dreamed" possible.[13] That young ladies from the upper-middle class engaged in work among the poor in the East End of London is also stated as a well-known fact by Marian Ramelson.[14]

What Shaw achieved in his drama, however, was not only the creation of two striking characters intensely alive, but a statement of his opinion of the Salvation Army creed and the futility of its activities, as long as "the crime of poverty" was not abolished. His main object in *Major Barbara*, as in earlier plays, is to attack contemporary badly organized society, where the rich become still richer, and as a consequence poverty, slums, dishonesty and alcoholism are inevitable.

In *Getting Married* (1908), the most important of his discussion plays about marriage and divorce, Shaw introduced two more emancipated women: Edith, the bride, and Lesbia, the spinster. Both object to conventional marriage unless their own conditions are respected: economic independence for Edith, and for Lesbia a nonsmoker for a husband, whom she can also get rid of for two years when a child is born and needs her mothering. Shaw characterizes Edith as a person of "impetuous temper and energetic will . . . imperious and dogmatic." She has read an article on the indissoluble marriage and realizes how dependent on her husband she will be for the rest of her life. She refuses to enter into any contract unless her husband specifically consents to giving her a regular salary as his housekeeper, and liberty to continue her struggle for the exploited and maltreated factory girls, whom she supports against their dishonest and inhuman employers.

Lesbia is also unwilling to marry. She declared: "I am a regular old maid. . . . I am proud of my independence and jealous for it. I have a sufficiently well-stocked mind to be very good company for myself if I have plenty of books and music." To the stupefied General, her suitor of many years, she declares that she is ready to enter into an alliance with him in order to realize her "right to maternity." Lesbia's problem can be solved neither in a conventional way by marriage nor in an unconventional way by a *liaison*. She belongs to the "superfluous women" whose potential as wives and mothers is lost in society. Lesbia expresses this point of view thus: "Just because I have the qualities my country wants most, I shall go barren to my grave; whilst the women who have neither the strength to resist marriage nor the intelligence to understand its infinite dishonor will make the England of the future." In some respects Lesbia is related to Vivie in *Mrs Warren's Profession*: both are cool, self-controlled, reserved and strong-willed, independent of men and sexual relationship with them; both despise marriage and prefer not to meddle with men except as friends. But whereas Vivie is a hard-working woman, preparing herself for her career, Lesbia's future is unknown. The interest she first awakens is not maintained; the characterization is incomplete.

The discussion in the play, however, is continued among the assembled wedding guests, the Bishop and other persons, and they try in vain to formulate a reasonable marriage contract. The arguments for and against marriage cross and run counter to each other in the general discussion, in which topics such as monogamy, polygyny and polyandry occur, an example of adultery with "hotel-evidence" and "brutality" as reasons for a divorce, free love—a farcical treatment of serious problems, spotlighting many current matrimonial problems in which the characters are involved. The critics were disgusted, but what would the effect have been if the farcical treatment had been left out? Most certainly an unendurably dull "conversation."

The English marriage was practically indissoluble, except in cases of adultery, until the Matrimonial Causes Act of 1937. Thus in 1931 Henderson could state about *Getting Married*: "The play is sometimes said to be obsolete; and in America and many European countries it does not fit facts; but in England it is as topical as ever."[15] "Hotel-evidence" had been the usual expedient for obtaining divorce in most cases of adultery. But if the offense of collusion was suspected, an oath had to be sworn by the petitioner that no collusion between the parties existed; otherwise the situation might become disastrous. Both the Church and the State considered the institution of marriage of great importance. Before World War I, women were seldom granted an absolute divorce; this happened only in cases of aggravated adultery. In a divorce suit the wife, unlike the husband, could neither be plaintiff, defendant nor witness. As Wanda Neff states: "Before the law, then, a married woman was a chattel, an infant, made helpless by a system designed for primitive society."[16] Consequently, divorces were infrequent, but after the war the number steadily increased, as is evidenced in *British Political Facts*: 1910, 81 cases; 1920, 3,747; 1940, 8,396; 1950, 32,516 cases. The Act of 1937 added three new grounds for divorce: cruelty, desertion and incurably unsound mind. Before that date, a husband was legally entitled to beat his wife, provided the stick he used was not thicker than his thumb. Reports from police courts, however, often noted savage assaults on wives by husbands, in which the loss of an eye was common.[17]

In the fourteen years that separate *Mrs Warren's Profession* from *Getting Married*, very little had happened to forward the emancipation of women or to improve their working conditions. With the two different types of the New Woman, Edith, the emotional and humane woman, and Lesbia, a rather audacious construction of a modern woman—the most strikingly Unwomanly Woman that Shaw had presented on the stage so far—he emphasized his view on the necessity of Woman's emancipation by revolt against the conventional marriage of the middle classes.

After *Getting Married*, Shaw continued creating strong-willed women. Fanny O'Dowda, the alleged author of the play within *Fanny's First Play* (1910), and its heroine Margaret, Fanny's *alter ego*, were the next. They are delineated against a background of contemporary events. They too rebel against their conventional environment, according to Shaw's advice in the preface to young people: "Do something that will get you into trouble." That would teach them how life is led among common people whom they otherwise would know nothing about, as outward respectability and conventional behavior counted more than individual integrity and self-respect for women. Such new experiences, Shaw maintains, overstepping the bounds of class distinctions and even decorum, would develop them into thinking and compassionate fellow-men and fellow-women.

Fanny O'Dowda rebels against an old-fashioned environment and her escapist eccentric of a father by writing and producing a play that gives him a severe shock. Fanny is a modern radical undergraduate at Cambridge, testing her ability as a playwright with her play that introduces an entirely "new" heroine, Margaret Knox, who sharply accuses the old generation of always putting respectability before everything else—"pretending, pretending"—instead of facing realities. After her prison stay she has found that reality can be brutal, filthy and revolting, and her new experience has released her from inhibitions that were due to her environment and education. Her enlightenment now includes realities of which her parents are ignorant. She had been set free from all the silly pretenses of her former life and is ready to start a new, independent life with a man who, like her, has experienced a new environment that has developed him. Some of the suffragette spirit is found in Margaret. Like many suffragettes, she rebelled against an old-fashioned society in which a young woman was not allowed to choose her own way of living.

There is no doubt that *Fanny's First Play* refers to topical events that concern the contemporary emancipation movement in England. In 1910, when the play was written, the suffragette movement entered into an increasingly militant phase, of which Shaw was well aware and which he supported in the newspapers. There is a striking resemblance between Margaret's tale of her prison experiences and the narratives of the suffragettes suffering in jail.[18] When "Darling Dora" in the play describes her exit from prison, it is exactly like the reception that the suffragettes received from their friends in the movement when they had been released. This can in fact be seen in a newspaper photo in *The Daily Mirror*, 22 August 1908.[19] Darling Dora's and Margaret's descriptions are topical but pale compared to contemporary events, the treatment in prison of militant suffragettes. Lady Lytton is a name mentioned in Shaw's play; she was in reality a famous and courageous suffragette who in 1910 was put in the Third Division of a prison, the severest treatment, and suffered irreparable heart damage as a result of forcible feeding when hunger-striking. Protests were raised by 100 M.P.'s, by university staffs and by a number of organizations abroad, where the rumor about the treatment of hunger-striking women had spread. A protest containing the signatures of such famous persons as Madame Curie, George Brandes, Ellen Key, Selma Lagerlöf, Maurice Maeterlinck and Romain Rolland was presented to the English authorities.

One of the most horrible cases was that of Emily Wilding Davison, who in 1909, after the hideous procedure of forcible feeding, barricaded herself in her cell. The magistrate ordered a hose-pipe to be turned on her through the window. The prisoner, who had sustained five days' hunger-strike, gasped for breath when the heavy stream of water began to fill the cell. At last the magistrate ordered the cruel procedure to be stopped and the victim to be taken to a hospital. The authorities were declared guilty of "a grave error of judgment." Among other colleagues, Dr. Forbes Ross stated in *The Observer* that the methods employed for forcible feeding were "an act of brutality beyond common endurance." In fact, it brought many women to complete collapse, as was the case with Mrs. Pankhurst, "the greatest public figure" of the suffragettes, a cultivated lady who was sent to prison fourteen times. Some methods of great cruelty were the use of handcuffs day and night; forcible stripping of clothes; "frog-march" (mentioned in *Fanny's First Play*), that is, the carrying of the victim face downwards, by hands and feet; besides the use of the feeding tube with its sharp point of steel.[20] Shaw protested in the *Manchester Guardian* and declared that the vote must be given to women and become their means of getting into Parliament: "The only decent government is a government by a body of men and women. . . . I have sat on committees both with women and without them, and emphatically I say that there ought always to be women on public bodies. Decency demands it."[21] When World War I broke out, the militancy stopped, and the suffragettes went out to do their duty as nurses or factory hands.

Such was the social and political situation of English women at the beginning of the twentieth century. The relationship between Shaw's drama and the suffragette movement, as well as his support of it, is evident. It may be somewhat surprising that, loyal as he remains to the democratic principle of equality between men and women and keen advocate of women's education and emancipation that he was, Shaw should have restricted himself to using the suffragette movement merely as a background for his heroines, instead of using the highly dramatic subject matter that contemporary events afforded in a serious play. He may have found it too complicated and painful to handle. The only play he wrote about the suffragettes was the burlesque *Press Cuttings*, but whereas there is a message about another kind of emancipation—the emancipation of young girls—in *Fanny's First Play*, there is only high comedy in *Press Cuttings*.[22]

In *Pygmalion* (1913) Shaw created a heroine entirely different from the middle-class young ladies rebelling against their conventional environment: Eliza, the flower girl from the slums, a vulgar and dirty "guttersnipe." Like Pygmalion's statue in the myth, she was transfigured by Pygmalion-Higgins into a West End lady by learning to speak the King's English as a new language and at the same time acquiring good manners and a superficial education—all in six months. Depicted as emerging from poor people in the slums, she is a sample of the New Woman in Shaw's sense. There is also a minor character who is that sort of woman: Clara, the upper-class girl who finds satisfaction in work in an old furniture shop, according to Shaw's "epilogue," instead of the futility of the idle genteel life with its "husband-hunting." Eliza is energetic and intelligent enough to take the opportunity to improve herself in the hope of becoming an assistant in a florist's shop. Her progress in society is balanced by Clara's and Freddie's unwilling descent of the social ladder—a sample of the class circulation that Shaw recommends here as in *Fanny's First Play*, implying the abolishment of class discrimination and the "crime of poverty."

But *Pygmalion* also serves another purpose: it preaches the importance of the education of women. That was a lifelong interest of Shaw, whose first literary achievement, *My Dear Dorothea*, was actually an epistolary presentation of the twenty-two-year-old author's views on women's education. *Pygmalion* is no doubt the most outspoken of Shaw's plays as concerns women's right to have an education and to become independent human beings. A woman must have the right to choose her own career and should never be a mere appendage to a man; she must be treated as a person with a soul and not as a slave and slipper-fetcher, trod upon as dirt and abused in bad language by a man with an uncontrolled temper. Eliza realized that she must get some education, but what in reality were the chances of education for Eliza and those like her? A poor girl in the slums did not get more than a minimum of the elementary stage and possibly a basic training in housewifery. Through the Education Act of 1870, attendance at elementary school was made compulsory. Still there were many children who either did not go to or spent a very short time at school, because of the poverty of their family. There was a great difference between the standard of teaching and subjects taught at schools that poor children attended and those of primary and secondary schools attended by children of wealthy parents. This was roughly the situation for poor girls as it existed when Shaw wrote *Pygmalion*. For all its farcical entertainment, its didactic purpose is evident: *Pygmalion* provides the climax of Shaw's pleading in his plays for the education of women.

Even if the farcical element in the description of the two female ministers in *The Apple Cart* (1929) is prominent, still, underlying the bantering depiction of these unique women, there is the implication that career women could reach the highest possible rank in society. The introduction of female cabinet ministers was without counterpart in English political life before 1929 when Margaret Bondfield took her seat in the Cabinet as the first woman minister. Lysistrata in the play is too ambitious in her profession to allow her personal interests and the desire for pleasure and happiness to interfere with the demands and duties of her high office. "I love my department," she exclaims, "I dream of nothing but its efficiency." Lysistrata is an excellent specimen of the Unwomanly Woman as a career woman in Shavian drama.

Among the Unwomanly Women, Joan in *Saint Joan* (1923) occupies a conspicuous place. A rebel against the society of her own time, Joan was preceded by Annajanska (in a minor play, *Annajanska, the Bolshevik Empress*, 1917), a purely fictional amazon who is depicted as a royal princess turned revolutionary leader in the Russian revolution in 1917-18. Joan, with her demand for individual integrity, was a dangerous threat to the established temporal and eccleciastical authorities of the Middle Ages, and was therefore "diabolically inspired." Joan caused not only political problems but social problems by her stubborn refusal to adapt herself to the conventional habits of medieval women: she insisted on wearing men's dress and having her hair bobbed as men did. At the historic trial this was judged as a sin and was one of the reasons for her excommunication as a heretic.

Joan is depicted as Shaw conceived her after reading Murray's translation of the trial and the rehabilitation reports. What particularly appealed to Shaw was an extremely interesting woman, an extraordinary historical personage, who was "very capable; a born boss," and who "had Joan not been one of those 'unwomanly women,' . . . might have been canonized much sooner." Joan is depicted in the play as an individual with an iron will, able to inspire both soldiers and officers to fight against the enemy. She never doubts the mission she has to perform and she never hesitates to protest against all authorities. Shaw's peasant girl as soldier demonstrates incredible courage. Her behavior and demands are audacious; her magnetic personality influences all who come into contact with her. She has enormous self-confidence and presumption and a compulsion for masculine life as a soldier. "You have the makings of a soldier in you," Dunois comments, and she answers, "I am a soldier. I do not want to be thought of as a woman." Joan is, beyond comparison, the most Unwomanly Woman in the Shavian canon.

"I have always stood up for the intellectual capacity of women. I like to see the combative spirit in them," Shaw wrote.[23] His drama reveals his intense involvement with women's education and emancipation in order to attain an ideal: woman as an independent individual with the same political and social rights as man. By creating his suggestive and entertaining plays of ideas with their focus on the Unwomanly Woman, in contrast to the conventional heroine on the English stage, Shaw influenced large audiences and made them recognize their discrimination against women.

Notes

1. As quoted in St. John Ervine, *Bernard Shaw, His Life, Work and Friends* (1956), p. 255.

2. Ervine, p. 256.

3. Louis Simon, *Shaw on Education* (1958), p. 195.

4. Stephen Grecco, "Vivie Warren's Profession: A New Look at *Mrs Warren's Profession*," *Shaw Review* 10, no. 3, 93.

5. As quoted in Steven Marcus, *The Other Victorians* (1967), pp. 5-7.

6. See Act of 1885, Kester, "The Legal Climate of Shaw's Problem Plays," p. 74.

7. "The Unmentionable Case for Woman's Suffrage," *Englishwoman* 1 (March 1909), 120.

8. G. Kerchener-Knight, *The White Slave Traffic* (1910), pp. 6-7.

9. Full membership and the right to receive degrees were not conferred on women by Oxford until 1920 and by Cambridge until 1948. (Sources: *Handbook to the University of Oxford*, 1964, pp. 308-9; *Commonwealth Universities Yearbook*, 1974, p. 301.)

10. As quoted in *Playboy and Prophet*, p. 808.

11. Hulda Friederichs, *The Romance of the Salvation Army* (1907), p. 12.

12. Herman Lagercrantz, *I Skilda Varldar (In Different Worlds)* (1948), pp. 6-8, 70, 74-76, 93-95.

13. Bernard Watson, *A Hundred Years' War: The Salvation Army, 1865-1965* (1964), p. 9.

14. Marian Ramelson, *The Petticoat Rebellion: A Century of Struggle for Women's Rights* (1967), p. 135.

15. *Playboy and Prophet*, p. 560.

16. Wanda Neff, *Victorian Working Women: An Historical and Literary Study of Women in British Industries and Professions, 1832-1850* (1966), p. 210.

17. Ramelson, p. 53.

18. E. Sylvia Pankhurst, *The Suffragette Movement* (1931), pp. 438-54.

19. Pankhurst, p. 308. Consult also Judith Kanzantzis, *Women in Revolt: The Fight for Emancipation,* Jackdaw, No. 49 (1968).

20. Pankhurst, pp. 385, 390-91.

21. "G.B.S. and a Suffragist," *Tribune,* 12 March 1960, p. 1.

22. See Michael Weimer, *"Press Cuttings:* G.B.S. and Women's Suffrage," p. 84.

23. As quoted by Blanche Patch, *Thirty Years with G.B.S.,* p. 63. For further information about Shaw's New Woman see Sonja Lorichs, "The Unwomanly Woman in Bernard Shaw's Drama and Her Social and Political Background" (Ph.D. diss., Uppsala, 1973).

III

SEX ROLES OR TRUE VOCATION?

THE NEW WOMAN AND
THE NEW COMEDY

Barbara Bellow Watson

When Shaw thinks about women, something remarkable happens. He makes no assumptions. It would be wonderful enough to make no assumptions about what women are fitted for, what their place in society should be. The real wonder is to begin thinking about women without assuming that there is any mystery at all. Shaw does so and instead of wearing himself out trying to solve a mystery that does not exist, sets to work observing the life around him. Experience indicates that if man is not mysterious, woman is not mysterious either. If woman is an enigma, isn't man? "I always assumed that a woman was a person exactly like myself, and that is how the trick is done."[1]

The trick is Shaw's creation of a long list of interesting characters who happen to be females, and that contribution alone should make him a patron saint of the women's movement. Beginning nearly a hundred years ago with the independent and intelligent women in his novels, and continuing through his last plays, Shaw turned out a distinctive product, the Shavian woman—the quintessence of the New Woman. But the full significance of this Shavian woman emerges only as an element in a larger pattern in which the woman as character and the woman as theme are largely interchangeable. And in changing the treatment of women, in placing women as subjects at the center of the dramatic structure, Shaw changed radically the structure of comedy itself. The Shavian comedy of ideas is full of ideas on all kinds of subjects, but the revolutionary aspect of its comic structure is tied most essentially to its ideas on women.

If conflict is at the center of drama, the enduring themes of drama in our culture have been conflicts between the needs or conscience of the individual and the requirements of social institutions, political, religious or sexual. In comedy the pattern has been even more specific. A funny thing happens on the way to the wedding. There is conflict between the sexual wishes of the powerless young and the restrictive rulings of the unreasonable old. It is understood that there is only one happy solution for such a conflict. When lovers marry, comedies can end. In Greek, Renaissance and Restoration comedy, and in the sentimental plays that mark the decline of the comic spirit after the Restoration, this pattern manifests itself in various ways, but remains essentially an expression of the social values of a relatively stable society. In some sense, Shakespeare may indeed be our contemporary. In another, our age, beginning in the eighteenth century, is no more like Renaissance England than it is like ancient Greece, and since comedy is so specific to the values of a particular culture, Shakespeare is less our contemporary in the comedies than in the tragedies and histories. It is probably significant that comedy fell into a long coma during just the period when this fundamental change in social expectations was beginning. Social stability, the reliable repetition of the patterns of life, could no longer be counted on. And once a new consciousness had been shaped by the conditions of modern life, it was no longer possible to construct any comedy with real vitality upon the old pattern. In Shavian comedy the pattern has shifted radically. Instead of the conflict between the individual with state and church, specifically in comedy the conflict between the lover and the laws and mores of marriage, Shavian drama deals preeminently with the conflict between the individual woman's humanity and the rigidity of the sex role assigned to her. This shift in subject matter represents also a profound shift in the structure of the comedy, reflecting an essentially changed society.

The revolutionary structure of Shaw's comedy is not, of course, an isolated phenomenon. The new drama of Ibsen, Strindberg and Checkhov is one in which the woman is not only more important but important in a quite different way. Woman has changed from being primarily an element in the plot to being primarily an element in the thought of the play. Her part in the action becomes less a matter of circumstance, less external, and more a matter of her own personality and volition, more internal and psychological. Literature in general during this whole period (beginning before the French Revolution with the rise of the romantic consciousness) shifts its center of gravity from exterior to interior events, reflecting the individualism, the egalitarianism, and the psychological preoccupations of the time, and it is not surprising that the man of action should begin to be replaced at center stage by the woman of awareness. The man of sensibility is there also, but it is obvious that the possibility of having a woman as hero increases when the heroism is inner. The young man adventuring his way to success never disappears in fact or fiction, but his story begins to convey less to both men and women than that of the woman who cannot adventure against the world but does struggle, lighting up in the hopelessness of her attempt the whole landscape of the struggle that each one is puzzling out alone. Since every woman has, in addition to personal conflicts of her own, the universal conflict of the individual female with the expectations of a sex role that is made to fit everyone and no one, the woman's struggle for self-realization has a special weight. This is not yet the Shavian woman, the "woman of action," but it is the same atmosphere that will produce her at a later stage. Even outside the realm of literature, public debate on "the Woman Question" has more than a hundred years of tragicomic history. Here too, though the outer conflicts with the world of men and laws have been monstrous and ludicrous enough, the inner conflicts have been the distinctive mark of this particular liberation. The cant concerning women has been institutionalized into a prison and internalized so thoroughly that every outward conflict exacerbates an inner war, the war of the born self against the assigned self. Melodramatic, tragic, pathetic in other fictions, this war undergoes a transformation in Shavian comedy, where it becomes funny, trium- phant and profound.

In this new kind of comedy the revolutionary nature of the new era is given its artistic expression. If the traditional pattern of conflict is between the spontaneous desires of the young and the stiff resis- tance of the old, with the marriage of young lovers as the goal and the triumph, the relation of this theme to traditional society is easy to see. The desired conclusion is simply wedding, a reciprocal pro- cess by which society accedes to lovers and they to society. At this point the young ones begin to become old ones; the very triumph by which they have forced society to accept and legitimize their union integrates them into the structure of legal and social insitutions. The young lover, once wedded, becomes a shareholder in the status quo, an old father in the bud. There could be no more perfect ex- pression of traditional society than this ending that implies an eter- nal recurrence of the same patterns generation after generation. There is always a Polonius to remind us that in his time he suffered much for love and to prove that this makes no difference to his deeds. The order of society, in this view, is tantamount to an order of nature. That is where Shaw breaks off from the tradition, and that is where the unromantic woman, the individualized woman of his plays, becomes by her very existence a revolutionary theme. Shaw sees society, and even nature, as capable of genuine evolution, of an escape from recurrence, and his comedy reflects that view in its very structure. Both the nature of the conflict and the nature of its resolution differ in Shaw from the traditional comic pattern, even when the events of the plot seem most conventional.

Both thought and character in the Shavian drama proclaim the possibility of radical change, for they defy law itself, not just some abuse of the law. They defy custom itself, not just some perversion of custom. They are, in fact, essentially criminal, in the sense R.P. Blackmur, in his discussion of *Madame Bovary*, suggests that beauty and vitality are essentially criminal in their disturbance of conformist social being. Shaw's heroines and the vital geniuses among his heroes are criminals of the triumphant genus revolutionary. All subscribe to Andrew Undershaft's motto, "Unashamed," and all, unlike the tragic nonconformists of nineteenth-century fiction, Emma Bovary, Tess, Anna Karenina, know how to emerge as winners in the battle of life. Their secret is simple: it is total subversion. Instead of being punished for breaking one law while keeping others, they succeed by overturning the whole code. Criminality, in Shaw, is an intellectual thing. The illusions that harm you are the illusions you believe, and our laws are a codification of our illusions.

In comedy the most complete rejection of tradition is a play that ends with its leading characters *not* getting married and treats this ending as a rapturous fulfillment. There is one whole category of Shavian courtships in which the woman escapes from marriage and from the tyranny of love with the same swoon of relief that drops other women into a lover's arms. In *Captain Brassbound's Conversion*, Lady Cicely, a gifted moralist and tactician, finds herself almost mesmerized into marriage in the last minutes of the action but, reprieved for the final curtain, cries, "How glorious! How glorious! And what an escape!" Shaw calls the thesis of the play "trite," and of course its revenge motif and its celibacy motif have both been dealt with in the New Testament, but in modern comedies both are unusual.

In regard to *Pygmalion*, the issue has been sharply drawn by the desire of directors to sweep Eliza into the arms of Professor Higgins in an illogical and irrelevant final embrace. Shaw resisted this in his lifetime and wrote a full explanation showing the logic of the true ending, but there is more to it than logic. Like the ending of *King Lear*, which has also given offense, this one has poetry. The curtain falls on a new kind of consummation, a woman finding herself.

These endings in which a woman (sometimes a man) finds herself instead of losing herself, even though they fit the standard Shavian pattern of reversal or paradox, are highly significant. In all the rest of literature there are few such findings. Colette ends *La Vagabonde* this way, but the ending carries far less conviction than Shaw's because Colette goes to great lengths to establish the reality of the love that has to be rejected in favor of the woman's self-realization. In realistic fiction the more strongly this point is made the more difficult it is to believe. The artistic problem is solved more satisfactorily in Kate Chopin's novella, *The Awakening* (1899), in which a nineteenth-century woman who has every advantage life can offer her, except for illusions about her feminine role, recognizes suicide as the only escape from her conflicts. The cold passion of this suicide makes it as different from those of Emma Bovary and Anna Karenina as such an act can be, but it hardly answers the question women are asking now: can a woman find herself (herself—not somebody's wife) without incurring death or disfigurement in doing so? Shaw's comedies say yes. They also say of course. They also say everybody knows it. Here, as in so much of contemporary writing about women, comedy is the mode that works best.

Even where the classic conclusion of comedy in a wedding takes place, the Shavian vision differs radically from tradition. None of these weddings is the simple ritual solution expected in comedy. To each the Shavian comedy of ideas imparts some meaning that gives comfort to the woman in rebellion against the marriage panacea. The question is met most explicitly in *Getting Married*. Here the subject of the play is actually the question: to marry or not to marry and why? In one sense the pattern is standard enough. An obstacle is placed in the way of the engaged couple, and that obstacle is eventually cleared away. Although Shaw claimed in a newspaper interview before the play opened that there is no plot but only an argument, the argument in this case functions as a plot and does just what a letter, an abduction or a mistaken identity would do in another play: it brings about the awaited wedding. But the wedding that follows this long exposition of the various impossibilities of marriage is accomplished with symbolic fitness away from all the ritual prepared for the other wedding that was to have taken place. It is as though the young couple had become different people after reading the pamphlet on the laws governing marriage that has so horrified them on their wedding morning, as though they had actually been prevented from marrying each other in the sense they first intended. Having lost their illusions before instead of after the wedding, the couple marry with less ceremony, and the changed meaning of that rite is made unmistakable by its changed position in the play. The announcement of the event is brief and prosaic; coming as it does just after Mrs. George's rhapsodic apostrophe to love (and complaint to men), it has a minimal effect, and the argument goes on for fourteen pages more. The final word on marriage in this play is Mrs. George's: "Hm! Like most men, you think you know everything a woman wants, dont you? But the thing one wants most has nothing to do with marriage at all." The question of what this is remains very properly suspended in the air among the many requirements the women in the play would like to make of marriage if they are to consent to it at all. The men, interestingly enough, find the status quo less intolerable. The bride has a Christlike objection to letting marriage interfere with her work for justice and salvation. Lesbia wants children but no husband. Leo wants a ménage à trois ("Well, I l o v e them both.") or better: "I should like to marry a lot of men. I should like to have Rejjy for every day, and Sinjon for concerts and theatres and going out in the evenings, and some great austere saint for about once a year at the end of the season, and some perfectly blithering idiot of a boy to be quite wicked with. I so seldom feel wicked; and, when I do, it's such a pity to waste it merely because it's too silly to confess to a real grown-up man." And the bishop's opinion is that "most imaginative and cultivated young women feel like that."

Mrs. George, the mystic and philanderer, wants her marriage to stand like a rock while she flits off with various lovers and writes passionate letters to the Bishop about meeting him in heaven. Finally, the greengrocer's wife, the only woman in the play who accepts marriage and motherhood on the usual terms, is so thoroughly a wife and mother that her husband cannot talk to her and her children leave home as soon as possible.

When a wedding takes place in the midst of these discussions, it has very much the same effect on the meaning of the play as if no wedding had taken place at all. Interest has been focused on what will come after, and not on resolving the tangle that comes before. This is comedy of argument with a vengeance, and the subject of the argument is marriage, primarily woman's need to preserve a self in spite of marriage.

Man and Superman seems to be the chief stumbling block for feminists approaching Shaw. Here, of course, the outline of the plot is conventional to the point of parody. The curtain does indeed come down on one engagement announced, one secret marriage accepted. Ann does employ feminine wiles to get her man. And the author does in the Epistle Dedicatory speak of Woman as mother and say that "Ann is Everywoman." All this looks like male chauvinism and also like classic comedy. But not quite. Without taking the technical out provided by the author's saying this is "not a play, but a volume which contains a play," it is still possible to see an essential difference from traditional comedy, the very difference that the inclusion of the woman's viewpoint makes.

The pursuit of matrimony, running but never smooth, is again the center of the comic pattern. Octavius woos Ann, who woos Jack Tanner, who regards marriage as apostasy. Violet and Hector are secretly married and wooing Hector's father for support. Feminists naturally object to the implication that marriage is the natural goal of a woman's life, ignoring the fact that both Octavius and young Hector are as dedicated to that goal as the women, and that even Tanner, eloquent as he is on the subject, is no very reliable narrator of his own feelings on marriage or on the more pertinent subject of his feelings about Ann herself. The fact that both male and female are all for love is no departure from convention, but the nature of the obstacles certainly is. The resistance of Tanner, the Don Juan of the piece, is notorious, and his reasons are not very different from those of Shakespeare's Benedict. The resistance of Ann is less evident and more significant. Octavius is the man for whom Ann would be destined in a simpler story, as we know from *Don Giovanni* and from indications supplied by Shaw in his stage directions: "Mr. Robinson is really an uncommonly nice looking young fellow. He must, one thinks, be the jeune premier; for it is not in reason to suppose that a second such attractive male figure should appear in one story." Ann herself creates the complications without which there would be no play when she rejects this romantic whole-hearted lover. She does so because she is no longer the heroine of all female flesh and feminine caprice, but a person with ideas and conscious choice, a modern woman. Leaving aside the question of whether "Woman Immortal," one very provoking example of Shavian gamesmanship, is speaking through Ann, as Saint Joan's voices speak through her own unconscious mind, the mere mortal has quite decided ideas as distinct from simple impulses. Another unconventional touch is leaving the attractive Octavius unmated, in spite of the existence of a convenient sister whom any conventional plotting would have worked up into a fiancée. Besides, the subplot, with its suitably crasser subtheme (money), acts as a foil for the high ideas behind the figure of Ann. Violet, named for a flower that is a symbol of feminine modesty but actually grows like a weed, simply wants her Hector and his father's money, which is standard and all right. Empty and attractive, Violet and Hector are the pristine stuff of comedy. Their simplicity hints at the complexity of Ann's motives, which are explained in the Epistle Dedicatory.

Not only are the men as bent on marriage as the women, Tanner always excepted, but they are relegated to a passive role. This, of course, fits Shaw's reiterated view that women are the aggressors in sex, but it does reverse the sexual stereotypes, and in this respect Tanner is quite like Octavius and Hector and even the sentimental devil Mendoza. His moves are all reactions to Ann's actions. The women are enterprising, audacious, aggressive and self-assured, and it is they who secure all the desired outcomes through their wit and daring. Violet prevails against both her husband and his father to set up the marriage on her own terms with the necessary income. Ann prevails against both the man who says he wants to marry her and the one who says he does not, setting up just the arrangement that is best for all three. This Ann explains in the scene in which she rejects Octavius:

> ANN. [*with conviction*]Tavy. I wouldnt for worlds destroy your illusions. I can neither take you nor let you go. I can see exactly what will suit you. You must be a sentimental old bachelor for my sake.
>
> OCTAVIUS. [*desperately*] Ann: I'll kill myself.
>
> ANN. Oh no, you wont: that wouldnt be kind. You wont have a bad time. You will be very nice to women; and you will go a good deal to the opera.

A moment later she is explaining to Octavius why she does not dread disillusioning Jack: "I cant: he has no illusions about me. I shall surprise Jack the other way. Getting over an unfavorable impression is ever so much easier than living up to an ideal. Oh, I shall enrapture Jack sometimes!" There is every reason to believe in Ann's accuracy here. She does prevaricate, but she does not mistake.

A second feminist complaint against *Man and Superman* is that Ann employs feminine wiles to gain her end. What else can she do in her social context? Shaw's point here, as in his defense of Mrs. Warren's choice of profession, is that society is to blame for offering no workable alternative. Shaw says, with Tanner, "Forgive my brutalities, Ann. They are levelled at this wicked world. not at you." In this case as in others, criticism directed at action, character or any other dramatic element without regard to the social context and the thought has little or no validity. The act itself has no meaning. The act related to its occasion, its intention, its effects, its limiting context, does have meaning. Ann's deviousness is determined by society, which penalizes other methods in a woman, not by any feminine nature. Besides, Ann does not find deviousness congenial nor fool herself about what she is doing. She says:

> But I have a great respect for Violet. She gets her own way always.
> OCTAVIUS. [*sighing*] So do you.
> ANN. Yes; but somehow she gets it without coaxing—without having to make people sentimental about her.

Here Ann is voicing exactly the feminist objection to methods that trade on sexual attraction or the secondary sexual characteristics of helplessness, modesty and the like. The meaning of her behavior is therefore the opposite of what a simple plot summary would imply.

The third and most serious accusation of male chauvinism in this play rests on the idea of the mother-woman and the artist-man advanced in the Epistle Dedicatory. Shaw does set up the two goals in opposition and speaks of one as the man's and the other as the woman's. But to assume that he takes this to be an eternal principle is wrong, and to assume that woman is meant to be limited to this one role is equally wrong. In making Ann the mother-woman, he is speaking of "modern London life, a life in which as you know, the ordinary man's business is to get means to keep up the position and habits of a gentleman, and the ordinary woman's business is to get married." But this is the temporal and ordinary thing. He makes explicit reference to the complicated case in which the genius is a woman. I must admit that he goes on to say: "I state the extreme case, of course; but what is true of the great man who incarnates the philosophic consciousness of Life and the woman who incarnates its fecundity, is true in some degree of all geniuses and all women." This hyperbole seems to be part of the polemical rhythm, not of the real argument. Shaw's work argues always for freeing motherhood, not for forcing it, and even in this same Epistle there is a correction worth noting: "As I sat watching Everyman at the Charterhouse, I said to myself Why not Everywoman? Ann was the result: every woman is not Ann; but Ann is Everywoman." Then there is Tanner's little-noted question as he yields to destiny: "What have you grasped in me? Is there a father's heart as well as a mother's?"

Ann is taken too seriously most of the time. It is no wonder, considering the Everywoman business, but it does throw things out of kilter to take her more seriously than any other character in the play. She is a vital genius. The author says so. Yet she has her being in the light ironic mode, and her deviousness, her feminine wiles, the whole catalog of her faults must be interpreted accordingly. Look, for the parallel case, at Jack Tanner. Surely this parlor socialist, this talker, this ludicrously unconscious prey is not meant to represent the highest mark the philosopher-man can reach? Yet it is equally sure that his follies are not meant to discredit the tract he is supposed to have written. It is naive to forget that Ann is just as much a comic version of certain selected qualities, that though she is an incarnation of the divine spark she is a comic incarnation. She no more detracts from the value of the maternal function than Tanner detracts from the value of socialism, but she is a reminder that the Life Force may assume strange shapes to get its work done in our time.

The Millionairess, a late play that also ends with an engagement, shows the same kind of disparity between an apparently traditional comic pattern and an actually revolutionary and feminist structure. Its heroine is a walking catalog of the virtues the radical women's movement believes in. She is Boss incarnate and was created to be just that, as the Preface argues. Her methods are blunt and tough and by no means exclude physical violence. She has no scrap of modesty, guilt or dependence. She is in full possession of her own sexuality. Her first husband, whom she dumps without ceremony, is a handsome athlete without interest of mind or character, chosen primarily as a sex object. "He stripped well, unlike many handsome men," she says. But, as she explains to her lawyer: "I have made a very common mistake. I thought that this irresistible athlete would be an ardent lover. He was nothing of the kind. All his ardor was in his fists." Consigning him to the care of his mistress, she remarks, "His good looks will give you a pleasing sensation down your spine."

The Egyptian doctor on whom this free spirit fastens for her next husband, pursuing him by direct assault, without any feminine wiles, is finally undone, against his will, by her sexual vitality, as ruthless as her appetite for power, unless I entirely misread the capitulation that comes when he feels her pulse: "Ooooh!! I have never felt such a pulse. It is like a slow sledge hammer. . . . It is the will of Allah. . . . You are a terrible woman; but I love your pulse. I have never felt anything like it before." The courtships in *Village Wooing* and *Too True To Be Good* are even more explicit on this point. Again it is the woman as individual, full of force and particularity, that transforms the meaning of marriage as a conclusion. Conventionally, woman as female is passivity, a sex *object*, whereas Shavian woman is activity, a *subject* in sexual as in other matters. For the woman as female in literature, marriage and procreation have been treated as ends in themselves. In *The Millionairess*, the marriage is a goal, but it is only one goal, subsumed under the woman's main goal of having her own way about everything. Love never makes her forget herself or her principles. Here, as in most of Shaw's work, marriage may be part of a woman's life, as it may be part of a man's life, but it is destiny to the same extent for both.

Most of Shaw's plays make an even more complete break with the conventions of comedy. Weddings and matings recede from the center of interest and take their place along with other human concerns including social change and the survival of the species. In Shaw the assumption that society can and must change is as pervasive as the assumption in traditional comedy that the wheel will continue to go round. And that change is both embodied and symbolized in the new relation of woman to herself, to other people and to the universal. A glance at five plays having different emphases may indicate how the pattern plays itself out against different backgrounds.

Saint Joan might seem to be a fortuitous example of the importance of woman in transforming Shaw's drama, but I do not mean to argue from the simple fact that Joan was a female. In any case, plays like *Major Barbara, Pygmalion, Mrs Warren's Profession* and *Misalliance* show that the woman protagonist is no historical accident. And there are elements in Joan's drama that show very well the conflict of the woman with her feminine role and the way that conflict epitomizes the drama of a new age. Her accusers dwell on witchcraft and unfeminine behavior. Her defense against these charges shows how necessary it is for women to unsex themselves to succeed in great enterprises, how the woman's role is a trap to be wary of and is, furthermore, the best example of the way all such traps as stereotypes work. These stereotypes claim to be roles but in fact are denials of role. Soldier is a role, bishop is a role, shepherd is a role (although shepherdess turns it into a mythological fancy), even saint is a role, but woman is an antirole and therefore a woman must be a rebel or nothing. The supposed role of woman is either a fiction or a negation. Mother is a role, cook is a role, typist is a role, but woman means only that one cannot be a soldier, cannot be a boxer, cannot be a bishop, cannot be a thousand other things without coming into conflict with the illogical role of woman. A real element in Joan's martyrdom is her inability to conform to the role assigned to her as a woman. Obedience to her father, domesticity, marriage, obedience to her husband—a different kind of martyr is made this way, but a woman like Joan has only a choice of martyrdoms. And to have any real role at all, she has had to learn the techniques of total subversion, for in her time no girl broke away with less.

In *Major Barbara* the initiative, the anguish and the enlightenment are primarily a woman's. Barbara Undershaft will have won her way through to be her father's heiress by right of her struggle, not by right of birth. She will marry Cusins, admittedly, and he will become the nominal heir, but only through her, through her rebellion, clearsightedness and courage. As a man, he had his role, professor of Greek. But as a woman, Barbara has had to blast her way out of the woman's role in order to have any real life at all. Having broken out of the old illusions, she is quite prepared to break out of any new ones that threaten her love affair with reality, and the impossibility of every last sacred cliché is the ironic heart of the play. Undershaft has succeeded because he does not confuse morality with business. Cusins will succeed because he does not confuse purity with virtue. Barbara succeeds because she does not confuse femininity with selfhood. The stories of the two men are rightly subsidiary to hers. Here, as elsewhere in his theatre, Shaw's socialism is subsidiary to his feminism. The woman, struggling through a swamp of deceptions and irrelevancies toward an idea of what she has to do in the world, is the heroic heart of the comedy.

As a test case, consider *Candida*. On the surface, a love triangle: married woman, romantic lover, dramatic confrontation, return to husband. Symbolically, the woman a Renaissance madonna, motherhood spiritualized at one period, again made flesh at another, and revived in the new religiosity of art—evidently a protean thing. The husband a pillar of society, in no ironic sense, a solid man. The lover an artist, fire and air. Such a triangle seems to promise a problem play, its real action in the interplay of forces like liberty, law, earth-mother, its outcome a lesson in the ranking of abstractions. Instead, the force of the play sheers off again to the issue of woman and the conflict with her ascribed role, a conflict to which the other characters acting upon her are only incidental. Candida has known and lived with her dilemma long before her husband and her lover duel verbally to possess her. There is no melodrama, no problem play, only an adroit comedy, yet a comedy of the new kind: centered in a woman, with inner conflict replacing outer obstacles, and with a smell of revolution in the air. In the climactic scene that plucks out the heart of the mystery, Candida reveals all the traditional relations in a strange new light. The husband's strength is weakness; the lover's weakness, strength. This paradox settles the outward events, which have ceased to matter. Whether she goes with one or remains with the other is no longer an interesting question. The interesting question is why. In writing his own version of *A Doll's House* and reversing the outcome, Shaw proves also that the importance of Nora's leaving is not the leaving itself but the reasons for it. In *Candida,* strength and weakness, principles of honor, all the used furniture of ideas about wifehood and motherhood and Love have been superseded by Candida's question: "Oh! I am to choose, am I? I suppose it is quite settled that I must belong to one or the other," and by Marchbanks, who translates: "She means that she belongs to herself." Whatever the secret in the poet's heart, that is the secret in the woman's.

In one way or another, that is the message of the plays. In *Heartbreak House* any mystical work is done by an old man aided by the Seventh Degree of Concentration (a rum concoction), but his daughters, Hesione and Ariadne, both declassicized versions of a feminine principle that once could redeem a male world, dominate the middle generation, their men being devoid of all epic quality. The entering wedge into the future, as a lost society founders, is the young Ellie Dunn, who falls in love with the handsome and false Hector Hushabye, plans to marry Boss Mangan and his millions for the sake of her helpless father and her expensive soul, and finally discovers her soulmate in old Captain Shotover's mad mysticism and sane questions. The women are without fear, as though masculine wars were only another football game, and they are hoping, as the curtain goes down, for the terror and beauty of another air raid.

It should be admitted that the dominance of the sisters over their weak men is one of the elements of decadence in *Heartbreak House,* yet the dominance is clearly healthier than the vacuum of submission that draws it forth. The women may prop up or tyrannize over the men, but the men have first been destroyed by something other than the women. Shaw never flinches from strong women. Where most men see in strong women a threat to themselves, Shaw sees in them a hope for the world. The destructive women, as Shaw recognizes, are the weak ones. Certainly in *Heartbreak House* the hope for any revival in a dying world lies in Ellie's quest for a sensible grail. The play again breaks the comic pattern without abandoning it, for the influence of Chekhov goes only so far. The woman sets aside romantic love to marry for money, sets that aside for a mystical marriage to reality in the old captain, and finally chooses danger, excitement and her own spirit. This pattern is radically different from the traditional comedy in which awareness of human folly, along with the right pairing off, can set a wobbling world spinning prettily again, but the Chekhovian pattern is not really followed either. The old world and its choices may be vanishing, but the self is still a reality and a source of strength. The new world that may emerge is evidently one in which the human spirit is androgynous. In this play, as in the Christian heaven, there is neither marrying nor giving in marriage, but there is redemption.

There is also a sense in which a play like *The Apple Cart* bears out my theory of a changed comedy and its relation to a changed role for women. The comedy is political and the vital genius a man, but the deployment of women is interesting. The scene moves from politics to playful love and back again, but King Magnus keeps the frivolity of his mistress firmly bracketed in the interlude. He returns almost on time to his work and his placid maternal wife whom Orinthia calls an old cabbage, with a remark no male chauvinist could have dreamed up: "Besides, all these old married cabbages were once roses; and, though young things like you dont remember that, their husbands do." In his cabinet King Magnus has only two dedicated, intelligent, honest public servants among the rabble of egotists, fools, frauds and babies. These two are the only two women.

> ORINTHIA. And then you go back to your Amandas and Lysistratas: creatures whose idea of romance is a minister in love with a department, and whose bedside books are blue books.
>
> MAGNUS. They are not always thinking of some man or other. That is a rather desirable extension of their interests, in my opinion. If Lysistrata had a lover I should not be interested in him in the least; and she would bore me to distraction if she could talk of nothing else. But I am very much interested in her department. Her devotion to it gives us a topic of endless interest.

These women are not the central characters in the comedy, but they are more important to it than the King's wife or his mistress, and they are effective because they have surpassed the feminine roles attributed to them. The main idea of the play is actually a variant on this feminine rebellion. One of the few men born, like a woman, with a role ready made for him is a constitutional monarch. Magnus is told over and over that he is supposed to be a rubber stamp, a figurehead. But this attributed character does not fit the man Magnus, and his refusal to accept it is exactly parallel to a woman's refusal to accept the role offered her by birth. Being a kingly king is like being a womanly woman: all right until it gets in your way.

On the womanly woman Shaw said the last word early in his career in *The Quintessence of Ibsenism*, and King Magnus is the proper test of those ideas, for Shaw recognized that woman's rebellion against her attributed role would be the model for all such rebellion against roles, against duty, against cant. He predicted then that the woman's revolt would come first because the woman's enslavement was more complete, but that man would learn subversion and come to understand the impossibility of "duty" in due course. But the exemplary case is that of the woman of spirit whose choice is to rebel or to die, and the particular comedy of our time is that in which a woman pits her spirit against a set of deadly mythologies, as in another age a man would pit his body against physical death, or a couple their desires against laws and fathers. Shaw is the creator of this kind of comedy, in which the emphasis is on fighting free of cant, and the implication is that by learning to see through one kind of cant women show men how to see through others. Seeing through newcant (the cant of one's own generation) is an art achieved only by the masters. Yet that is the art Shaw means to teach. Roebuck Ramsden, in *Man and Superman*, speaks with all the pride of middle age when he says, "I was an advanced man before you were born." With his name so weighted with masculinity, and a style so ineffectual in dealing with anything feminine, Ramsden is a perfect representative of the patriarchy, and his dedication to the newcant of his youth is typical of patriarchal illusions. Looking through the whole list of Shavian characters, it seems fair to say that most of the realists, those who have a grasp of the secret and need not repeat the nightmares of the past, are women. The only female equivalent of Ramsden seems to be Mrs. Clandon in *You Never Can Tell*, who liberates herself in the wrong direction by becoming more masculine. She has tried to reduce life to a science, but at least she has given birth to the fey twins and to Gloria, who finds out how to fall in love even though no one has ever taught her anything. Anyone who thinks to make life a science is no realist in Shaw's view.

Perhaps something of what Shaw values in woman can be deduced by looking at the men he selects to play Vital Genius in some plays. They are seldom husbands in the true sense. Husbands tend toward the bombastic or uxorious. Fathers and grandfathers come off much better. In *Major Barbara*, *Heartbreak House*, *Cashel Byron's Profession*, *The Millionairess*, and elsewhere, fathers show a certain verve. It is only a step from father to Caesar, who is paternal toward the infantile Cleopatra. Like the paternal, encouraging, instructive manner of King Magnus, his power, which is his detachment, which is his wisdom, is part of an androgynous consciousness. No conventional masculine traits like aggression, vengefulness, violence appear in the vital genius, just as no conventional feminine traits appear in the vital woman. Androgyny appears to be the key to the new humanity.[2]

If so, the remaining question would seem to be why women, so much more locked in a stereotyped sex role than men, should seem to represent the hope for the future. Perhaps because outsiders get a better training in realism. For them it has survival value, and miraculous attention goes into the lessons of survival. Also, where a culture places a high value on masculinity, repudiating that role is harder than repudiating the role of inferior. Whatever the reason, Shaw took the theme of woman's fate wherever he found it (and he found it everywhere) and made of it a mythogenic center.

Notes

1. "As Bernard Shaw Sees Woman," *New York Times Magazine,* 19 June 1927, p. 2.
2. For a valuable discussion of androgyny in literature and a distinction between feminist and androgynous works see Carolyn G. Heilbrun, *Toward a Recognition of Androgyny.*

WHATEVER HAPPENED TO SHAW'S MOTHER-GENIUS PORTRAIT?

Susan C. Stone

G.B. Shaw is often hailed as an early advocate of women's rights, both as a writer of speeches and prefaces and as a dramatist who portrayed sympathetically the unwomanly woman, the liberated woman, the new woman. He also, however, presented womanly women, old-fashioned women, women trapped by their social and religious codes. Those who exult in the Shavian portraits of Lina Szczepanowska or Saint Joan as incarnations of the goals of the women's movement are inclined to overlook the definition of woman's role proclaimed in *Man and Superman*. A number of studies of Shaw's characterizations of women have been done, and usually these involve some sorting of Shaw's women into types. Thus we have the Womanly Woman, the Mother Woman, the New Woman, the Manly Woman and any number of others.[1] Among all this variety of female types, one, a woman defined by Shaw himself, seems to be missing from the Shavian canon, or when she appears she is not what Shaw's definition leads us to expect.

In the Epistle Dedicatory to *Man and Superman* Shaw defines the roles of man and woman in the service of the Life Force. The men who are most effective in furthering the work of the Life Force are "men of genius: that is, men selected by Nature to carry on the work of building up an intellectual consciousness of her own instinctive purpose." While man is employed in the area of intellectual consciousness, woman's work is a kind of instinctive regeneration of the race. It is her job not only to continue the race, but to carry out genetic experimentation (unconsciously) by selecting and pursuing the man who most appeals to her—presumably the man who will be the best one to father her children.

Having introduced the concepts of genius-man and mother-woman, Shaw pauses briefly to admit the possibility of a cross between the two roles; there is no reason why the genius could not be a woman. (The fourth possibility, the man who devotes himself to pursuing choice mates and fathering superior children, is not mentioned.)

Man and Superman portrays the *conflict* between woman in her traditional role and man in his. Shaw notes in the Epistle Dedicatory that "we observe in the man of genius all the unscrupulousness . . . of Woman. . . . Here Woman meets a purpose as impersonal, as irresistible as her own; and the clash is sometimes tragic. When it is · complicated by the genius being a woman, then the game is one for a king of critics: your George Sand becomes a mother to gain experience for the novelist and to develop her, and gobbles up men of genius, Chopins, Mussets and the like, as mere hors d'oeuvres." Here Shaw sees the combination of the mother-drive and the genius-drive as a complication; the two forces are in competition, with the genius-urge surpassing the mother-urge. At the same time the combination seems to strengthen the rare being who possesses it, for she "gobbles up men of genius . . . as mere hors d'oeuvres." Since Shaw conceives of the two Life Force drives in conflict with each other, the internal struggle of a character possessing both would surely be an interesting subject for drama, yet Shaw never developed such a subject in a play. He depicts women who exhibit the genius-drive, women who exhibit the mother-drive, women who exhibit neither in any marked degree, and some women who *might* have made good subjects for a drama focusing on the clash between the two drives, but whose dramatic lives are otherwise occupied. Finally, in some later plays, Shaw does give us the mother-genius, but surprisingly, she is not at all in conflict with herself. She is the complete woman, purposeful, powerful and serene, not a being divided by conflicting drives.

Many of Shaw's most attractive women are predominantly neither mothers nor geniuses. They are just realistic, witty, sensible, forthright—and often quite feminine. Lady Cecily of *Captain Brassbound's Conversion* belongs in this group, as does Candida and some of the liberated women such as Fanny of *Fanny's First Play* and the Eliza Doolittle who has emerged by the end of *Pygmalion*. What these women are not is of more interest than what they are; they are part of Shaw's iconoclastic vein. As Joseph Molnar observes of the type he labels "the Emancipated Woman," "she is concerned mainly with rebellion, with asserting her individuality and winning her freedom" (p. 21). Hers is a negative orientation; the positive drive of genius to serve the Life Force characterizes a different woman. However attractive the Cecilies and Candidas of Shavian drama may be, they are not practicing geniuses—nor are they incarnations of the mother-urge.

The woman in whom the mother-urge is predominant is the one who has a sense of being driven by something beyond herself to mate appropriately and produce superior offspring. Z, when she has finally captured A in *Village Wooing* by unremitting perseverance, says, in reflecting on the audacity and tenacity of her pursuit, "I'm not a bit like that, you know, really. Something above me and beyond me drove me on. Thats why I know it will be all right." Gloria in *You Never Can Tell* also seems to be a sort of mother-woman, though she tries most earnestly not to be, and in this play it is the man, Valentine, who is the aggressor, and he who expresses the feeling that they are driven "as if Nature, after letting us belong to ourselves and do what we judged right and reasonable for all these years, were suddenly lifting her great hand to take us—her two little children—by the scruffs of our little necks, and use us, in spite of ourselves, for her own purposes, in her own way."

Still, Gloria, in her unsuccessful struggle against the force of the mother-urge in herself, demonstrates the strength of that force almost as conclusively as Ann Whitefield does, more obviously and positively, in *Man and Superman*. Gloria describes herself as "driven almost mad with shame by the feeling that all her power over herself had broken down at her first real encounter with—with—." She cannot finish, but she means love or sex or what Valentine in this early play calls Nature, what Shaw would later call the Life Force. Once she has given in to this force, which is stronger than her power to resist it, Gloria becomes the aggressor, clinching the match despite Valentine's panicky protests.

It is in *Man and Superman*, of course, that Shaw deliberately worked out the incarnation of the mother-woman in Ann. Shaw gives Valentine's cunning pursuit tactics, his determination, his alternation of assurance and anguish to Ann, having decided that these characteristics are truly found in the female of the species, though they are traditionally assigned to the male. Ann exhibits the resourcefulness, the zeal, the urgency of the "vital genius"; she is the epitome of the mother-woman, though the verbalization of the greater purpose which impels her to pursuit is given to Jack. To Ann, the "Life Force" might as well be the "Life Guards." The interplay between Ann, the mother-woman, and Jack, the genius-man, is depicted as a conflict in which Jack fights for his freedom while Ann fights to capture him. The implication is that since Ann is victor, Jack's loss of freedom, his responsibilities as a family man, mean the diminution of his effectiveness as the Life Force servant who strives to use his genius to make life ever more conscious of its own struggle to improve itself. Ann's purpose, her mode of service to the Life Force, shows every promise of being gloriously realized at the end of the play. She is mother-woman, triumphant in the clash with genius-man; however, she has certainly nothing in herself of the genius.

There are many women in Shaw's plays who in some way step into man's role. But from Vivie Warren through Lina Szczepanowska to Epifania di Parerga, they generally possess masculine traits other than that power to make life understand itself which Shaw called genius. They may smoke cigars and wear masculine attire, they may be physically vigorous, aggressive, domineering—but for the most part they are not noticeably in the service of the Life Force, either as genius or as mother.

Joan is the obvious exception. Shaw describes her in his preface to *Saint Joan* as a genius, one who "seeing farther and probing deeper than other people, has a different set of ethical valuations from theirs, and has energy enough to give effect to this extra vision and its valuations in whatever manner best suits his or her specific talents." While this definition differs from the one offered in the Preface to *Man and Superman*, the two are not incompatible. Though Joan does not understand Creative Evolution, Shaw sees her as an agent of the Life Force inspired by a force greater than herself, which drives her to fulfill the needs of the race instead of only personal ones. By championing nationalism and protestantism—however unconsciously—against the orthodox forces of the church and feudalism, Joan is acting to satisfy "an appetite for evolution."

If one can overlook the unconscious quality of Joan's genius, she qualifies as the genius half of the mother-genius who ought to appear in Shaw's drama, but as an incarnation of the mother-drive, she fails. She exhibits the sort of masculinity displayed by other Shavian women, rejecting feminine attire and codes of behavior. She has apparently no interest in men except as comrades and no especially feminine traits. When Joan wishes Dunois were one of the village babies so she could nurse him, he declares her "a bit of a woman after all," but she protests, "No, not a bit. I am a soldier and nothing else. Soldiers always nurse children when they get a chance," and Dunois concedes the point. Lacking the mother-urge, Joan is but one half of the complete portrait of woman; Ann Whitefield is the other half. Where is the woman who combines the two?

There are several women among Shaw's characters who *could* qualify as the complete woman—Lavinia in *Androcles and the Lion* and Major Barbara are examples. For each a case for the genius-urge can be made, and for neither is there any evidence that the mother-urge is *lacking*—these ladies are not among Shaw's masculine heroines—but neither is there any evidence that the maternal instinct is present. Simply, in each of these plays Shaw's focus is on something other than the Life Force, and the question of Lavinia's or Barbara's maternal urge does not arise.

Lavinia is Shaw's model Christian: laughing, witty, broadminded, kind, thoughtful of others, firm in her adherence to the spirit of her religion, if not to the letter of its laws. She repudiates the "Christian fairy stories" as the reality of death approaches, but she is convinced that she "must die for something greater than dreams or stories," for God, whom she cannot define. When we know what God is, she believes, "we shall be gods ourselves." At the end of the play, her resolution is to "strive for the coming of the God who is not yet." For the Creative Evolutionist, this is a statement of the intent to strive for improvement of the self and the race, for God is within us; God evolves as life does.

Lavinia qualifies as a servant of the Life Force in her dedication to the struggle to understand and advance the best in life. But the question of her sexual service to the Life Force is neither clearly asked nor answered. The relationship of Lavinia and the Captain is important, but the handsome Captain is apparently introduced to give Lavinia an articulate opponent in religious discussions and to allow her to refuse the traditional happy ending, to *resist* the temptation of the desirable marriage. Still, though her efforts are hardly directed toward capturing him, the future of their relationship is left open:

> THE CAPTAIN. May I come and argue with you occasionally?
> LAVINIA. Yes, handsome Captain: you may.

One can hypothesize that if Lavinia can convert him spiritually (or intellectually), then he might be a fit mate for Life Force service, but the play itself does not focus on any maternal impulse in Lavinia.

Major Barbara presents a heroine who is similar to Lavinia in every respect. Barbara too is the sort of Christian Shaw admires, with the same wit and gaiety Lavinia displays to soften her religious zeal. Barbara undergoes even more obviously than Lavinia a spiritual-intellectual struggle which brings her, at the conclusion, closer to the truth of how most effectively to go about doing God's work, "the raising of hell to heaven and of man to God," which is, again, the evolutionary process of improving mankind.

Barbara, like Lavinia, is provided with love interest, but through-out it is Cusins who is depicted as the pursuer. Barbara seems well content to have him around, but not consciously active in keeping him interested. She reveals that if Cusins had decided against taking over Undershaft's empire, she would have given him up for the man who did accept the empire. This might still be advanced as an argument for seeing Barbara as a seeker after the fittest man to fa-ther her children, except that it is treated rather as the means to secure for her the position in which she can most effectively pursue the "genius" work of the Life Force, rather than the "mother" work.

In these plays, by more or less ignoring the biological branch of the Life Force service, Shaw is tacitly admitting that the genius work is more interesting, more dramatic, more worthy of his favorite women characters than the mothering work. There is no indication of struggle between the genius and the mother in Lavinia or Barbara (or Joan); if there ever was any such struggle in these characters, the genius impulse apparently won easily.

It is in two later plays, *Back to Methuselah* and even more clearly in *The Simpleton of the Unexpected Isles*, that Shaw finally depicts the mother-genius. *Back to Methuselah* contains two focuses of interest: one is the evolving women characters who appear variously in the different plays of the cycle as Eve, Savvy, Mrs. Lutestring, and fi-nally Zoo, the Oracle, and the She-Ancient. The other is Lilith, re-ferred to in the first play of the cycle, but presented only in the last, in a sort of epilogue.

The physical resemblance between Savvy in the second play, and Zoo in the fourth is explicitly noted in the stage directions. The con-nection between Savvy and Eve in the first play is suggested in Savvy's belief in reincarnation: "I suspect I am Eve. I am very fond of apples; and they always disagree with me." Shaw's reason for suggesting a line of characters who resemble each other can be guessed from Conrad's response to Savvy: "You are Eve, in a sense. The Eternal Life persists; only It wears out Its bodies and minds and gets new ones, like new clothes. You are only a new hat and frock on Eve." The resemblance among the women is a symbol of the relationship of one generation of life to another. In some sense all the women in the play are "a new hat and frock on Eve," as all the men are variations on Adam.

One can think in terms of two groups of women characters in the cycle, as Shaw suggests in discussing doubling possibilities. A dif-ferent actor for each part, he wrote to Lawrence Langner, who pro-duced *Back to Methuselah*, "would be extravagant and would spoil the unity of the show." Among "a few doublings which suggest themselves" are "Eve, Mrs. Lutestring, the Oracle, the She-Ancient (dignified leading lady)" and "Savvy, Zoo, the Newly Born."[2]

The youth and effervescence of Savvy, Zoo, and the Newly Born, as well as the note on Zoo's resemblance to Savvy, constitute a link among these three characters, and they are all associated with Eve through Savvy's verbal reference to her. The older, more responsible, more awe-inspiring women form another group, one which includes Eve in Shaw's note about doubling, so that the physical associations among them would be conveyed in a stage presentation. The descriptions of these characters, however, emphasize not individual traits, but generic traits. Mrs. Lutestring is a "handsome woman, apparently in the prime of life, with elegant, tense, well held-up figure, and the walk of a goddess. Her expression and deportment are grave, swift, decisive, awful, unanswerable. . . . Her dress . . . is not markedly different from that of the men." Here Shaw is depicting the mature woman of 274 years in contrast with the childlike creatures of a few decades' age; individual characteristics do not matter greatly. The description of the She-Ancient is similarly designed to portray generic characteristics rather than individualizing ones: "She is like the He-Ancient equally bald, and equally without sexual charm, but intensely interesting and rather terrifying. Her sex is discoverable only by her voice, as her breasts are manly, and her figure otherwise not very different. She wears no clothes, but has draped herself rather perfunctorily with a ceremonial robe." Both these women, as well as the Oracle of the fourth play, whose description is brief, but whose function is primarily to awe Shortlivers, are more important as representatives of a mature and responsible race than as individuals.

I should like to focus on Eve and the She-Ancient of the first and last plays in my approach to this composite woman character of *Back to Methuselah*. Eve is certainly the race mother, epitomizing the maternal urge in her service of the Life Force. Her joy in the serpent's revelations about birth and creation, her enthusiasm about creating new life in the first act of "In the Beginning," marks her as the mother-servant of the Life Force. By the second act, some centuries later, Eve's maternal enthusiasm has been partly replaced by boredom with the sameness of her sons, her sons' sons and her sons' sons' sons. Yet she still feels hope, and the genius impulse comes to the fore as she exults in the poets, the musicians, the artists, the scientists, the inventors and the prophets among her progeny. "When they come, there is always some new wonder or some new hope: something to live for. They never want to die, because they are always learning and always creating either things or wisdom, or at least dreaming of them." Her concluding speech, "Man need not live by bread alone. There is something else," anticipates the goal of the Ancients in the final play: to dispense with matter and exist as a whirlpool of energy. Of the characters who actually appear in this first play of the cycle, Eve comes closest to exhibiting "an intellectual consciousness of [Nature's] own instinctive purpose," thus suggesting the combination of mother and genius.

In the last play, "As Far As Thought Can Reach," the She-Ancient is representative of mature womanhood. She is not different from the He-Ancient except in voice; she is apparently no longer distinguishable in terms of reproductive function. Man has become oviparous, and apparently the matter of producing the egg is a scientific, nonsexual concern. This means that the mother-urge is no longer a necessary part of the Life Force service, and woman as well as man can devote herself to the consciousness-molding or genius form of service. The She-Ancient is concerned with children, but no more than the He-Ancient. She does preside at the birth, but there is no indication that this is routinely her duty; she may have this scene just to balance her role with that of the He-Ancient, who has a scene with the children at the beginning of the play. Both appear to be on call in case of emergency, and both participate in instructing the children informally whenever they happen to come in contact with them. But for the most part each is away from the children, absorbed in his/her own contemplation of life, in his/her own self-creation. The She-Ancient is an impressive character, but she is not individualized, even sexually; she is simply representative of the race of mature Ancients in contrast with the children, who are much more similar to ourselves. The She-Ancient (like the He-Ancient) combines the function of mother—the child-rearing part—which requires minimal involvement, with that of genius, which commands most of her time and attention. There is some suggestion of conflict between the two roles, since the Ancients are bored by the children; they can comfortably tolerate only a limited amount of time with them before they turn again to their genius-pursuits.

Lilith, another character of *Back to Methuselah*, even more clearly combines the mother and genius functions, and there is no indication whatever of conflict between the two; in fact, one is a necessary part of the other. Lilith is even more the primordial race mother than Eve, since it was she who conceived both Adam and Eve. At the end of Shaw's "metabiological pentateuch" Lilith has the closing speech, a pronouncement on life's progress and its promise for the future. Lilith is a supernatural figure who has the power to give life and to take it away. She revels in the accomplishments of her progeny:

> The impulse I gave them in that day when I sundered myself in twain and launched Man and Woman on the earth still urges them: after passing a million goals they press on to the goal of redemption from the flesh, to the vortex freed from matter, to the whirlpool in pure intelligence that, when the world began, was a whirlpool in pure force. . . . I gave the woman the greatest of gifts: curiosity. By that her seed has been saved from my wrath; for I also am curious; and I have waited always to see what they will do tomorrow. . . . Let them dread, of all things, stagnation; for from the moment I, Lilith, lose hope and faith in them, they are doomed.

Lilith is both giver of life (the mother force) and judge of life's progress (the genius force). She is the supreme example of the woman who combines the two modes of Life Force service. Yet she is not really a woman, not a character. She is an abstraction personified sufficiently to have lips from which words may issue. It is an indistinct, mythical being, not a real woman, who personifies the combined modes of Life Force service better than any of the more realistic, individual women characters of *Back to Methuselah*.[3]

A later play which offers the combined mother-genius urge in a single "real" character is *The Simpleton of the Unexpected Isles*. Though the play's title suggests that Iddy Hammingtap, the "simpleton," will be the central character, and though the six parents or the four children of the play's eugenic experiment might seem to have equal importance as a group, in fact, the priest and priestess, Pra and Prola, are the dominant characters, and though their roles are equal in size, Prola comes by the end of the play to command the center of the stage. It is she whom the children nominate to be Empress of the Isles, and Pra concedes that "Prola has always been the real ruler here." The children are eager to place on her shoulders the burdens of thought, knowledge, righteousness, justice and mercy, and Prola acknowledges the partial appropriateness of this desire with her comment, "These are not burdens to me: they are the air I breathe." Prola's wisdom, practicality and beauty rightly earn her the admiration and respect of everyone who knows her.

Significantly, Prola's Life Force service is a closely interwoven combination of the genius and mother functions. She and Pra have carefully calculated a eugenic experiment which is consciously designed to improve the race by the creation of "superchildren." The six-parent family designed to mingle the blood of the East (Pra and

Prola) with that of the West (the Farwaters and Hyerings) is the first phase of the experiment. The resulting four "superchildren" are apparently superior in every way except for a damning total deficiency in moral values or conscience. The second phase of the experiment draws Iddy into the family group in the hope that his excessive endowment of conscience will compensate in the next generation for the girls' deficiency. Clearly, the eugenic experiment directed by Pra and Prola involves both the consciousness of the genius function and the mating drive of the mother function. Equally clearly, there is no conflict between the two urges in this case. Prola is anything but a character in conflict with herself; she is confident, serene, determined, self-assured, everything that the complete woman might be. Though like the first, the second phase of the eugenic experiment fails when Iddy proves sterile, Prola faces the future with hope and enthusiasm, planning to continue her efforts. Pra feels that they are failures, but Prola answers, "Let men despair and become cynics and pessimists because in the Unexpected Isles all their little plans fail: women will never let go their hold on life."

Though Prola's role in the life of the Unexpected Isles has not been clearly distinguishable from Pra's during the play, certainly not in the way that Ann's is distinguishable from Jack's in *Man and Superman*, there is some attempt at establishing a distinction in the concluding speeches of the play. Prola's speech quoted above about women's optimism is a part of this distinction; so is the following exchange:

> PROLA. . . . For me every day must have its miracle, and no child be born like any child that ever was born before. And to witness this miracle of the children I will abide the uttermost evil and carry through it the seed of the uttermost good.
>
> PRA. Then I, Pra, must continue to strive for more knowledge and more power.

Prola's next speech is about their joint approach to the future; the predominant pronoun is "we." But it concludes with:

> I, Prola, shall live and grow because surprise and wonder are the very breath of my being, and routine is death to me. . . . The fountain of life is within me.
>
> PRA. But you have given the key of it to me, the Man.
>
> PROLA. Yes: I need you and you need me. Life needs us both.

This mode of defining the distinction between man and woman is reminiscent of *Man and Superman*, yet nothing in the play indicates that Prola's function is different from Pra's except biologically (a point which is minimized to the extent that it is never mentioned, just assumed). One could defend the interchangeability of Pra's and Prola's roles in the service of the Life Force; one could also defend Prola's superiority. It is she who has the courage and confidence and curiosity necessary to carry on at the end of the play, she who commands the greater share of attention even before the end of the play.

The view of woman we get from Prola in *The Simpleton*, however contradictory it seems in suggesting both a sort of interchangeability of man's and woman's roles and at the same time an almost indefinable superiority of woman, is consistent with the view developed through a number of other plays, particularly in *Back to Methuselah*. The special fascination of woman, the creator of life, is apparent in the mystical superiority of such women as Prola and Lilith. Lilith is never anything but a myth; no attempt is made to humanize or individualize her. Prola has about her an aura which awes even the other characters of the play. A sense of Eastern mystery is deliberately set against the all too mundane reality of the Britons in the play: Iddy, the Farwaters and the Hyerings. The characteristic which Prola and Lilith share, the one which Shaw is most explicit about in defining the woman's difference from and superiority to the man, is not her biological child-producing function. It is the curiosity, the wonder, the surprise, the delight in life which each expresses in concluding speeches. By contrast, man is more frequently depicted as cynical and pessimistic. This view of woman is a kind of idealized version of her as creator of life, minus the biological inconveniences.

The more customary, more rational view of woman offered by Shaw is that expressed in a 1927 speech: "A woman is really only a man in petticoats, or, if you like, . . . a man is a woman without petticoats."[4] This assertion is followed by his revelation of his secret for characterizing women: "I have always assumed that a woman is a person exactly like myself." Even in Shaw's early plays a suspicion of the interchangeability of men's and women's roles exists, as we see Valentine in *You Never Can Tell* playing the part Ann plays in *Man and Superman*. Jack's line at the climax of *Man and Superman:* "What have you grasped in me? Is there a father's heart as well as a mother's?" also suggests this interchangeability. Where Shaw acknowledges or even emphasizes sexual differences between man and women, he is seeing people in practical, temporal terms, as a product of their particular society. When he depicts the ideal, or nearly ideal state, sex fades to insignificance. Even in *Man and Superman*, where sexual differences are most emphasized, the ideal state is suggested in Don Juan's description of heaven, a description which bears a marked resemblance to the ideal world of the Ancients that Shaw created years later in *Back to Methuselah*. Heaven, Don Juan claims, "is the home of the masters of reality," earth "the home of the slaves of reality." In *Back to Methuselah* "reality" is translated as "flesh" or "matter"; the Ancients' goal is to be free of the slavery to their bodies which imprison them, and it is only in terms of this prison that woman differs from man. In the heaven of *Man and Superman*, as Don Juan hears to his great relief, there are no beautiful women; "they might be men of fifty." In the world of *Back to Methuselah's* Ancients too, the sexual differentiation is minimal.

In *The Simpleton* Shaw gives us not a futuristic drama but a fantasy. The Unexpected Isles are apart from the everyday world of political and material concerns. Though the real world threatens to intrude, with the arrival in the harbor of the boats and officials from many nations, the threat is quickly vanquished by Pra's inspired smallpox rumor. The practical concerns, such as legal and financial matters which dominate other Shaw plays, are not important here; consequently Prola is not limited by her sexuality but free to realize her full potential as a human being. In contrast is such a play as *Getting Married* in which marriage laws are a problem of such proportions that Lesbia is barred from fulfilling her maternal instinct by the social necessity of tying herself to a man for life in order to become a mother at all.

Shaw depicts woman on three levels. The first, a practical, temporal and social view of her, shows her distinctly handicapped by her biological function or by restrictions society has imposed on her because of this function. Shaw regards the purely instinctive mother-urge as inferior in interest to the conscious genius mode of service to the Life Force, and in the practical terms of society as Shaw presents it, the two come into conflict. On the second level, woman is equal to man and their roles are, in fact, interchangeable. Lilith is man *and* woman, seen in this light—man and woman are Lilith "sundered in twain." On this level, there is no conflict between the genius and the mother; the two combine to serve the Life Force in harmony. The third level is the mystical one which idealizes woman beyond man for her devotion to Life. Though Lilith, personification of the Life Force, is explicitly described as bisexual, she appears as a woman. These three levels, all of which exist simultaneously in Shaw, are not incompatible or contradictory; they represent the range of views from the immediate and practical to the ideal and mystical which are to be found in Shaw's work.

Notes

1. See, for example, Joseph Molnar, "Shaw's Four Kinds of Women"; Nethercot, *Men and Supermen.*

2. Quoted by Lawrence Langner, *G.B.S. and the Lunatic* (1963), p. 42.

3. For a possible psychological explanation of this mystical elevation of woman, see Watson, *A Shavian Guide to the Intelligent Woman,* p. 24.

4. "Woman—Man in Petticoats," *Platform and Pulpit,* ed. Dan H. Laurence (1962), p. 174.

MR. SHAW'S MANY MOTHERS

Andrina Gilmartin

Bernard Shaw loved the ladies and created great roles for them. His consideration of woman—her plight and position—was a lifelong preoccupation. He tells that when he was a little boy, women looked like great spreading mountains to him. One day a friend of his mother came to call. "Crinolines were going out; and she had discarded hers. I, an innocent unprepared child, walked bang into the room and suddenly saw for the first time, a woman not shaped like Primrose Hill, but with a narrow skirt which evidently wrapped a pair of human legs. I have never recovered from the shock, and never shall."[1]

As a young man in search of himself, he discovered the fascinating means by which an author could play surgeon to ailing man, using his words as scalpels to uncover the festering sores and ugly diseases beneath the Prince Albert coat. With his penchant for standing things on their heads and turning them inside out, it is not surprising that his first serious piece of writing, at age twenty-one, should be a letter to a make-believe little girl, *My Dear Dorothea: A Practical System of Moral Education for Females Embodied in a Letter to a Young Person of that Sex*. In it he distinguishes three kinds of mothers: those who are always kind, those who "having long since exhausted the novelty of having a child . . . think of [it] only as a troublesome and inquisitive little creature," and those "wicked women who beat their children."[2] This was written in 1878, before any of the plays. Forty-four years later, in 1922, reviewing Chesterton's book *Eugenics and Other Evils*, he says: "We are confronted with the children of three mothers: the first a model of maternal wisdom and kindness, the second helpless by herself but quite effective if she is told what to do occasionally, and the third an impossible creature who will bring up her sons to be thieves and her daughters to be prostitutes."[3] In "The Menace of the Leisured Woman" (1927), he says: "I have known a fair number of women in my time. Some of them produced splendid children and were totally unfitted to have charge of them in any way. Others were born mothers; they had a genius for it. Between them come a certain number of people who, with a little assistance and guidance, can get on fairly well."[4]

It is pertinent that the seventy-year-old Shaw did not retract the opinions of his twenty-one-year-old predecessor. "The wicked women who beat their children" (1878) are the "impossible creatures who bring up their sons to be thieves and their daughters to be prostitutes" (1922) and "are totally unfitted to have charge of the splendid children they bore" (1927).

E.B. White has said that "whoever sets pen to paper writes of himself, whether knowingly or not."[5] Shaw has said that no great writer uses his skill to conceal his meaning; so it seems fair to assume that what he wrote about mothers is what he thought about mothers, though not necessarily what he thought about his own mother. What an unknown young man writes at twenty-one may be autobiographical, but it is not likely to be contrived just to deceive future critics. Shaw knew the value of exaggeration and admits that he used overstatement habitually and deliberately. *My Dear Dorothea* may be overstatement, but we cannot doubt that Shaw believed what he wrote. Some critics find his plays full of rancor, with a "hatred of mothers and motherhood."[6] They see his stage mothers as unpleasant and impossible females. Many of them are certainly unpleasant, but we cannot condemn the artist for his model's image. If we grant the playwright the dramatist's license to create stage people for stage plays who will express dramatically his outrage at the cruelty and hypocrisy he sees, we will accept Shaw's stage mothers for what they are: types, but nevertheless real; overdrawn, but still believable. He would not have written his "System of Moral Education" telling a little girl that she must not act injuriously to others, that she must learn to bear sorrow without any pitiful display of grief and that she must never hurt those weaker than herself, and then spend his lifetime as a genius vilifying his own mother.

Victorian morality extolled "the home," "the wife," "the mother." Shaw spent his writing life impishly pricking these unrealistic bubbles, clowning to mask his despair at what he considered dangerous illusions. He was a practical man of the theater; he was also an artist of integrity who never tailored his ideas to fit an audience, but deliberately and invariably presented what he thought and exposed the folly of what everybody else accepted. He explains how Victorian men denied women their humanity:

The men looked at one another, and did not like each other very much; and that sort of feeling that you must have something to adore, something to worship, something to lift you up, gave them a curious notion that if they took the women and denied that they were human beings; if they dressed them up in an extraordinary manner which entirely concealed the fact that they were human beings; if they set up a morality and a convention that women were angels; then they would succeed in making them angels.[7]

Shaw was not fooled, and with his better-than-average vision and his growing skill with scalpels, he showed an unbelieving audience what the Victorian mother was really like underneath her mound of petticoats.

The first mother in his *dramatis personae* is the unforgettable Kitty Warren of *Mrs Warren's Profession*. Ready to assume her role as mother, Kitty promenades about giving orders to adults as if they were children in the nursery. "Come! sit up, George; and take your stick out of your mouth." When Praed suggests that Vivie may be sensitive about being treated so cavalierly, Kitty, unacquainted with both subtlety and consideration, is genuinely amazed. "Respect! Treat my own daughter with respect! What next, pray!"

Nor does introspection trouble Kitty. She assumed that the act of childbirth automatically made a woman a mother, and she is confident that mother knows best. Children, like chairs, belong to the people in whose house they live; she believes she can possess as she has been possessed—for the British pound sterling.

Shaw says Kitty is "spoilt and . . . decidedly vulgar," but she is not—at first—either stupid or vicious. She does not lust after men, she lusts after that nineteenth-century staple, respectability. It is impossible to think of Kitty uttering "the harlot's cry from street to street";[8] it seems much more likely that she ordered the gentlemen up to her room just as she ordered Sir George to take his stick out of his mouth; that she welcomed them with boisterous *joie de vivre* and sent morality skulking to the cellar. For Kitty not only knew how to please a man, she learned to dominate. She is not a hypocrite about how she earns her living. When Vivie asks her if she was never doubtful or ashamed, Kitty answers: "Well, of course, dearie, it's only good manners to be ashamed of it; it's expected from a woman. Women have to pretend to feel a great deal that they dont feel." But she has overcome the sin of poverty. The price was the surrender of fastidiousness and chastity; she paid it for the greater good, life. She has avoided the Shavian hell of drifting and has steered her course by determination and thrift.

Kitty is a second-class mother in Shaw's category; "helpless by herself [perhaps], but quite effective if she is told what to do occasionally."[9] She is not a misguided Frenchwoman thinking, even for a moment, that a brothel is a suitable place to bring up a young girl. She has money, so she entrusts Vivie's education and upbringing to the people whose business it is to make distinguished scholars and proper young ladies out of even such unlikely material as a prostitute's illegitimate daughter. Kitty's ambitions are conventional; she wants Vivie to take tripos in math and prods her with an offer of fifty pounds.

Kitty has not been a wicked mother who beat her child. She is not bored with having a child. Instead she worked and saved to become a regular mother, but Kitty's imagination didn't carry her beyond the last entry in her bank book and being "good to some man that could afford to be good to her." Her experience was so harsh, she was self-deceived into thinking parents own their children; she imagined she could impose her will on a young woman she had done everything to make independent and self-sufficient. In her ambition for respectability, Kitty created a misalliance of classes between her child and herself. She is not a bad mother until the last act. Then, wild at being crossed, seeing her expensive pearl eluding her grasp, she reverts to shrew, "the echo of the slums in her . . . voice." She cries, "Do you know what I would do with you if you were a baby again? aye, as sure as there's a Heaven above us. . . . I'd bring you up to be a real daughter to me."

The most respectable Victorian mother might have spoken so to a pregnant, unmarried daughter. Shaw gives the line to a prostitute whose daughter is eminently respectable. Kitty is condemned by her own admission. In her tragic lesson of discovery, she becomes a third-class mother, "an impossible creature who would bring up . . . her daughter to be a prostitute."[10]

Catherine Petkoff in *Arms and the Man* is the second of Shaw's stage mothers. She aspires to be a Viennese lady and affects elaborate tea gowns for every day, but she has the peasant's ingrained thrift and makes her worn-out fancy dresses do duty for mornings in the scullery. The handsome Sergius whom Raina has kept waiting a whole year before she would be betrothed to him is the hero of the evening's battle. Catherine is confident that this will bring her intractable child to reason, and she is very romantic describing the "gallant . . . Bulgarians with their swords and eyes flashing," but underneath she is a harassed, practical mother faced with the knotty problem of saving her daughter's reputation and getting her suitably married.

Catherine knows that things are seldom what they seem. She also knows it is better not to ask the awkward questions Raina asks. A woman's life is full of compromise; the sooner Raina learns to accept illusions as antidote for the pain of everyday reality, the sooner she will marry and "live happily ever after" and not be that embarrassing liability, an unmarried daughter.

Mrs. Petkoff is not just a second-class mother who has exhausted the novelty of having a child; she's human and she's tired. Raina is difficult and the business of finding her a husband is exhausting. Catherine's crime as a mother is that she is an accomplice in perpetuating the romantic myth of love and war. She keeps vacillating between acting the way she wishes things were and behaving the way she knows they are. She urges Raina to worship Sergius, but she doesn't worship her husband. When Major Petkoff says Raina always makes her appearance at the right moment, Mrs. Petkoff says impatiently, "Yes; she listens for it. It is an abominable habit."

Raina, of course, is fighting her battle of filial independence. Catherine's truths are not hers, and mother and daughter more often meet as peers and contemporaries than as mother-superior and daughter-apprentice. Sergius, who suspects that it was Raina and Catherine who helped Bluntschli escape, says the old lady was fascinated by the enemy soldier. Catherine draws her skirts about her in fastidious hauteur. "If such women exist, we should be spared the knowledge of them." In almost the next breath, alone with Raina, she says, "A nice mess you have got us into!" Raina is hazy about the details of the man-in-her-room episode, and Catherine storms: "Will anything ever make you straightforward? If Sergius finds out, it will be all over between you."

Catherine preaches honesty, practices hypocrisy, and is paid in candor, for Raina is a truth-loving realist. She says, "Oh, I know Sergius is your pet. I sometimes wish you could marry him instead of me. You would just suit him. You would pet him, and spoil him, and mother him to perfection." This is true, and Catherine knows it, but Catherine can't resist "dangerous illusions." Her romantic imagination pictures things-as-they-might-be: herself as mother-wife to the dashing Sergius instead of *hausfrau* to barbarian Petkoff. For a moment she is caught unawares. "Oh, if you were only ten years younger!" she threatens.

She might have been a wicked mother who beat her child, but she wasn't. Though motherhood has worn a little thin for her, she won't quit until she's finished her job. She is not a monster mother, and she's only a phony in the parlor. Below stairs, in her heart, she's very real and she wants what most mothers want for their daughters: a good marriage. Valiant may not be the word for Catherine, but she bumbles through to victory.

Having sung his song of *Arms and the Man*, Shaw examined the "lived happily ever after" myth. *Candida* presents the seemingly ideal married couple. There's "a boy for you, a girl for me,"[11] but there are no cradles or lullabyes. The babies are in the country with nursemaids. Candida is her husband's mother, and this is tea for three because the young poet, Marchbanks, nephew of an earl and "stranger within their gates," is madly in love with her. Morell's secretary complains that "a man ought to be able to be fond of his wife without making a fool of himself," but Morell equates love with Christian Socialism, and his marriage to Candida with a "foretaste of . . . the Kingdom of Heaven . . . on earth." The biblical "comfort me with apples: for I am sick of love" would be incomprehensible to him. He has been swaddled in love all his life and made fatuous by it.

Candida has *"the double charm of youth and motherhood"* and is *"clever enough to make the most of her sexual attractions for trivially selfish ends."* She looks at men with *"amused maternal indulgence."* She is practical about flannels and aprons and onions; she was probably radiant in her pregnancies—one of the women who "produce splendid children"—but it is not the little baby that makes her arms yearn to comfort and protect. It is the big boy baby, her husband. To him she is tiger-mother; though she cuffs him occasionally, she claws anything that threatens him. Like Mrs. Warren, she is competent and has learned to dominate. She controls her husband as his mother before her had controlled him: by creating "a castle of comfort and indulgence and love for him." But this kind of maternal care belongs to babies and little children. The wife who plays mother to her husband robs him of adulthood. The husband who submits to mothering by his wife, who lets her stand between him and "the tradesmen who want their money," between him and reality however harsh, forfeits his right to steer his own course through life and is committed to the Shavian hell of drifting.

Candida is intelligent. She knows that Morell is spoiled with love and worship, that he gets far more of it than is good for him, and she tells him so. She knows that Marchbanks is right in his thinking, that he understands Morell, and her, and Prossy, and she tells Morell that too. But she cannot stop there. She must finish. She says "and you, darling, you understand nothing." It is her terrible matter-of-factness that is so frightening. That she tells her husband she is thinking of offering herself to Marchbanks as "I would give my shawl to a beggar" is shocking; that she expects poor, besotted, cant-preaching Morell to understand is staggering. She is shrewd and she is cruel. She has not outgrown the pretty girl's excitement over the tremendous power she wields because she is sexually desirable, and she is not above humiliating those who have made themselves vulnerable by professing their love for her.

She is intelligent, but her intelligence has been squandered in the penny-pinching of every day. Her value is that her tyranny acts as catalyst and startles genius into maturity. The aristocratic Marchbanks family's way of throwing their young to the wolves of chance has produced a man. Eugene has learned that "it is a horrible thing to see one person make another suffer." This truth does not change Candida. She goes right on talking, heedless of Shaw's advice that "unpleasant things which you may know about people should never be mentioned."[12]

Shaw goes from Candida's kitchen to Mrs. Clandon's kindergarten. *You Never Can Tell* is a farcical comedy, but instead of the conventional philandering husband, Shaw presents the abandoned husband; instead of the wronged, deserted wife, he portrays the new woman in rebellion against the old idea of marriage as the union of male-master and female-slave. Mrs. Clandon is a woman of conscience and courage. Unlike Mrs. Warren, she does not see "good" as merely economic good. A marriage that violates a woman's common humanity is legalized prostitution. So, to preserve her self-respect, she gathers up her children and leaves. They are human beings, future adults. She will not have their spirits broken by their father's vile temper.

At the seaside hotel with potted palms, paper lanterns and William, the perfect waiter, the only clouds in the picture-postcard sky are Dolly's toothache and the little problem of father, father, who is our father? Mrs. Clandon treats Gloria and the twins with consideration and respect, but when Philip says they feel she should take them into her confidence, tell them about their father, Mrs. Clandon says, "I never ask you questions about your private concerns." The answer would be idiotic if this were not drawing-room comedy and if she had not already arranged for M'Comas to explain Crampton to the children because she doesn't trust herself to be unprejudiced.

Mrs. Clandon is an instinctive mother, "a model of maternal wisdom and kindness,"[13] but she is flaky and Shaw is deliberately overstating the holiday world of moonlight and soft music. Catherine Petkoff erred in prescribing romantic love as the end-all; Mrs. Clandon's fault is in ignoring it so completely that she has not prepared Gloria for being "swept off her feet." But it's a sin of omission, and it is not fatal.

Having dealt with mothers devoted to *Kinder* and *Kuche*, Shaw

turned to the *Kirche* mother. *The Devil's Disciple* satirizes the melodramatic, nick-of-time reprieve, a man's laying down his life for love,
and exposes crimes committed in the name of Christianity. Mrs.
Dudgeon worships religion, not God. Neither loving nor loved, she
is incapable of maternal kindness, and it is not surprising that "one
son's a fool, and the other a lost sinner." Jesus's command to "suffer the little children to come unto me" is not part of her creed. She
beats them with her vicious tongue. Christopher, whom she compares to a stuck pig, deplores her brutal treatment of luckless Essie.
Dick, the apostate, is gentle and kind to Uncle Peter's "irregular
child" because "children suffer enough in this house." Mrs. Dudgeon no doubt believed that "if thou beatest [the child] with the rod,
he shall not die," yet she, of all people, should have known about
death in the heart. She is typical of those "people who are always
winning victories over themselves [and so] . . . always enslaving
themselves."[14] She exchanged her cheerful maiden name, Annie
Primrose, for the married name, Dudgeon, but, because Puritan
preachers rushed in where God himself might hesitate, she let old
Eli Hawkins convince her "that the heart is deceitful . . . and desperately wicked." She renounced Peter, whom she loved, and married
Timothy, his brother, who was God-fearing and soft-headed. Their
loveless mating produced Richard of the hard heart and loutish
Christopher, and transformed Annie into the diabolical Mrs. Dudgeon who distorts scriptures to support her perverted religion of
self-denial.

Preacher Hawkins did Annie's thinking for her, and she in turn is
determined to think for her sons. Because Dick is strong and Mrs.
Dudgeon cannot break him to her will, he becomes her mortal
enemy, the devil's disciple. Because Christopher is stupid and weak
and easily cowed, he earns her contempt. Mrs. Dudgeon learns too
late that she too has sacrificed "all for nothing," yet she castigates
Anderson because he didn't make her mistake, that he followed his
heart and married pretty Judith.

Shaw suspected that the clergyman might be "the worst man in
church,"[15] and he told Dorothea in his letter to her that she "need
not think about religion"[16] until she was grown-up. Mrs. Dudgeon
was born too soon to benefit from this sane advice; what she got
was the penetrating, devastating honesty of an autopsy on her
heart.

Mrs. Warren was an erring mother judged by her high-principled
daughter; Mrs. Dudgeon is an outwardly pious mother judged by
her outwardly irreverent son. Kitty, the sinner, has the instincts of a

natural mother; Annie, the God-fearing, Bible-quoting Puritan, is a man-made martyr, a monster mother, grinding her spiteful resentment into the hearts of her children.

Nature and Shaw were in a mischievous mood when they made Mrs. Whitefield mother of the superwoman Ann in *Man and Superman*. She has been described as a "bleating old sheep,"[17] and it is true that she has been delivered of a splendid child she is totally unfitted to have charge of, but the problem is not that she is such a poor mother but that Ann doesn't need a mother. She needs a man to father the superman. Poor Mrs. Whitefield, whose *"faded flaxen hair looks like straw on an egg,"* is always being elbowed into ambiguous corners, but she is not a little dog yipping up at her graceful greyhound daughter. She knows perfectly well that she is no match for Ann; she just keeps talking in an attempt to keep the record straight.

Mrs. Whitefield is a conventional mother, and she is probably adequate for her conventional daughter, Rhoda—she asks Jack to take Rhoda "out for a run occasionally." For Ann she is merely an available convenience. When Jack tells Ann she's an incorrigible liar and has poisoned Rhoda's mind about him, Ann says, "Mother made me." Jack counters with "to lie and slander . . . that is what obeying your mother comes to," and Ann says circuitously, "I love my mother, Jack." When Octavius declares his love for her, Ann says reasonably, "Whats the good, Tavy? You know that my mother is determined that I shall marry Jack." Mrs. Whitefield is determined about nothing, but she is not a fool, and she sees Ann more clearly than anyone else. She says to Jack:

> [Tavy] is in love with her himself, though what he sees in her so wonderful, goodness knows: *I* dont. It's no use telling Tavy that Ann puts things into people's heads by telling them I want them when the thought of them never crossed my mind. . . .
> You would tell her the truth about herself. She wouldnt be able to slip out of it as she does with me.

With what talent she has, Mrs. Whitefield is a sensible and good mother to exasperating Ann. Since even that would-be realist, Jack Tanner, author of *The Revolutionist's Handbook*, could not hold out against her, it is not surprising that her mother is putty in the hands of so much Life Force. It is to her credit that she keeps fighting to the end.

Lady Britomart of *Major Barbara* is another of Shaw's dominant women. She is the arrogant aristocrat living her life of unearned leisure on undeserved wealth; her only concern is to perpetuate the system for herself and her children. She tells her son Stephen that "Sarah will have to find at least another £ 800 a year for the next ten years." "Barbara will need at least £ 2000 a year . . . and I am trying to arrange something for you." When Stephen learns that his father's fortune comes from munitions, he is shocked, but Lady Britomart says, "It is only in the middle classes, Stephen, that people get into a state of dumb helpless horror when they find that there are wicked people in the world. In our class, we have to decide what is to be done with wicked people; and nothing should disturb our self-possession."

Kitty Warren wants to provide for herself decently; Lady Britomart expects to be provided for handsomely, but she does not have even Kitty's sense of obligation to earn her support, "to be good to some man that could afford to be good to her." Lady Britomart demands and commands; she is without conscience or scruple. Having beaten timid Stephen into submission with her tongue-lashings, she then demands that he act like a man and advise her because she is only a woman and can't be expected to act as the head of the family forever. She is a combination of Kitty's insensitivity, Mrs. Dudgeon's irrational determination, and Ann Whitefield's scheming without Ann's honesty. She is arbitrary and unprincipled, yet her children are delightful and independent. It is not Lady Britomart's ways but Andrew Undershaft's means that are the answer.

Lady Britomart is greedy and inconsistent; she lives on her husband's munitions money, but she refuses to live with him. She is not a hypocrite, yet she cannot forgive Andrew for not being one. She says accusingly, "You got on because you were selfish and unscrupulous." She does not see that that is precisely how she has gotten on. She says with equanimity the outrageous things she thinks: "Really, Barbara, you go on as if religion were a pleasant subject. Do have some sense of propriety," yet she denies Andrew this freedom. She admits she does not censure him because he did wrong things, but because "he said them and thought them." She explains to Stephen: "Just as one doesnt mind men practising immorality so long as they own that they are in the wrong by preaching morality; so I couldnt forgive Andrew for preaching immorality while he practised morality." Lady Britomart declares for hypocrisy and pretense. Hers is the Victorian philosophy of wealth at any price.

Snobby Price, born to poverty, and Stephen Undershaft, born to wealth, were both brought up by mothers who "beat" them, physically or mentally. Snobby becomes a liar and a hypocrite; Stephen's ideas of right are almost overrefined. Shaw is saying that it is not the mother, but the money that makes the difference. "He is willing . . . to throw even morality overboard, if in so doing, he can hit hypocrisy and timid conventionality on the head."[18]

Mrs. Tarleton of *Misalliance* is a clear-eyed, realistic mother. She has settled for one-tenth of a superman husband, and spends her days on the three-way tightrope between his reading recommendations, her son Johnny's unprepossessing talents in father's underwear business, and her daughter Hypatia's escapades as virgin-vessel of the Life Force. Mrs. Tarleton thinks "a girl should know what a man is like in the house before she marries him," so the aristocratic Bentley Summerhays is their guest; but she explains to Hypatia, "You neednt be afraid of the aristocracy, dear: theyre only human creatures like ourselves."

She is the soul of hospitality, the help of the helpless, and the dash of cold water on the overextended. When the men are trying to salvage Patsy's honor and force poor Julius to sign the retraction, Mrs. Tarleton says, "Tear up that foolish paper, child. . . . You ought to be ashamed of yourself, Patsy; and so ought you, too, Mr. Percival, for encouraging her." Percival says, "I give you my word of honor—" Mrs. Tarleton says, "Oh, go along with you and your word of honor. Do you think I'm a fool? I wonder you can look the lad in the face after bullying him."

She is neither an ideal nor a perfect mother, but since her children aren't perfect either, she tends her maternal garden sensibly, pruning this, cultivating that, and hoping for the best.

To Mrs. Eynsford Hill in *Pygmalion*, Eliza Doolittle utters the prostitute-of-the-English-language cry when she says, "Wal, fewd dan y' dəooty bawmz a mather should, eed now bettern to spawl a pore gel's flahrzn than ran awy athaht pyin." And it is this protest that brings her to Henry Higgins's attention. As that tantalizing tidbit, an eligible bachelor, Higgins brings out the maternal in all women. He maintains cordial, independent relations with his civilized, outspoken and equally independent mother. They live in handsome, but unlike, flats, enjoy each other's company, and respect each other's privacy. There is neither pretense nor hypocrisy between them. When Henry comes uninvited to her at-home, Mrs. Higgins tells him to go, that he offends all her friends. She scolds him for never falling in love with any woman under forty-five, and he flatters her with "My idea of a lovable woman is somebody as like you as possible."

This remark has earned Higgins the reputation for having a

mother fixation, but it is the obvious reply of the bachelor who wants to get his mother off the subject of why he does not get married. Mrs. Higgins is indeed that remarkable thing, an uncommon mother, but she is not so much Henry's mother as she is Eliza's godmother, a mother-essential for Pygmalion testing his Galatea.

Denny O'Flaherty's mother (*O'Flaherty, V.C.*) does everything wrong for the right reasons. She's a third-class mother who beat her son "from the time he could feel to the time she was too slow to ketch him," but she didn't bring him up to be more of a thief than was necessary for them as poor Irish tenants to get the rent together for their English landlord. She made a brave man of a timid boy by bringing him up "to be more afraid of running away than of fighting." Now he wants to spare her the humiliation of finding out that he's fighting for—not against—the English, and explains his predicament to Sir Pearce. "It's that I'm fond of her, and cant bring myself to break the heart in her. You may think it queer that a man should be fond of his mother, sir . . . but I'm fond of her; and I'm not ashamed of it."

Mrs. O'Flaherty makes the ignorant peasant's mistake of thinking she knows more than her son just because she is his mother. Kitty Warren and Lady Britomart made the same mistake with less excuse. Mrs. O'Flaherty's treatment of her son has not made him bitter or resentful as Mrs. Dudgeon's made Dick. She knows that unless a mother teaches her boy what he needs to know to protect himself in this world, he will always need her protection, and she will be defenseless in her old age. If the English do not understand the difference between cruelty and Irish jousting on the green, Shaw is not surprised. The English never have understood the Irish.

Shaw's gallery of mothers is long, and the portraits are varied. He would be the first to admit that a stage mother can never be an altogether real mother, since a play is not real life but a moment of life compressed into dramatic form, and a stage mother is never a free agent. It is true also that the artist often creates more than he intends, and between the mind of the maker and the pen on the paper, however swift the transference, a character, brushed by freedom, picks up a little life of its own.

Shaw lived with his mother until he was forty-two years old. "Absolutely without the smallest friction of any kind," he says, "Yet when her death set me thinking curiously about our relations, I realized that I knew very little about her."[19] Mrs. Shaw was an unusually free woman for her time; she seems to have been part Mrs. Clandon who refrained from asking her son too personal questions and part Mrs. Higgins who maintained cordial, independent relations with her equally independent son.

In play after play Shaw decried the Victorian myth of woman's goodness, purity, supremacy. He offered in its stead reality, truth. Women were human beings, he insisted, equal and responsible members of the human family. Mothers, too.

Notes

1. Shaw, "Woman—Man in Petticoats," p. 173.

2. Shaw, *My Dear Dorothea*, pp. 16, 19.

3. Bernard Shaw, "Chesterton on Eugenics and Shaw on Chesterton," in *Pen Portraits and Reviews* (1949), p. 101.

4. *Platform and Pulpit*, p. 170.

5. E.B. White, *The Second Tree from the Corner* (1954), p. xi.

6. Rossett, *Shaw of Dublin*, p. 347.

7. *Platform and Pulpit*, pp. 172-73.

8. G.M. Trevelyan, *Illustrated English Social History*, vol. 4, *The Nineteenth Century* (1952), p. 26.

9. *Pen Portraits*, p. 101.

10. Ibid.

11. Irving Caesar and Vincent Youmans, "Tea for Two," from *No, No, Nanette*, published by Harms, Inc., 1924.

12. *My Dear Dorothea*, p. 37.

13. *Pen Portraits*, p. 101.

14. I.A. Richards, "Science and Poetry," reprinted in *Criticism: The Foundations of Modern Literary Judgment*, ed. Mark Schorer, Josephine Miles, and Gordon McKenzie (1958), p. 512.

15. *My Dear Dorothea*, p. 13.

16. Ibid., p. 22.

17. Constance Barnicoat's article in the *Fortnightly Review* (March 1906), quoted by Watson, *A Shavian Guide to the Intelligent Woman*, p. 18.

18. William Irvine, *The Universe of G.B.S.* (1949), p. 33.

19. "Parents and Children," *Collected Plays with their Prefaces*, vol. 4, p. 109.

FEMINISM AND FEMALE
STEREOTYPES IN SHAW

Elsie Adams

"I say, Archer, my God, what women!" exclaimed Robert Louis Stevenson of *Cashel Byron's Profession* in 1888.[1] Since then, it has become a critical cliché that Bernard Shaw is the creator of startlingly original fictional women, an opinion that is echoed in the first full-length study of Shaw and women, Barbara Bellow Watson's *A Shavian Guide to the Intelligent Woman*. This book, dealing at length with Shaw's treatment of women in his political theory and fictional practice, emphasizes Shaw's departure from convention in his creation of domineering, clever, sensible, good-humored, sexually aggressive—in short, "unladylike"—women.[2] Undeniably, Shaw portrays arresting and powerful women. But in spite of his departure from the nineteenth-century stereotype of the demure, fragile, "womanly" woman, he more often than not creates women characters who belong to types familiar in Western literature. In play after play he presents us with various combinations of the traditional figure of temptress, goddess, or mother (usually with a capital *M*); and even when he creates a woman who has broken out of a traditional "female" role, he tends to draw on another literary type—the "emancipated" woman.

In sharp contrast with such traditional treatment of women in his plays, Shaw's political statements about women challenged (and continue to challenge) tradition. Shaw was an early and vigorous exponent of female/male equality, insisting "that a woman is really only a man in petticoats, or, if you like, that a man is a woman without petticoats."[3] His essay on "The Womanly Woman" in *The Quintessence of Ibsenism* can still stand as a revolutionary feminist document, with its analysis of the social conditioning causing women to sacrifice self for others; its view of a male-ruled society dictating that women minister to male appetites; its argument that "the domestic career is no more natural to all women than the military career is natural to all men"; and its insistence that female rebellion is the first step to emancipation.[4] With these pro-feminist statements in mind, we might reasonably expect to find women in Shaw's plays who are men in petticoats, or who are in rebellion against traditional definitions and roles. But what we in fact find are permutations of basic literary types: temptress, mother, goddess.

The temptress in Western tradition is, like Eve, the cause of man's fall from grace or, like Pandora, responsible for unleashing evil on the world. She inspires awe and terror, for though she fascinates, she is manipulative, destructive, sometimes deadly. She is *La Belle Dame sans Merci*, who seduces the knight and then leaves him wandering, psychically devastated, in a symbolic wasteland. She is the serpent-lady (the "Dragon Lady" belongs to the type), the *femme fatale*, or in some literature the castrating bitch. This type appears throughout Shaw's work, often associated metaphorically with the "tiger cat" or "viper." We see her in Blanche Sartorius's animal ferocity in love-making; in Raina Petkoff's attack after discovering Sergius's flirtation with Louka; in Ann Whitefield's tightening boa-like grip on Tanner. Shaw's fullest treatment of the *femme fatale* is Cleopatra, the kitten turned tiger, who against Caesar's advice stains her hands with her enemy's blood.

There is a sense in which all of Shaw's strong-willed, dominating women are variations of this dangerous but attractive type. Certainly men are no match for these women: "Dont hit us when we're down," Tanner pleads with Violet after she delivers a tongue-lashing to everyone for assuming she is a "fallen woman." When Sergius calls Raina a "tiger cat!" and Raina objects, Bluntschli explains to her, "What else can he do, dear lady? He must defend himself somehow." Even the male-dominated Eliza Doolittle shows her claws and threatens to scratch when Higgins and Pickering ignore her after her triumph in Act IV.[5]

For the most part, however, the women in Shaw's plays do not threaten men through tigerish displays of temper; more characteristically they dominate through kittenish "feminine wiles" (i.e., deceit and cunning). Lady Cicely, for example, controls everyone around her while ostensibly deferring to male authority and superior knowledge. She protects and nurses her baby-men—she even mends their clothes!—all the time arranging their lives and doing as she likes.

Lady Cicely exemplifies another major type in Shaw's plays: the mother-woman. This type is, of course, also as old as Eve, the mother of us all, and appears in mythology in various forms of the fertile Earth Mother. Without rehearsing the case for Shaw's "mother fixation," we should note that his plays abound with women for whom maternity is a calling. They are women who instinctively offer maternal protection and control, as when Raina maternally coaxes and shakes her "chocolate cream soldier" when he is too tired to stay awake or when Major Barbara bosses her "dear little Dolly boy." Candida is one of the best examples of Shaw's mother-women: throughout the play she babies and bullies her two "boys," Morell and Marchbanks, and the boys take turns sitting in a child's chair at her feet. Doña Ana (and presumably Ann Whitefield in Act IV of *Man and Superman*) becomes another archetypal mother as she leaves the dialogue in hell searching for a father for the superman. What these women have in common is an instinct for mothering, an ability to manage others, and a tendency to brook no interference with their own plans. In their will to prevail, they have affinities with Philip Wylie's "mom," except that we condemn "mom" and are forced to admire—even if grudgingly—the tremendous vitality of Shaw's mothers.[6]

In his attitude toward women and the Life Force, Shaw—who in theory advocates sexual equality—makes rigid sex role divisions. According to the argument of *Man and Superman*, it is man's function (as thinker, philosopher) to create new mind, while woman's function (as childbearer, mother) is to create new life. Surprisingly, even in the midst of an attack on marriage as an oppressive institution (in "The Womanly Woman") Shaw says that motherhood is a means by which a woman regains the self-respect she loses through marriage.[7] And such reverence for motherhood leads, ironically, to an idealization of woman: "Sexually, Woman is Nature's contrivance for perpetuating its highest achievement."[8] As not only the creator of life but also the nourisher and sustainer of it, the Life Force woman becomes Shaw's version of the Great Mother, traditionally revered but also feared. In "Symbolic Figures and the Symbolic Technique of George Bernard Shaw," Margaret Schlauch argues that this Mother-Goddess is a recurrent symbolic figure in Shaw, and cites as examples Lady Cicely, Candida, Mrs. George (*Getting Married*), and Mrs. Hushabye (*Heartbreak House*). She further notes that "in their most elaborated forms . . . Shaw's goddess-figures serve as clear allegorical vehicles for his theory of the Life Force, as incarnations of consciously creative evolution."[9] Thus we are presented with the paradox of a man who can argue against the romantic idealization of woman, but who nevertheless personally worships the mother-goddess figure he artistically creates.

As agents of the Life Force, such women as Candida, Lady Cicely, Barbara Undershaft or Saint Joan are as self-sacrificing as the most fanatic Victorian martyr-woman. Even as these women avoid the stereotype of the "womanly woman" and are aggressive, often manipulative, no-nonsense women, they finally are not self-serving; they are instead always working for some "higher purpose." Candida, for example, sees herself as the supporter of male achievement and gives herself to the man who needs her most. So too Lady Cicely's secret of command is to lose the one "little bit of self" left in her; she is seen as totally selfless in her motives, and is called a "saint" by Marzo (*Captain Brassbound's Conversion*, in *Three Plays for Puritans*). Major Barbara is likewise a savior of others, as is Saint Joan. As Watson notes, "the quality to be extracted from all Shaw's willful women and from some of the men, is saintliness."[10] Curiously, Shaw attacked the women-are-angels morality, but himself liked to portray women as saints.

Shaw's greatest portraits of women are complex and do not belong to a single type. Candida, for example, is portrayed as a seductress, planning to initiate Marchbanks into a knowledge of "what love really is." At the same time, her primary instinct is for mothering; the phrases "silly boy" or "my boy" punctuate her speech to both Morell and Marchbanks. And in the comparison of Candida to "the Virgin of the Assumption over her hearth" and the reverence both men have for her (Marchbanks kneels for her blessing before he exits at the end of the play), she can be seen as a Shaw Madonna, in a play which he called "THE Mother play."[11] The interfacing of types in such a complex portrayal adds depth and texture to Candida and to the play.

So too Ann Whitefield is a combination of literary types. When we view her through Tanner's eyes we see the dangerous huntress, the *femme fatale*: "a cat," "a boa constrictor," "the lioness," "a Bengal tiger," "Lady Mephistopheles." At the end of Act II Tanner flees from her in terror, realizing that he is "the marked down victim, the destined prey." And by the end of the play he feels trapped, caught. In contrast, Ann is seen by Ramsden as the epitome of female propriety and innocence: "a wonderfully dutiful girl," "only a woman, a young and inexperienced woman at that." Octavius shares this mistaken view of her and also worships her as archetypal goddess; she reminds him, a stage direction tells us, of *the whole life of the race to its beginnings in the east, or even back to the paradise from which it fell. She is to him the reality of romance, the inner good sense of nonsense, the unveiling of his eyes, the freeing of his soul, the abolition of time, place and circumstance, the etherealization of his blood into rapturous rivers of the very water of life itself, the revelation of all the mysteries and the sanctification of all the dogmas."* Here she is linked with Eve and the very source of life (Shaw himself seems caught up in this description of her), and thus comes to embody some of the mother-woman's characteristics. Like Candida, she babies men: she tells Tanner that he is "a perfect baby in the things I do understand," and she calls "Ricky-Ticky-Tavvy" "a nice creature—a good boy." By the end of the play she is identified, through Doña Ana's dialogue in hell, with the creative maternal impulse of the Life Force. Shaw describes Ann as "one of the vital geniuses" who inspires "confidence . . . also some fear." He regards Ann as "Everywoman" (Epistle Dedicatory); and, significantly, Everywoman is a composite of traditional types.

There is a last type which Shaw presents which is neither traditional nor composite; this is the contemporary figure of the emancipated woman who has rejected typical "female" roles. The literary treatment of this type has been a portrait of a woman who is unmarried, plain and "masculine" in dress and manner. (We know her in the twentieth century as the stereotyped "career girl" and very recently as the "women's lib freak.") There is a *Punch* cartoon of 1880 which graphically depicts the late nineteenth-century version of this woman: she wears a white shirt and tie and a simply cut suit (resembling a man's) and wears her hair short or severely pulled back. The title "Man or Woman?—A Toss Up" makes the editorial comment. When Shaw created Vivie Warren, he created a similar type. Admittedly, Vivie has all the characteristics of a character—male or female—representing Shaw's values: like Shaw, she has no use for the beauty worshipers or the idealizers of love; she believes in free choice and turns her back on the capitalist exploitation represented by Mrs. Warren and Crofts; and in one sense she can be said to fulfill Shaw's explanation that "the secret of the extraordinary knowledge of women which I shew in my plays" is that "I have always assumed that a woman is a person exactly like myself, and that is how the trick is done."[12] But for those of us who find it refreshing to read about a literary heroine who is "permanently single . . . and permanently unromantic" (*Mrs Warren's Profession, Plays Unpleasant*), it is a disappointment to see her resembling a *Punch* cartoon, her "masculine" qualities emphasized as she smokes her cigars, carries her fountain pen and paper knife on a chain, and cripples hands with her handshake.

In saying that Vivie Warren—or Ann Whitefield, or Candida—or any of the other of Shaw's magnificent portraits of strong women belong to literary types or are composites of them, I am not denigrating the art of the plays. We take for granted that good—and great—art can be produced by artists who utilize character types rather than "real life" models; and we know that typing belongs especially to the comic mode. Furthermore, we do not expect characters to embody the complexity of real people; art by its very nature simplifies.

And in defense of Shaw's realism, we can point out that even stereotypes have some basis in reality. Shaw knew real women— e.g., his mother, his sister Lucy, Jenny Patterson, Ellen Terry, Mrs. Patrick Campbell—who served as partial models for some of his characters and who apparently in their real lives embodied aspects of the tiger cat, the mother-woman, or the self-sacrificing saint (as we no doubt have known women who share some of Candida's mothering, or Ann's man-chasing, or Lady Cicely's manipulative expertise, or Vivie's independence). But the artistic defense is, finally, the only defense of Shaw's characters: there is no question that the plays are interesting and theatrically, structurally and stylistically effective. As literary critics we admire Shaw's art.

Otherwise, we have to deplore his failure to create female characters who reflect his expressed opinion that women must be regarded as equal to men and must seek personal identity—an identity separate from traditional roles. An examination of the portraits of women in literature reveals, almost without exception, rigid role definition: as the Enemy (destroyer, temptress), as the Goddess (purity, sanctity, selflessness personified), as the Mother, and—recently—as the "Working Girl." Had Shaw not written so eloquently against stereotyping women, we would hardly be surprised to find these types in his work since they are prevalent throughout Western literature. That the types do appear, however, suggests the need to reexamine all Shaw's female characters. And as a beginning point, we should stop exclaiming about their originality and make a clear distinction between Shaw's traditional treatment of women in the plays and his feminist politics.

Notes

1. Letter to William Archer, quoted in its entirety in Archibald Henderson, *George Bernard Shaw: Man of the Century* (1956), p. 128.
2. Watson, p. 19, et passim. Other studies of Shaw's women include Joseph Molnar's "Shaw's Four Kinds of Women," which proposes the types of the Womanly Woman, the Shavian Emancipated Woman, the Life Force Woman, the Shavian New Woman; Toni Block's "Shaw's Women," which

offers real life sources for the female characters; and Betty Bandel, "G.B.S. and the Opposite Sex." Arthur H. Nethercot, in "The Female of the Species," *Men and Supermen: The Shavian Portrait Gallery,* pp. pp. 77–126, lists the Womanly Woman, the Pursuing Woman, the Mother Woman, the New Woman, the Younger Generation, and the Manly Woman.

3. "Woman—Man in Petticoats," p. 174.

4. *The Quintessence of Ibsenism,* in *Major Critical Essays* (1932), pp. 32–41.

5. The three scenes occur, respectively, in *Man and Superman, Arms and the Man* and *Pygmalion.*

6. See Andrina Gilmartin's "Mr. Shaw's Many Mothers," p. 143 in which Shaw's mothers are divided into three types: the "kind" mother: the "bored" one (who can nevertheless do an adequate job of mothering with assistance and guidance), and the "wicked" one.

7. *The Quintessence of Ibsenism,* p. 38.

8. Spoken by Don Juan, *Man and Superman.*

9. *Science and Society* 21 (Summer 1957), 210–21. Schlauch's examples of the Life Force goddess-figures: Dona Ana, Prola *(The Simpleton of the Unexpected Isles),* Eve and Lilith *(Back to Methuselah).*

10. Watson, p. 77.

11. Letter to Ellen Terry, in *Bernard Shaw: Collected Letters 1874–1897,* p. 641.

12. "Woman—Man in Petticoats," p. 174.

A WHORE IN EVERY HOME

Germaine Greer

The most curious aspect of *Mrs Warren's Profession* is that profession itself. A profession is better than a *trade* and something manifestly more solid than a *game*. The audience of the play is involved in a conspiracy with the actors in understanding what Mrs. Warren does or has done without its ever being described, to such an extent that one feels an utter ninny for being unsure. The disgust expressed by the other characters, even by so sensible a girl as Vivie, is apparently not excited by Mrs. Warren's venality or by her financial success but by the sexuality of her way of life, a sexuality which, if we are to take her pass at Frank as any indication, she rather enjoys.

Shaw considered himself several cuts above the authors of aphrodisiac plays and even boasted in his preface that he had shown the worse side of the lives of glamorous courtesans which so often graced the Victorian stage. But what is bad about Mrs. Warren's profession is as efficiently repressed as its unspeakable name. Shaw refrains from making his spectators desire his heroine, but the whole structure of the play relies upon their prurience for its interest. He rings the same change as his master Ibsen does in *Ghosts* by hinting at possible consanguinity between Frank (or Praed or Crofts) and Vivie, possible coincidences which have a great deal to do with the plot and not much to do with the theme.

In his preface Shaw argued that if his play were to "cause an increase in the number of persons entering the profession or employing it, its performance might well be made an indictable offense," a safe challenge because there could be no way in which information upon the point could ever be collected. Indeed, the basic assumption of the play, that vice is the only way that a poor woman can "better herself," that is to say, grow richer and even rise into the hypocritical middle classes, while virtue (considered as chastity) can do no better than vice at its worst—i.e., "end in poverty and overwork"—is the most effective incentive to prostitution that can be imagined. Mrs. Warren's success seems inevitable within the context of the play and the unpleasantnesses no more than those which might occur within holy wedlock—"having to try and please some man she doesn't care two straws for—some half-drunken fool that thinks he's making himself agreeable when he's teasing and worrying and disgusting a woman so that hardly any money could pay her for putting up with it." The middle-class prostitute - *entrepreneuse* may be comfortable and idle, but a good deal of prostitution is carried on at the same time as backbreaking toil in the laundry or the sweatshop or the fields, and never leads to riches at all. Only the tiniest minority of successful prostitutes has ever *died* rich.

The lot of the prostitute has probably deteriorated since Shaw's time. Growing sexual license has meant a decline in the market value of sexual favors. The weakening of the supports of the "marriage hearse" has not lessened the poignancy of the "youthful harlot's curse." Kept women would not now consider themselves part of the sisterhood, and the house of ill-fame, the only shelter and protection that many whores ever knew, has been banished from most cities, with the result that prostitutes must ply their trade in the street. Refusing to recognize the existence of professional prostitution has merely decontrolled the trade, not abolished it. Nowadays more haphazard arrangements prevail, door-to-door prostitutes, prostitutes with their own cars, clients using their cars as bordellos, blow-jobs in office hours, half-hours in Paddington hotels. The permissive society favors the rich, the handsome and the successful: the old, the ugly and the poor must still pay for what their "betters" get for free. Prostitutes are more likely to cast their lot with immigrants, criminals, cripples, old men and nut-cases. More and more they need physical protection—and for that they must pay.

Prostitutes often define themselves as a public service, when being questioned by those who love to study them, because they draw off from decent women the "filthier" demands which cannot be made of amateurs. They are even more frequently bashed and murdered than little girls. What does Mrs. Warren know of this? She may not be as flamboyant and as seductive as Camille, but she can conduct herself in a solid businesslike way. Her demeanor is consistent with that of any businesswoman, say a pastrycook, who has risen in the world and put a daughter through Newnham. Moreover she is pretty, the one necessary condition for her escape from a life of brutalizing drudgery. Shaw's argument seems to be that all working-class girls are whores who can be. The rest are the plain losers.

What is the Dreadful Truth which (in the play) is only written down on pieces of paper, one torn up and the other passed about like obscene words in a court-case? "Whore and Procuress?" & "Prostitute and Bawd?" "Slut and Pander?" Sticks and Stones. Even Mrs. Warren's rejection by her child is no more than virtuous and well-meaning mums have to suffer. Can this be the whole or any part of the truth about a way of life beset by police persecution, illness, exploitation by pimps and protection rackets, clients who exact humiliating and pain-ful liberties and then refuse to pay, landlords who rack-rent to the trade, and the prostitutes' own guilt and shame? Can Shaw's play have been written by a man who had ever known a prostitute? What would he have made of Bengali Rose and Jane the Urdu who relieve the total sexual deprivation of whole households of Pakistanis in an hour, for a pound a head? Are they better or worse than Mrs. Warren because they service so many for so little?

So the mystery remains—what is prostitution? What is it more than practicing upon sexuality for gain? It need not involve indiscriminacy, or even sexual intercourse, or even money, but simply *gain*. If health officers complain that *amateur* prostitutes are spreading disease, it must follow that prostitution need not even be professional to be so defined. If gain is what makes a prostitute, then prostitution is univer-sal in a society where all contributions are tainted by an ulterior motive. Marriage itself is legalized prostitution, for legitimate sex is as fre-quently deployed for advantage as any other sort. The wife who is trained as laboriously as any Geisha in the arts of keeping her hus-band, and keeping him contented and successful, is a sanctified whore. The colder a woman the more successful she is in manipulat-ing male susceptibility from dating to mating. The dating-mating female is playing for higher stakes, for a long-range subsidy on more favorable terms than Sir George gave Mrs. Warren. Alimony is the ultimate testimony. There are many wives who capitulate as ably as the professionals to their husbands' fetishistic demands in return for the guarantee of security.

Men often complain about the indignity of monogamous whoremas-tery as if they were its only victims, but these same men are fascinated by straightforward prostitution. They themselves are bound up in the cash value of sex, the notion that girls are sitting on a fortune and have the world in their laps, if they would only exploit it. But women are not better off in this world where sex like everything else is a commodity. However desolating it is to make love to a woman who cooperates out of greed or kindness or pity or laziness, it is as desolating never to know the innocence and spontaneity of sexual desire. The most spectacular whores in our society of impotent voyeurs are those who never have to put out at all. Mrs. Warren's modest competence and her solid family firm pale into insignificance and respectability beside the millions made by women who sell not their bodies but the image of them, not desire but the imitation of it; theirs is prostitution at a second remove, they sell the image in order to be paid for selling something else.

Many a common prostitute whom the million-dollar purveyors of pussy would spit upon would rather lavish all her earnings upon the one man she desires than grow rich in such frigidity. It is not vice at its worst or virtue at its best which exploits men and women, but the profit motive, which is indifferent to ethics and has no sex at all. Shaw could get no nearer the correct etiology of whoredom than the feeble Fabian diagnosis that women were overworked, undervalued and underpaid so that they were powerfully tempted to a way of life falsely represented as easier.

The ambiguity of the apportionment of blame in *Mrs Warren's Profession* does leave us, however, with an inkling of the truth, that prostitution is universal in a capitalist society in that all talent, all energy, all power is a commodity with a cash value. All contributions, material or spiritual or carnal, are marketable and will be marketed willy-nilly. Artists, teachers, craftsmen, lovers all hope to keep their faculties separate from the marketing of them, and none of them has more than Mrs. Warren's chance.

IV
SHAW'S LIBERATED WOMEN

VIVIE WARREN:
A PSYCHOLOGICAL STUDY

Marlie Parker Wasserman

Shaw's early advocacy of equal rights for women has long been well documented. When Shaw wrote *Mrs Warren's Profession* he portrayed Vivie Warren as an intelligent, aggressive, independent woman, a fact which has been emphasized in recent articles. Sonja Lorichs labels Vivie as Shaw's first Unwomanly Woman.[1] Savitri Khanna considers her an example of the Shavian New Woman.[2] It is pleasing to see Shaw again recognized for his progressive views, but the full extent of his achievement is not yet appreciated. He did not take the easy path of making a point through the usual means of a stereotyped character. I can only partially agree with Elsie Adams in her claim that Vivie Warren represents a literary type—the emancipated woman.[3] Certainly Vivie's portrayal has many elements of a stereotype, as is illustrated by her tailored clothing. But Shaw's characterization of Vivie goes far beyond a literary type. His portrayal is a psychological one, probing Vivie as a living woman, not just typing Vivie as a liberated woman.

Shaw's use of psychology in his characterizations is seldom discussed by critics and is often denied if it is mentioned at all. Arthur Nethercot studies this matter in his article "Bernard Shaw and Psychoanalysis." "It is disillusioning to discover," he reports, "that, of all the myriads of Shaw's biographers and critics, only a tiny minority have thought the subject of Shaw's opinions on the mental science of psychoanalysis even worth mentioning."[4] After studying Shaw's very limited use of psychological terminology, Nethercot concludes, "The whole particular situation almost leads one to speculate seriously on whether Shaw had actually read anything specific by Freud."[5] Joseph Wood Krutch is even more condemnatory in his generalization that "human psychology is something with which Shaw never bothers."[6]

The critical trend toward minimizing Shaw's familiarity with psychology has met with scattered opposition. Barbara Bellow Watson prophesies that "it may some day become clear that Shaw created an early parallel of Freudian psychology."[7] Unfortunately, she does not elaborate. A stronger challenge to Nethercot and Krutch is presented by Sidney P. Albert in his cogent article, "Reflections on Shaw and Psychoanalysis." After offering thorough and convincing proof that Shaw's knowledge of psychology was at the least more than anyone has given him credit for, Albert concludes that "Shaw offered us his own distinctive insights and perspective on human life and its psychological conditions."[8] Albert's research is invaluable in its reassessment of Shaw's attitude toward psychoanalysis, but a careful study of each play is beyond the scope of his purpose. Only one critic, Bernard Dukore, discusses Shaw's use of psychology in *Mrs Warren's Profession*. In a study limited to Kitty Warren, Dukore admits Shaw was concerned with psychological causes, but believes Shaw considered these less important than social and economic causes.[9] There appears to be no study recognizing Shaw's use of psychology in his portrayal of Vivie Warren.

It is almost certain that Shaw was unfamiliar with Freud when he wrote *Mrs Warren's Profession* in 1893 and 1894; most of Freud's major works were not even published at this time. From a review of Shaw's writings, Albert estimates that 1911 was probably the beginning of Shaw's familiarity with Freud.[10] Moreover, in 1894 the dramatist was as ignorant of psychoanalysis as he was of its founder. The earliest instance Albert notes where Shaw referred to psychiatric theory was in 1895.[11] It is reasonable to conclude that when Shaw wrote *Mrs Warren's Profession*, he was unaware of both Freud and developing psychological theories. But he *was* aware of the motivating influences of human nature. It does not take a student of Freud to observe and record, and this is precisely what Shaw did in his portrayal of Vivie Warren. Even though he was not familiar with psychoanalysis and could not possibly have known of recent studies of the correlation between institution children and the recurrence of specific personality traits, Shaw nevertheless was able to instinctively sense the effects of institutional life upon Vivie's character.

The reader learns of Vivie's institutional upbringing early in the first act of *Mrs Warren's Profession*. As the play opens, Mr. Praed comes to visit Vivie and her mother in their home. Minutes after meeting Praed for the first time, Vivie tells him, "I hardly know my mother. Since I was a child I have lived in England, at school or college, or with people paid to take charge of me. I have been boarded out all my life. My mother has lived in Brussels or Vienna and never let me go to her. I only see her when she visits England for a few days." According to the dialogue, at this point Praed has already expressed to Vivie his desire not to "appear intrusive." Perhaps because of his respect for privacy, Praed becomes *"very ill at ease"* after Vivie has finished the above speech. Vivie is remarkably eager to volunteer the story of her childhood to a guest who was a stranger a minute before and who makes a noticeable effort to avoid meddling in the affairs of others. It is logical to conclude that Vivie's impersonal upbringing was of great significance to her and, at least in this instance, was in the forefront of her thoughts.

Shaw was careful to make Vivie's institutional upbringing understood early in the play, since so many of the personality traits which she would exhibit later are dependent on this background information. As Vivie herself may have sensed, her upbringing was crucial to the "abnormal" development of her personality. A comparison of Shaw's characterization of Vivie with recent psychological studies will demonstrate the playwright's intuitive understanding of the dependent relationship between boarding school life and recurring personality traits.

Some of the best research on this correlation has been done by Anna Freud and Dorothy Burlingham. In their 1943 publication, *War and Children*, they observed that "The ability to love . . . has to be learned and practiced. Wherever, through the absence of or the interruption of personal ties, this opportunity is missing in childhood, all later relationships will develop weakly, will remain shallow. The opposite of this ability to love is not hate, but egoism."[12] Vivie's decision in the final act of *Mrs Warren's Profession* is a perfect example of such egoism. She terminates her relationship with her mother Kitty and her suitor Frank, deciding in favor of pure self-reliance. When Vivie defies her mother, she insists, "In the future I shall support myself. . . . From this time I go my own way in my own business and among my own friends. And you will go yours. . . . I dont want a mother; and I dont want a husband."

In *Infants without Families*, published in 1944, Freud and Burlingham continued their studies.

> Lack of family setting produces serious qualitative changes. The basic emotional needs of the institutional child are, of course, the same as those of the child who lives at home. But these needs meet with a very different fate. One important instinctual need, that for early attachment to the mother, remains as we

know more or less unsatisfied; consequently it may become blunted, which means that the child for a while ceases to search for a mother substitute and fails to develop all the more highly organized forms of love which should be modelled on the first pattern.[13]

Vivie never indicates any capacity for a "highly organized form of love." She appears to be capable only of a sexual relationship, which Freud and Burlingham would presumably consider a "lower form." Since Vivie never had a model for love, Frank's courtship represents for her the only kind of relationship she is aware of—the sordid affair—and of this she wants no part. When Frank asserts his love for her, she retorts, "The same feeling, Frank, that brought your father to my mother's feet. Is that it?" Frank's father was a customer of Vivie's prostitute-mother.

In 1949, William Goldfarb further elaborated on the correlation between institution children and the recurrence of specific personality traits. "Institution children," wrote Goldfarb, "present a history of aggressive . . . behavior."[14] Vivie's physical aggressiveness is obvious; she smokes cigars, lifts chairs with ease, and shakes hands too firmly for a turn-of-the-century woman. Moreover, her decisions are also aggressive. Only a very venturesome young lady would be strong enough to break off relations with her suitor and her mother.

John Bolby's report to the World Health Organization in 1951 is another study which almost seems like an analysis of *Mrs Warren's Profession*. He describes the typical reactions of a child who is raised by a mother-substitute and occasionally visited by his mother:

> Those [reactions] most commonly observed are . . . a hostile reaction to the mother on her return, which sometimes takes the form of a refusal to recognize her . . .; a cheerful but shallow attachment to any adult within the child's orbit; and . . . an apathetic withdrawal from all emotional entanglement, combined with monotonous rocking of the body and sometimes head banging.[15]

Vivie's reaction to her returning mother approaches hostility. When Praed suggests that they go to the station to meet Kitty, Vivie replies "[coolly] Why? She knows the way." When Kitty returns after an undoubtedly long absence, Vivie's reaction is far from affectionate. "How do, mater," she says. "Mr Praed's been here this half hour waiting for you." An even more startling resemblance between Bowlby's description and Vivie's actions occurs when Frank and Vivie rhythmically rock one another in the third act. Frank nestles against Vivie who tries to lull him asleep. Shaw's stage directions for

Vivie read, *"rhythmically, rocking him like a nurse."*

Shaw's psychological insight is further evidenced by Harry F. Harlow's research with infant monkeys separated from their mothers and raised by surrogates. Harlow's numerous studies demonstrate the emotional disturbances of motherless monkeys. Three characteristics of these disturbances are especially pertinent to a study of Vivie Warren. First, Harlow found that peer group affectional responses were underdeveloped among motherless monkeys. According to his studies, "the mother-raised babies appeared to interact more freely and subtly and have more social awareness than the surrogate-raised infants. . . . From early life onwards the real-mothered infants show superiority in social play responses over the surrogate-mothered babies."[16] Secondly, infant-mother relationships were also harmed by separation. It is evident from Harlow's research that even a "brief period of motherlessness inhibits the formation of a fully developed infant-mother attachment."[17] Finally, monkeys were more inclined toward rocking motions if they were raised with a wire surrogate than with a cloth surrogate which more closely approximates a real mother.[18]

Although human behavior is not a perfect reflection of simian behavior, Harlow is confident that there is a distinct parallel. A parallel is certainly apparent in Vivie's behavior; her weakly developed relations with Frank and her mother have already been cited, as has her inclination toward rocking. In *Mrs Warren's Profession*, Shaw anticipated Harlow's primate research by seventy years.

Shaw's observations are not as detailed as the above studies, but they do illustrate that he was aware of the effects of an institutional upbringing. An examination of other Shavian works besides *Mrs Warren's Profession* further substantiates Shaw's cognizance of a child's psychological reaction to an institution. In his preface to *Immaturity* he recalls, "I was never in a school where the teachers cared enough about me."[19] He becomes increasingly antagonistic in the chapter "Socialism and Children" of *The Intelligent Woman's Guide to Socialism and Capitalism:*

> Our eyes are being opened more and more to the fact that in our school system education is only the pretext under which parents get rid of the trouble of their children by bundling them off into a prison or child farm which is politely called a school. We also know, or ought to know, that institutional treatment of children is murderous for infants and bad for all children.[20]

It is clear, even from this limited study, that Shaw was able to observe and record a cause and effect relationship. True, he does not use psychologese or explicit analyses, but his understanding of psychological motivation is nevertheless evident. The opportunity for Shavian criticism to demonstrate Shaw's intuitive use of psychology in his characterizations should not be ignored. An awareness of the depth of his characterizations of women can even further enhance his reputation as a supporter of equal rights. A woman with understandable weaknesses as well as understandable strengths is likely to be more convincing than a stereotype.

Notes

1. Lorichs, "The Unwomanly Woman," p. 250. See also p. 100.

2. Khanna, "Shaw's Image of Woman," p. 257.

3. Elsie Adams, "Feminism and Female Stereotypes in Shaw," *Shaw Review* 17 (January 1974), 17-22. See also p. 156.

4. Arthur H. Nethercot, "Bernard Shaw and Psychoanalysis," *Modern Drama* 11 (February 1969), 366.

5. Ibid., 368.

6. Joseph Wood Krutch, *"Modernism" in Modern Drama,* (1953), p. 57.

7. Watson, *A Shavian Guide to the Intelligent Woman,* p. 132.

8. Sidney P. Albert, "Reflections on Shaw and Psychoanalysis," *Modern Drama* 14 (September 1971), 194.

9. Bernard F. Dukore, "The Fabian and the Freudian," *Shavian* 2 (June 1961), 10.

10. Albert, "Reflections on Shaw and Psychoanalysis," 173.

11. Ibid., p. 172n.

12. Anna Freud and Dorothy T. Burlingham, *War and Children,* Medical War Books (1943), p. 191.

13. Anna Freud and Dorothy [T.] Burlingham, *Infants without Families,* War Books (1944), p. 27.

14. William Goldfarb, "Rorschach Test Differences between Family-Reared, Institution-Reared, and Schizophrenic Children," *American Journal of Orthopsychiatry* 19 (1949), 625.

15. John Bowlby, *Maternal Care and Mental Health* (1951), p. 25.

16. Harry F. Harlow, "The Maternal Affectional System," in *Determinants of Infant Behavior,* vol. 2, ed. B.M. Foss (1963), pp. 12, 13-14.

17. Harry F. Harlow and Robert R. Zimmerman, "The Development of Affectional Responses in the Infant Monkey," in *Determinants of Infant Behavior,* ed. B.M. Foss (1959), p. 80.

18. Harry F. Harlow and Robert R. Zimmerman, "Affectional Responses in the Infant Monkey," *Science* 130 (21 August 1959), 424, 426.

19. Bernard Shaw, *Immaturity,* in *The Collected Works of Bernard Shaw,* vol. 1 (1930), p. xxxii.

20. Shaw, *The Intelligent Woman's Guide to Socialism and Capitalism* (1928), p. 413.

SHAW AND WOMEN'S LIB

Gladys M. Crane

What characteristics does the Shavian female heroine have in common with today's liberated women? Their major goal is the freeing of woman from her traditional roles as wife, mother, housekeeper. Shaw, in expressing his outrage against the stereotyped thinking of his day, took up the cause of woman who was expected to embrace her role as an inferior, dependent being confined to childbearing and housekeeping. Shaw's creation of women characters who were real people, who escaped the confines of the stereotype to triumph as individuals in the outside world, was his blow for the emancipation of women. In a similar way today's women activists seek greater independence for woman in choosing her role, whether it be wife and mother, professional woman, or some combination of the two: in short, a life style which provides various options both professionally and socially. Further, the choice of career must be unconstrained by societal expectations of woman's role. Along with freedom of career choice is the freedom of thinking about herself as a woman. An accurate self-evaluation, self-awareness and sense of personal worth are also characteristics of the modern liberated woman.

Taking as our basic criterion, then, the desire of women for more independence, socially, economically and psychologically, let us look at the struggles of Shaw's heroines who sought greater independence. Since Shaw saw theatre as a means of awakening people about various phenomena in society, his women characters are consistently at odds with society's mores, either overtly in the roles they choose, or more subtly, as they are outwardly obedient but inwardly rebellious. Frequently they are superior to the male characters in intelligence, social skills, and maturity; in a few cases they have superior physical strength or mechanical skills, as in the case of Lina Szczepanowska, the Polish acrobat-pilot of *Misalliance,* or Mrs. Banger, who served as a trouper in the war in *Press Cuttings.* In any case, Shaw's women seem innately unsuited to the role of a dependent, inferior being. Each is put in the position of working out the conflict between a full expression of her true abilities and the repressive demands of society. Shaw's women characters exemplify their liberation primarily through their independence: socially, economically, psychologically. Of the six characters to be considered here, only two are fully liberated; the others are moving toward that freedom in all areas of their lives.

Epifania Fitzfassenden in *The Millionairess* has the economic independence of the millions which she inherited from her father; this money frees her from dependence on others such as a husband. Although the original source of her money is her father, she has maintained her income by careful management. Her business acumen and her ability to manage others is amply demonstrated in her experience of taking over the "sweat shop" and convincing the boss that he could make much more money by owning the means of production and dealing directly with the source of supply. Her logic and her dynamic way of presenting her ideas enable her to dominate the others quite fully. Epifania dominates, then, through the power of her money which in turn gives her a sense of personal power that others usually submit to. Her ability to analyze a business and diagnose the changes necessary to make it more profitable establish her superiority in a sphere usually dominated by males.

Comedy results from Epifania's sense of unlimited power over others, a phenomenon resulting from her prior success in bullying others. A primary source of humor is her use of insults to attempt to cow others verbally. When, for example, the Egyptian doctor refuses to take her injury seriously, even though she offers him money, her response is a classic of invective: "You are a pig and a beast and a Bolshevik. It is the most abominable thing of you to leave me here in distress . . . . You are an unmitigated hippopotamus."

Epifania's pride in her position, her dominant personality, her reincarnation of the father she idolizes, make her somewhat unattractive to men, apart from her fame and wealth. Her idea of herself as a desirable woman able to tempt men away from their serious pursuits is comically exploded by the Egyptian doctor who refuses her invitation to have a romantic fling. He characterizes her as having "enormous self-confidence, reckless audacity, insane egotism," and as "apparently sexless." Shocked, she asks him what he means. He replies: "You talk to me as if you were a man. There is no mys-

tery, no separateness, no sacredness about men to you. A man to
you is only a male of your species." Eventually she wins him
through the most impersonal and uncontrolled part of her; he falls
in love with her pulse.

Had Epifania decided against marriage, her "bad luck" in male
partners would have been eliminated. Her need to be married to
gain society's approval is apparent in her admission: "It is convenient to be married. It is respectable. It keeps other men off. It gives
me a freedom that I could not enjoy as a single woman. I have become accustomed to a husband. No: decidedly I will not divorce
Alastair—at least until I can find a substitute whom I really want."
In all instances, Epifania's ability to have a meaningful relationship
with a man is inhibited by her superficial evaluation of him, a direct
result of her father's valuation of people according to their wealth.

Thus, though Epifania has long enjoyed economic independence
and possesses knowledge and skills to continue in that freedom, her
submission to the societal demand for marriage coupled with her
inability to have a truly satisfying marriage indicates that she is not
fully liberated. Psychologically she is a female counterpart of her
father in her dependence on her wealth for prestige, affection and
power. Epifania is not fully liberated because she has not found her
unique personality apart from her father.

Lesbia Grantham in *Getting Married* fulfills the definition of a liberated woman in the sense that she is independent personally, socially and economically; she rejects the traditional woman's role of
marriage and motherhood. She is freed from the necessity to marry,
having determined for herself that the disadvantages outweigh the
advantages, but she is not freed for something better than the traditional women's role. In that sense, then, she too is incompletely
liberated. She has a definite desire for motherhood and a sense that
she would be an excellent mother; in response to Boxer's question,
"Don't you want children?" she states:

> I ought to have children. I should be a good mother to children.
> I believe it would pay the country very well to pay ME to have
> children. But the country tells me that I cant have a child in my
> house without a man in it too; so I tell the country that it will
> have to do without my children. If I am to be a mother, I really
> cannot have a man bothering me to be a wife at the same time.

Boxer, still unsatisfied with her answer, questions her natural desire
for sex, asking, "Don't you want a husband?" to which she replies:
"No. I want children; and I want to devote myself entirely to my
children, and not to their father. The law will not allow me to do

that; so I have made up my mind to have neither husband nor children."

Thus Lesbia desires motherhood and even admits that she has "natural appetites" but cannot stand the thought of having to live with a man in order to enjoy motherhood. Her reasons for abhorring the thought of marriage, however, render trivial her whole consideration of woman's role of marriage and motherhood. She declares to Boxer:

> I'm a regular old maid. I'm very particular about my belongings. I like to have my own house, and to have it to myself. I have a very keen sense of beauty and fitness and cleanliness and order. I am proud of my independence and jealous for it. I have a sufficiently well-stocked mind to be very good company for myself if I have plenty of books and music. The one thing I never could stand is a great lout of a man smoking all over my house and going to sleep in his chair after dinner, and untidying everything. Ugh!

Her decision to live a celibate life is a denial of her feeling that she would be a good mother; in comparing herself to Mrs. George who she feels is self-indulgent and undisciplined, she makes clear her sense of personal worth as a potential mother: "Just because I have the qualities my country wants most I shall go barren to my grave; whilst the women who have neither the strength to resist marriage nor the intelligence to understand its infinite dishonor will make the England of the future."

Lesbia, then, is liberated because she consciously chooses the life of an old maid for good reasons. She has resisted society's pressure to get married, yet she very much wants children and is convinced that she would be a good mother. In this she has a strong self-awareness and a sense of dignity and personal worth. She is only partially liberated, however, in denying herself the fulfillment of children because she cannot abide the institution of marriage that must go with motherhood.

Both women so far considered possess to some degree an independence of mind, a self-sufficiency both economically and socially, and a clear sense of who they are personally and in society. Eliza Doolittle, who makes perhaps greater changes than is usual for a comic character, seems at the end of *Pygmalion* well on her way to becoming a liberated woman.[1]

At the beginning of the play Eliza is an independent person, but her manner of coping with life is a pugnacious, defensive dealing with what she perceives as a hostile environment; hers is a lonely struggle for bare survival. In choosing to take speaking lessons for the purpose of improving her status in life, she gives up the independence of being in the lowest socioeconomic class, that which her father calls the "undeservin' poor." When she succeeds in convincing the upper-class people at the ball that she is one of them, she discovers that she has, in her thinking, moved out of her lower-class status and has begun to believe herself better than a flower girl. In seeking a recognition from Higgins of her changed status, she makes the shocking discovery that all of his attention to her was focused on building up his own ego and therefore was completely lacking in any personal regard for her. This precipitates an "identity crisis" for Eliza; she acts out her extreme disappointment with Higgins by running away from him. Higgins's attempt to get her to return, more from habit and convenience than any other motive, forces Eliza to deal with her feelings for him directly. What Eliza really wants from Higgins is acceptance of her new self, appreciation, recognition and affection. Higgins, incapable of responding to her demands, distorts her desire by saying that she wants him to make love to her. Eliza explains that if it were marriage that she wanted, she could marry Freddy, who is crazy about her. Higgins, disagreeably surprised, declares that Freddy is totally unworthy of her and could never support her. In her response, Eliza stumbles onto the tool of her independence from Higgins: she declares that she can support herself and Freddy by becoming an assistant to Higgins's rival and teaching what she has learned from Higgins. Eliza, then, is once more an independent, self-sufficient human being with a number of choices for her way of life. Shaw makes it quite clear that she will not marry Higgins; if she does marry Freddy, however, she will not be the traditional wife, dependent on and submissive to her husband. Since she is far more practical and competent than Freddy, she will most likely play the dominant role and be the breadwinner in the family. The self-assurance with which she departs from Higgins is a strong indication that she no longer needs anyone to prop up her new personality.

Eliza, then, has developed her independence first by giving it up in deference to a man superior to her in every way: wealth, position, knowledge. Transformed by Higgins's teaching to a charming, attractive, poised young woman whose training and experience open many doors to fulfillment for her, Eliza regains her independence by rejecting her mentor. We do not know which of the several options she chooses or if she has momentary lapses into her old ways, but clearly she is on her way.

Of the many fascinating women characters created by Shaw, the two who seem fully liberated are Vivie Warren and Lina Szczepanowska. Both young women are sufficiently attractive to have the choice of marriage or a career, since both have male suitors who would like to marry them. What then are their reasons for deciding against the traditional role of wife and mother? Both of them have unusual intelligence and the ability to use their minds for practical success. Although most of Shaw's women characters are intelligent, Vivie and Lina are especially so. Both are self-supporting, having chosen a profession for which they are eminently qualified. This removes them from economic dependence on a man, whether it be husband or father. In both cases, the woman's economic independence has been made possible by parental provision: Vivie's education in the best schools in England has been paid for by her mother's "profession" and Lina's training as an acrobat came from her family. Economic independence has made available the option of a career instead of marriage.

Shaw's characterizations of Vivie and Lina are far from subtle. Each creates a sensation on her initial appearance by some blatant social impropriety. Lina's entrance (when the plane she and Percival are flying crashes into the Tarleton greenhouse) is even more surprising than Vivie's. Dressed in male clothing with the helmet and goggles of a pilot, Lina is taken for a man. The discovery that she is "a remarkably good looking woman" creates a mild sensation and profuse apologies from the men for their lack of deference to her as a woman. Lina compounds her social deviation by refusing to borrow one of Hypatia's dresses so that she may be properly dressed for dinner at the Tarletons'. Another way that she reverses conventional womanly behavior is through her bluntness of speech. She states that she does not like to wear dresses because they make her feel ridiculous. Lina creates a further sensation by revealing that she deliberately risked her life by going up in an "aeroplane"; her purpose was the fulfillment of her obligation to her family of famous acrobats, whose tradition it is to risk one's life daily. Not only has she chosen an unusual profession for a woman but she is also very successful economically. These facts make a profound impression on the men who patronize her with their self-made wealth and position.

Both Vivie and Lina unnerve those who expect traditional womanly behavior from them by expressing themselves in a very straightforward and unequivocal way instead of being more subtle and even devious, as was expected of the Victorian woman. Vivie, after offering Praed a bone-crunching handshake, tells him he is "just like what I expected" and that she hopes he is disposed to be friends with her. Praed's surprise and delight is apparent in his statement, "You modern young ladies are splendid: perfectly splendid!" Praed remarks that the conventional behavior among strangers of the opposite sex was "nothing real," "always saying no when you meant yes"; to which Vivie's only comment is that it was a frightful waste of time, "especially women's time." Vivie's sense of values are revealed to be as unconventional as her initial response to Praed. Praed assumes that her achievement as third wrangler in the mathematics contest is an indication of her thirst for culture; she explains that her reasons for entering the contest were totally practical: she was offered fifty pounds to compete. She describes how limiting the study of mathematics has been: "Outside mathematics, lawn tennis, eating, sleeping, cycling, and walking, I'm a more ignorant barbarian than any woman could possibly be who hadnt gone in for the tripos."

Praed responds that the "wicked, rascally system" is "destroying all that makes womanhood beautiful." Vivie then explains that she is going to utilize her knowledge of mathematics to earn her living by doing actuarial calculations and conveyancing; to which Praed remonstrates, "Are you to have no romance, no beauty in your life?" Vivie responds that she cares for neither, explaining that she went to London on the invitation of an artistic friend and that three days of the art galleries and concerts was more than she could tolerate. Vivie then describes her ideal life style: "I like working and getting paid for it. When I'm tired of working, I like a comfortable chair, a cigar, a little whiskey, and a novel with a good story in it." Thus Vivie explodes thoroughly the notion that education creates a cultured human being.

Vivie and Lina, then, in their first scenes establish unique personalities, breaking the mold of ideal lady. In addition to revealing very unconventional choices of profession, both ignore the superficial "small talk" expected in social intercourse between strangers and say exactly what they mean. This directness of expression reaches its comic climax in their interactions with men who are romantically involved with them.

A candor similar to Vivie's telling Praed upon meeting him that she likes him and hopes he will like her is a source of surprise and humor in Lina's first encounter with Tarleton. Both Lina and Vivie manage to create misleading impressions of themselves which cause the men some embarrassment. Lina, because of her exotic career as a public performer and her total disregard of social amenities, creates the impression that she is equally free of moral restrictions. Tarleton, after learning from Summerhays that Lina is an acrobat, responds, "Good! . . . that brings her within reach." Tarleton's view of himself as a romantic figure, who in spite of his years possesses superabundant vitality, is evident in his ways of presenting himself to Lina. Lina's response to Tarleton's invitation to have an affair with him creates humor because she reacts so unconventionally to his somewhat obviously standard approach. Her initial response, "How much will you pay?" fails to daunt him; even her question about how he feels about his wife doesn't slow him down. Lina's final surprise, that he is unacceptable because he has not kept in good physical condition, explodes Tarleton's image of himself as possessing "super abundant vitality." Offered her friendship instead of her love, Tarleton breaks down in tears; Lina ministers to him by taking him off to the gym where she exercises him to the point of exhaustion. Lina's ability to see beneath Tarleton's self-delusion and her propensity for speaking the plain truth is a source of humor in all of her responses to the men in the Tarleton household.

Lina's reaction to the one legitimate proposal of marriage, from Johnny Tarleton, is both a brilliant exposure of Johnny's motives and a very contemporary vilification of the institution of marriage. Johnny gives as his reason that he will give her a home and position, because her present position is not one for a nice woman. In response, her description of her life sounds like a manifesto for the modern woman: "I am an honest woman: I earn my living. I am a free woman: I live in my own house. I am a woman of the world: I have thousands of friends . . . . I am strong: I am skilful: I am brave: I am independent: I am unbought: I am all that a woman ought to be." This she contrasts with the conventional attitudes toward women of the people in Tarleton household: "You seem to think of nothing but making love. . . . Your women are kept idle and dressed up for no other purpose than to be made love to. I have not been here an hour; and already everybody makes love to me as if because I am a woman it were my profession to be made love to." She then describes all that she would do in order to avoid marriage, ending her tirade with, "All this I would do sooner than take my bread from the hand of a man and make him the master of my body and soul. And so you tell your Johnny to buy an Englishwoman: he shall not buy Lina Szczepanowska." Lina's description of marriage as legalized prostitution, a kind of commercial selling of one's soul for financial security, has a very contemporary parallel in today's questioning of traditional marital arrangements.

It is important to note that Lina, though very independent in her thinking, blunt in speech and totally unsentimental, retains the essence of the feminine in being irresistible to the opposite sex. Clearly, by rejecting female attire she employs none of the outer trappings that attract men's attention. She is not coy and provocative, yet she has the entire male populace at her feet. She has a strong sense of her unique identity as a person and as a woman and enjoys thoroughly the adulation of her public. Her reasons for refusing the sexual encounters offered her, though she recognizes all but the marriage proposal as honorable, reflect her sense of personal worth and dignity, not prudery or coldness.

Lina rejects marriage to any man as ridiculous for her since she has a very satisfying life as an independent woman. Vivie, however, reacts negatively to the marriage proposal she receives because of the person proposing and his reasons for wanting to marry her. It is only after she learns her true heritage as the daughter of a procuress that she totally rejects marriage for herself.

Lina and Vivie surprise the men with whom they become involved by their honesty and bluntness of speech. Both, in their encounters with men, are more realistic and practical than the men; in the course of destroying the men's illusions, Lina and Vivie also deflate male egos very effectively. Sir George Crofts, old enough to be Vivie's father, is described by Shaw as "a gentlemanly combination of the most brutal types of city man, sporting man, and man about town." His cynicism as he approaches Vivie with the offer of marriage is apparent in his air. After sending Frank away he begins, "Pleasant young fellow that, Miss Vivie. Pity he has no money, isnt it?" Although Crofts is rather direct in his initial appeal to Vivie, she is even more blunt in letting him know she understands his meaning. She retorts, "I realize his disadvantages, Sir George." Crofts assumes that Vivie, like most people in the world, loves money and the security it means to her future. Vivie's response, after Crofts carefully explains his personal philosophy, which he assumes she shares, and his financial assets, is totally unsentimental and perfectly clear: "I am much obliged to you for being so definite and businesslike. I quite appreciate the offer: the money, the position, Lady Crofts, and so on. But I think I will say no, if you dont mind. I'd rather not." Not discouraged by Vivie's first refusal, Crofts then attempts to make her feel obligated to him for his initial investment in her mother's business. In the ensuing debate Vivie learns that the business is still thriving and Crofts learns that Vivie knows that the business is not hotels but brothels. Even Crofts's reminding Vivie that her entire livelihood has been supported by prostitution does not daunt her; she reviles him, her mother and "the society that tolerates" them. Crofts, infuriated and deflated, resorts to detaining

Vivie physically, but Frank's intervention rescues her.

The delight in Vivie's ability to stand up against a man like Crofts is similar to the joy in Lina's deflating the pompous Tarleton and her exposure of all the men who tried to seduce her. Both Vivie and Lina reject the mold created by men and triumph as individuals strong in self-respect and self-knowledge. The enticement of the male's superior financial status is a major argument in both scenes; both women are sufficiently self-supporting to be immune to that argument. In spite of Vivie's past financial dependence on her mother and Crofts, she has sufficient identity apart from her mother and the "profession."

Both Lina and Vivie face moral choices, but Lina's are infinitely simpler. With her many past experiences with men she has learned how to evaluate their motives, which enables her to solve the moral dilemma of an honorable versus a dishonorable offer. Her decisions, then, are primarily at a personal level, whereas Vivie's choice of her future involves the moral rot of the society in which she has unwittingly participated by accepting money from her mother.

Lina and Vivie very definitely and unequivocally win in their struggles against society's repressive demands on women. Both succeed in their encounters with men who are used to winning. A major factor in their success is their superior intelligence and knowledge; this includes an accurate self-knowledge. Because they see more clearly and are more practical than the men with whom they deal, they expose the self-delusion of the men. Another reason for their success is their clarity of purpose, their strong sense of identity in a world that creates confusion for the woman who does not fit society's mold. Both women have unusual strength arising from strong moral and ethical convictions. Both are enlightened about the pretenses of society: Vivie on the guilt of capitalist society that creates the paradox of women being forced into prostitution to obtain the finances necessary for their dignity and self-respect; Lina on the commercialism of marriage. Both, in their economic and social independence, in their moral and ethical consistency, in their dignity and self-respect, exemplify the ideal for modern free woman.

No consideration of women characters who transcend society's limitations upon them would be complete without including Joan of *Saint Joan*. Undoubtedly the bravest, the most consistent, the truest to her own nature and her unique destiny, Joan in her life and death represents a very complete fulfillment and self-realization of a human life. In contrast to the other women considered in this study, Joan's struggle is not an identity crisis, a search to find out who she is; rather her struggle is to survive a society that cannot absorb her uniqueness of thought and character. Her sense of her particular mission as a person, not as a woman, is established before she appears in the first scene.

Joan is unique too, in that her struggle is not on a personal or domestic level; she represents one individual in conflict with the power of the Church and the state. She rebels not against Victorian society as do Vivie, Lina, and to some extent Lesbia and Epifania, but against the broader restrictions of Church and society. She embodies the spirit of Protestantism in religion and nationalism in politics; her human suffering, though placed by Shaw in her own time, symbolizes the martyrdom of all saints whose vision transcends their own time and whose tenacity and conviction bring them to their own tragic death. Because her life and death transcend her particular society and also that of Victorian society, her suffering is removed from comedy which depends on a specific societal context. Her own character in her given circumstances causes her inevitable death. Even though her death accomplishes, eventually, her goal, it is the death of a tragic heroine. The action of the play deals seriously with the issues of profound changes in society; Joan's struggle, then, is against a background of man's inexorable movement toward greater personal freedom and individuality. She lives and dies at an entirely different and more profound level than that of the struggles of women to overcome the restrictions of Victorian society in their personal lives.

Note

1. See also Pederson, p. 14; Vesonder, p. 39.

SHAW'S LADY CICELY
AND MARY KINGSLEY

Stanley Weintraub

When Bernard Shaw in 1912 tried to account for the inability of his *Captain Brassbound's Conversion* (1899) to achieve a popular success, he took the strange position that its subject matter was too familiar to the theatergoing public. As an appendix to the first printing of the play he had attached notes which identified his confessed sources, notably the memoirs of his adventurer friend Robert Cunninghame Graham as related in *Mogreb-el-Acksa* (Morocco the Most Holy), which Shaw suggested had been "lifted into the second act." That had explained Captain Brassbound, but not the indefatigable Lady Cicely, a role he had written for Ellen Terry when she had complained after the birth of her son Gordon Craig's first child, "Now that I am a grandmother, nobody will ever write a play for me."[1]

The explanation for Shaw's reticence in the matter of Lady Cicely's prototype may have been that she was then still very much alive. (So was Cunninghame Graham, but he was a friend whom one thus had license to spoof.) Mary Kingsley's adventures had been in the newspapers in the middle 1890s, but only in 1897 had come the publication of her *Travels in West Africa*. Her *West African Studies* appeared in the year Shaw wrote *Captain Brassbound*, which at first he had intended to title, after the female lead, *The Witch of Atlas*—a Shelleyan suggestion as well as a reference to the Atlas range in northwest Africa.[2]

No witch, Mary Kingsley nevertheless prevailed in her African travels as if she were one, and Shaw pointed out in his 1912 program note that "the material" of his play had been spread before the public for some years by the sharply contrasted travels of explorers like Stanley and Mary Kingsley, which shewed us, first, little troops of physically strong, violent, dangerous, domineering armed men shooting and bullying their way through risks and savage enmities partly conjured up by their fear-saturated imaginations, and partly promoted by their own terrified aggressions, and then, before we had recovered the breath their escapes had made us hold, a jolly, fearless, good tempered, sympathetic woman walking safely through all those terrors without a weapon or a threat, and finding more safety and civility than among the Apaches of Paris or the Hooligans of London.

The saving grace of the Lady Cicelys and the Miss Kingsleys—and here the term can be applied quite literally—is their respect for the best qualities in human nature and their ability to discover such qualities in every individual they encounter. "I am quite sure," Miss Kingsley observed with her typical demure irony, "that the majority of Anglo-Saxons are good men and I am equally sure that the majority of Negroes are good men—possibly the percentage of perfect angels and calm, scientific minds in both races is less than might be desired but that we cannot help."[3] Lady Cicely confidently sees kind faces symbolizing kind hearts so often that she is—vainly—cautioned to "restrain your confidence in people's eyes and faces." But seeing the best in each man and announcing it publicly became a subtle form of coercion in encouraging even the unlikeliest to behave better than might otherwise have been expected.

Only privately had Shaw earlier indicated the depth of his indebtedness to a real-life prototype, and in the process his admiration for her achievement; for the resourceful Mary Kingsley was a "born boss" of the type Shaw would dramatize in later plays—an instinctive manageress who prevailed in a man's world through wile, wit and will. In July 1899 Shaw had finished *Captain Brassbound* and sent a copy to Ellen Terry. Her reaction was disappointing. "I believe it would never do for the stage," she wrote Shaw, dismissing the idea of her acting the Lady Cicely role. "I don't like the play one bit. Only *one* woman in it? How *ugly* it will look, and there will not be a penny in it."[4] Shaw responded on August 8 with a letter that was more a verbal lashing than his usual cajoling:

Send to your library for two books of travel in Africa: one Miss Kingsley's (have you met her?) and the other H.M. Stanley's. Compare the brave woman, with her commonsense and good will, with the wild beast man, with his elephant-rifle, and his atmosphere of dread and murder. . . . Have you found in your own life and your own small affairs no better way, no more instructive heart wisdom, no warrant for trusting to the good side of people instead of terrorizing the bad side of them. I—poor idiot!—thought the distinction of Ellen Terry was that she had this heart wisdom, and managed her own little world. . . .

I accordingly give you a play in which you stand in the very place where Imperialism is most believed to be necessary, on the border line where the European meets the fanatical African. . . . I try to shew these men gaining a sense of their own courage and resolution from continual contact with & defiance of their own fears. I try to shew you fearing nobody and managing them all as Daniel managed the lions, not by cunning—above all, not by even a momentary appeal to Cleopatra's stand-by, their passions, but by simple moral superiority.[5]

Like Shaw's heroine, Mary Kingsley was the exception to the Victorian rule, a lady brought up in the usual secluded fashion to manifest the diffidence and modesty, the tender-heartedness and self-abnegation of her sex and period, yet who confounded expectation by going exploring fearlessly where few white men trod, and doing so as a lady, in voluminous Victorian dress. According to Sir George Goldie, then director of the Royal Niger Company, Miss Kingsley "had the brain of a man and the heart of a woman,"[6] a summation that would fit Shaw's Lady Cicely Waynflete. When the death of her parents freed her at thirty from the conventional restraints of her sex and time, Mary Kingsley indulged the curiosity whetted by her reading books of science and travel in her father's library by a voyage to West Africa. An untrained amateur zoologist, she embarked with the aim of collecting fish and insect specimens for the British Museum, whose curator in the field was a family friend. Other friends expressed horror that she was going, and when she remained determined, showered on her advice, equipment and medicines. Shaw may have seen a kindred spirit in her published reaction to some of the advice. She had been referred to the missionaries for first-hand information. "So to missionary literature I addressed myself with great ardour; alas! only to find that these good people wrote their reports not to tell you how the country they resided in was, . . . but how necessary it was that their readers should subscribe more freely and not get any foolishness into their heads about obtaining an inadequate supply of souls for their money."

Shaw opens his play with a specimen missionary in his well-kept garden on the west coast of Morocco, a hearty Scot who has been at work in Africa for twenty-five years and for his pains has only one unlapsed convert, a derelict, alcoholic Englishman. But his lack of success among the natives fails to disturb him. "I hope I have done some good," he explains. "They come to me for medicine when they are ill; and they call me the Christian who is not a thief. That is something." It is to his door that Lady Cicely comes on her travels, dressed (in Shaw's stage directions) *with cunning simplicity not as a businesslike, tailor made, gaitered tourist, but as if she lived at the next cottage and had dropped in for tea in blouse and flowered straw hat.* Mary Kingsley had gone on her African travels almost the way she later went on her widely popular lecturing tours in England, in sweeping skirts and curious, old-fashioned hat. In her African kit she had made only one concession to the terrain, taking along an old pair of her brother's trousers, which she wore, when necessary, unseen under her "good thick skirt."

Like Lady Cicely, Miss Kingsley by choice traveled without another valuable article of masculine equipment—a husband. On her second voyage she had some difficulties with the colonial authorities, who had discovered that she was planning to explore the rapids of the Ogowe River, in the French Congo, in a native canoe. Uneasy about her crew of Igalwas, they observed that the only other woman who had visited the rapids, a French lady, had been accompanied by her husband. Mary Kingsley replied—she reported—that neither the Royal Geographical Society's checklist in its *Hints to Travellers* nor Messrs. Silver in their elaborate lists of articles necessary for a traveler in tropical climates "made mention of husbands." Nevertheless, she invented one when circumstances made it practical, for explanations to natives were fruitless. "I have tried it," she recalled, "and it only leads to more questions still." The best reaction, she noted, was to say that she was searching for her husband, and to "locate him away in the direction in which you wish to travel; this elicits help and sympathy." "The important thing," Lady Cicely observes when planning an expedition, "is . . . that we should have as few men as possible, because men give such a lot of trouble travelling. And then, they must have good lungs and not be always catching cold. Above all, their clothes must be of good wearing material. Otherwise I shall be nursing and stitching and mending all the way; and it will be trouble enough, I assure you, to keep them washed and fed without that." On the subject of husbands in particular she insists, practically, "I have never been in love with any real person; and I never shall. How could I manage people if I had that mad little bit of self left in me? That's my secret."

Shaw's understanding (it may have been instinctive in Miss

Kingsley) was that selflessness could exist, in advanced humans, in the form of complete selfishness. It is a concept which he explored in three successive plays—with Dick Dudgeon in *The Devil's Disciple*, Caesar in *Caesar and Cleopatra*, and Lady Cicely in *Brassbound*: his *Three Plays for Puritans*. Shaw described the quality as "originality" in his notes to *Caesar*:

> Originality gives a man an air of frankness, generosity and magnanimity by enabling him to estimate the value of truth, money, or success in any particular instance quite independently of convention and moral generalization. . . . Hence, in order to produce an impression of complete disinterestedness and magnanimity, he has only to act with entire selfishness. . . . Having virtue, he has no need of goodness. . . . The really interesting question is whether I am right in assuming that the way to produce an impression of greatness is by exhibiting a man, not as mortifying his nature by doing his duty . . . but as simply doing what he naturally wants to do.

Mary Kingsley has such "originality," which Shaw, it seems clear from a reading of *Travels in West Africa*, admired more than Miss Kingsley's "commonsense and good will." The very first sentence of her book even quotes his favorite author: "It was in 1893 that, for the first time in my life, I found myself in possession of five or six months which were not heavily forestalled, and feeling like a boy with a new half-crown, I lay about in my mind, as Mr. Bunyan would say, as to what to do with them." Thereafter her wit never falters. She reads a French book of phrases in common use in Dahomey which begins with "Help, I am drowning," and includes—exemplifying the white man's attitude toward the African—"Get up, you lazy scamps!" She "fully expected to be killed by the local nobility and gentry; they thought I was connected with the World's Women's Temperance Association, and collecting shocking details for subsequent magic-lantern lectures on the liquor traffic." And as a collector of "beetles and fetishes" she blithely brought into the houses of horrified settlers "abominations full of ants . . . or things emitting at unexpectedly short notice vivid and awful stenches." Lady Cicely, according to her brother-in-law, "from travelling in Africa, has acquired a habit of walking into other people's houses and behaving as if she were in her own." As she explains, "I always go everywhere. I know the people here wont touch me. They have such nice faces and such pretty scenery." But the seeming naivete masks a modern and methodical mind. Like Mary Kingsley, who was befriended by old chiefs and young cannibals alike, because she was uninhibitedly tolerant of their behavior among themselves, whether it be eating, marrying or praying, Lady Cicely claims to be "only talking commonsense" when suggesting that customs are relative and that respect works better than a revolver. "Why do people get killed by savages? Because instead of being polite to them, and saying How dye do? like me, people aim pistols at them. Ive been among savages—cannibals and all sorts. Everybody said theyd kill me. But when I met them I said Howdyedo? and they were quite nice. The kings always wanted to marry me." Later, when Brassbound warns her about a particularly dangerous trip into the interior, "You dont know what youre doing," she answers with confidence. "Oh, dont I? Ive not crossed Africa and stayed with six cannibal tribes for nothing. . . . Ive heard all that before about the blacks; and I found them very nice people when they were properly treated."

Lady Cicely's breezy indifference to Western shibboleths in Africa could be taken as having only coincidental resemblance to Mary Kingsley's memoir if we did not know that Shaw not only read it and admired it and even offered her as exemplar to the prospective stage Lady Cicely, but also that Miss Kingsley's prose reads as if she were a lady G.B.S. In places she sounds as if she had read Shaw's *The Quintessence of Ibsenism* (1891) in the years just before she had escaped her domestic cage. "One by one," she writes, summing up the lessons of her African experience, "I took my old ideas derived from books and thoughts based on imperfect knowledge and weighed them against the real life around me, and found them either worthless or wanting." Supporting her point by an anecdote, she told a story which would have been appropriate for the *Quintessence:*

> The difficulty of the [primitive] language is . . . far less than the whole set of difficulties with your own mind. Unless you can make it pliant enough to follow the African idea . . . , you will not bag your game. I heard an account the other day—I have forgotten where—of a representative of her Majesty in Africa who went out for a day's antelope shooting. There were plenty of antelope about, and he stalked them with great care; but always, just before he got within shot of the game, they saw something and bolted. Knowing he and the boy behind him had been making no sound and could not have been seen, he stalked on, but always with the same result; until happening to look round, he saw the boy behind him was supporting the dignity of the Empire at large, and this representative of it in particular, by steadfastly holding aloft the consular flag. Well, if

you go hunting the African idea with the flag of your own religion or opinions floating ostentatiously over you, you will similarly get a very poor bag.

Shaw's Lady Cicely, a compulsive nurse, gets her way in the play in part by managing to use her healing resources in pursuit of her larger goals. She emerges as unscathed as she does unmarried. Miss Kingsley in Africa protects herself as well as bargains to get her way by poulticing ulcers and disinfecting wounds; but after Shaw had written his play Miss Kingsley's nursing propensities were called upon in the Boer War. Although she sympathized with the plight of the Boers, her work was with her own people in a hospital in South Africa. Even there she was moved by the suffering of the enemy wounded as they paid the price for defending their land. "They want their own country, their very own," she wrote a friend in May 1900. "It works out in all their delirium—'ons Land, ons Land!' One of them held forth to me today, a sane one, how he knew every hill's name, every bend of the river's name, every twist in the road—his hills, roads, rivers, not England's, or Germany's, but 'ons Land.' It is a rocky problem for the future."[7]

A few weeks later she was sick herself—with enteric fever. Soon she realized that she was dying, and asked the other nurses to leave her alone, explaining that she wanted no one to see her in her weakness. Animals, she said, went away to die alone, and she felt like them. "It was hard for us to do this," a colleague recalled, "but we left the door ajar, and when we saw she was beyond knowledge [we] went to her."[8] On 6 June 1900 she died, and at her own request was buried at sea. Six years later, when a too-elderly Ellen Terry, at the Royal Court Theatre, finally played the role written for her, she could not remember her lines and worked instead at being charming. No one by then remembered Mary Kingsley well enough to connect anything in Miss Terry's mangled Lady Cicely with the indomitable authoress of *Travels in West Africa*. Yet Lady Cicely may be her monument.

Notes

1. Hesketh Pearson, *Bernard Shaw* (1963), p. 211.

2. Roland Duerksen, "Shelleyan Witchcraft: The Unbinding of Brassbound," *Shaw Review* 15 (1972), 21-25.

3. Mary Kingsley, *Travels in West Africa* (1897); all quotations from Miss Kingsley are from this edition.

4. Christopher St. John, ed., *Ellen Terry and Bernard Shaw: A Corre-*

spondence (1932), pp. 245 (3 August 1899), 241 (12 July 1899).

  5. *Collected Letters, 1898-1910,* pp. 98-99.

  6. Olwen Campbell, *Mary Kingsley* (1957), p. 15.

  7. Campbell, p. 179.

  8. Campbell, pp. 179-80.

V

INFLUENCE OF SHAW'S FEMINISM: THREE GENERATIONS

THE MAKING OF A FEMINIST: SHAW AND FLORENCE FARR

Josephine Johnson

One of the most important females in Bernard Shaw's life in 1889 was a quasi-professional actress, Florence Farr Emery. Shaw had become acquainted with her at a time when she was emerging from an unsuccessful marriage and attempting to bolster her ego by strongly identifying herself with the "new woman." G.B.S. was titillated by her forthright attitudes, especially her opinion that sex was merely a hygienic gymnastic, and that she personally preferred frank, intellectual companionship with men.

Shaw had already adopted the posture that women could not afford to become emotionally, sexually or intellectually free until society provided them with an opportunity for economic independence. But since Florence Farr was able to enjoy a minimal economic security, she was ready to discover other freedoms, notably, vigorous liaisons with men without the stifling bonds of matrimony.

Having relieved Shaw of the onus to court her in the established Victorian custom, Florence shortly embarked upon a steady companionship with G.B.S. They enjoyed evenings together at her rooms, teas at the A.B.C. shops, concerts, and "intimate" conversations. During the first year of their acquaintance, Shaw attended Florence's performances in the poetic plays of the Irish physician John Todhunter, and in spite of her weak performances, he concluded that Ibsen's *Rosmersholm* would be the perfect vehicle to expose her ideas of the "new woman" for public exhibition on the London stage. Actively coaching her for the role of Rebecca, he managed to influence her interpretation by his own vision of the quintessence of womanhood. Their collaboration brought forth a wife-destroying anti-heroine whose intellectual strength clearly mastered physical or emotional ardor. Moreover, Florence's portrayal made it clear that Rebecca had a perfect right to get rid of the "unwomanly" Mrs. Rosmer who was a "drag, a responsibility, a reproach, an everlasting and unnatural trouble with whom no really strong soul can live."[1] Shaw's description was a close approximation to Jenny Patterson, Shaw's first mistress, who was concurrently sharing him with Florence Emery.

The production of Ibsen's play at the Vaudeville proved a reasonable enough acting *coup* for Florence, but Shaw's carefully chiseled interpretation of a "womanly" woman required an explanation for the critics. Unable to say more than that Rebecca was attractive because she was so thoroughly "womanly," Florence decided to disclaim her own womanhood if there were further challenge to her role, and to declare herself "an abnormal development at the end of the century."[2] It was a position urged on her by Shaw, one which she was unable to undo for many years.

The work on *Rosmersholm* filled Shaw with an itch to create his own Ibsenish heroine for Florence to perform, one which in 1892 he thrust to the public "naked and shivering, for—inspection." Blanche Sartorius—played by Florence—appeared in his first play, *Widowers' Houses*, produced by J.T. Grein. Unhappy with Shaw's apparent lack of humaneness, William Archer questioned Shaw's feminist approach, wondering what evidence G.B.S. could manufacture to support the implication that passionate illusion was unknown in love, and that young men and women preferred "snapping each other's heads off instead of idealising each other." As for Florence's Blanche, in spite of her exotic costumes, there wasn't a remotest *"odor di femmina"* escaping over the footlights.[3]

Socialists, male and female, were often described as sexless by Victorian critics, and Florence Farr and Bernard Shaw did not escape this derision. Shaw saw it as only a seeming lack of passion while Florence blamed her distrust and ennui on the average, uxorious male. Yet how else could she hold Shaw's interest than to fulfill his quixotic fantasies of the behavior of a "womanly" woman on and off the stage? So with Blanche Sartorius barely forgotten by the press, Florence, without Shaw's coaching, decided to offer a treacherously "womanly" performance of John Todhunter's Lady Brandon in her own production of his *Comedy of Sighs*.

G.B.S. was horrified to see his pupil appear as "cold, loathly, terrifying, callous," and as "sexless" a devil as he had ever seen upon the London stage; her own "damns and devils" sounded to him like the "blasphemes of a fiend."[4] Undermining his estimation of her, Florence had clearly overreacted to G.B.S.'s womanly woman concepts, a failure which the taskmaster's vanity could not endure. Al-

though Shaw then wrote *Arms and the Man,* his first commercial success, to bail her out of her disastrous Avenue Theatre season, of
which Todhunter's play had been part, he began to question his
indulgent interest in one who did not seem to have the necessary
discipline to mold herself to his desire for her to become "powerfully beautiful." After all, he had committed himself to the statement that he could not "face the Judgment bar" at the end of his life
with her if he were unable to meet the question, "Why did you
suffer her to do her work badly?"

Shaw's words describe the inertia in the eventual dissolution of
their intimate relationship, which she compensated for with other
men, but Florence was wounded by the termination of the affair. An
opportunity to defend injured femininity occurred when she returned from a Yeats-inspired verse-speaking tour of the United
States over a decade later. In an article that she wrote for the *New
Age* in 1907, a Socialist journal largely financed by Shaw, Florence
experienced the joyous relief of publicly exorcising her resentment at
the private and not so proprietary rebukes she had long suffered
under G.B.S.'s tenure. Bursting out of what was left of the chrysalis
that Shaw had helped create for her, she lambasted the man and the
playwright. For nearly twenty years she had been unable to unravel
his secret hold on herself and the public. Now, after her visit to
Manhattan, she finally understood. G.B.S., surprisingly, was "New
York incarnate."

> Both of them ask questions, but will not listen to the answer.
> Both of them have the slightly metallic suggestion of a note of
> interrogation. Both of them have been brought up out of reach
> of the influence of a really venerable tradition. They have
> picked up such fragments as they could and turned them to
> strange uses. Both of them are feverish devotees at the altar of
> work. And even Mr. Shaw's religion scrapes the sky.
>
> To Mr. Shaw, as to New York, "doing nothing" is hell
> and damnation. This means that both the person and the place
> feel that they have not yet found their best expression. Play
> after play, preface after preface, pours from Mr. Shaw. He has
> been explaining himself for twenty years, but nobody under-
> stands. . . .
>
> Empty Mr. Shaw and New York of work and hurry, the man
> has a headache and closes his eyes in pain, he feels no reason
> for existence; and the city is a desolation.

As for his understanding of women:

He does not make hearts glow and expand before he analyses them. Cellini did not fix his model in a chair and copy her form. He chased her round the room giving her a severe drubbing, and no doubt his art got its quality from such behaviour. Mr. Shaw does not pose his model in the ordinary way either, but he seats her in a dentist's chair, puts a gag into her mouth, isolates a tooth as ruthlessly as any dentist and then takes her photograph. Therefore New York and Mr. Shaw in certain regions give us the impression of London backyards seen from the District Railway. They have as little pretension to anything but a stern recognition of the needs of life.[5]

Florence was well aware that in *The Doctor's Dilemma,* then Shaw's newest play, he had said that he believed in Michelangelo and Velasquez, but he could not have also mentioned Leonardo da Vinci. Shaw's dreams, to Florence, were not those of a "climber of the air, a dreamer whose dreams come true, a man who incarnates an ageless spirit that will haunt us and inspire us as long as we look into Mona Lisa's eyes." Shaw did not believe in the Mona Lisa; he was unable to "sacrifice to the Artemis who brings such spirits into being, whatever he may think he does." And there was definitely a "delicate brutality" that he shared with New York. When he wrote *Man and Superman,* Florence continued, he was obviously in the same humor as the New York youngster who, "after watching the habits of domestic fowls . . . said gloomily: 'If my wife lays an egg, I'll smash it.' " Shaw took the forces of nature and used them for his own amusement.

Impishly passing offprints of Florence's article to his friends, Shaw had to admit that her American tour had done her a "lot of good" and had added to her sense of female independence. He was even prepared to defend her attack on his work ethic. He could admit that he was "miserably" unhappy if his work were cut off, yet his "hideous" headaches were the result of work. He had made countless resolutions never to write after lunch, or only for two hours a day, but every day his craving again took possession of him. His passion for work forced him to dread holidays as he dreaded "nothing else on earth." Overworked and wasted by excess, how could the world know of his temptations, his backslidings, his orgies. How could it, "timidly munching beefsteaks and apple tart, conceive the spirit struggles of a young man who knew that Bach is good for the soul, and yet turned to Beethoven, and from him fell to Berlioz and Liszt for mere excitement, luxury, savagery, and drunkenness?" To be diabolically possessed with the finale of the Seventh

Symphony or the *Walkurenritt* was a worse fate than the life of a drunkard. Yet, "far from being an abstinent man," he was "the worst drunkard of a rather exceptionally drunken family," a "pitiable" example of one who craved something far stronger than alcohol: work.[6] (Another writer in the *New Age* chose to describe Shaw's lust otherwise. G.B.S.'s character, he wrote, was the result of self-intoxication with his own gastric juices which, "denied their proper sphere of action, have risen to his head in a deadly ferment.")[7]

Florence's attack on his seeming lack of humaneness, according to Shaw, was a misunderstanding. What he pretended to represent in his plays was about as real as a "pantomime-ostrich." Had he not taken himself to pieces for an audience "to shew the trick of him"? His whole point was that he was "unique, fantastic, unrepresentative, inimitable, impossible, undesirable on any large scale, utterly unlike anybody that ever existed before, hopelessly unnatural," and "void of real passion."[8]

With "G.B.S. and New York" accepted by the *New Age*'s editor as a "good tempered and truthful joke," Florence found herself to be a celebrated—and as a female, rare—member of an unpaid coterie of writers for Orage's paper, including Shaw himself. She therefore fulfilled a longstanding ambition to speak out on the intelligent woman's position—how and where she belonged in contemporary society. Articles on marriages of convenience, breeding and prostitution were not uncommon phenomena in the Edwardian press, but Florence managed to distinguish herself from other female writers after some shrewd guidance from Shaw, and by rephrasing relatively current ideas on feminism with her own special élan. Those who remembered her startling conversations when she first knew G.B.S. would have noticed that the passing years had honed a sharper edge to her opinions, and that middle age permitted her to speak as if slightly bitten by the "mad dog of modernity."[9]

Shaw had never trained Florence to be overly kind in her regard for women as a species, except for her concern about their economic independence. Her remark that New York women would rather scrub their own floors than vote did not suggest to her that she could stimulate an interest in the suffragism in her own country. The subject of "Man" was far more embracing, especially when she could insidiously direct the topic at G.B.S. After all, what was he but a cunning fox who had nearly outwitted nature and, by the pure art of deception, stolen the power of the serpent and the lion, causing his inferiors to serve him "by the magic of the eye and the roar of his voice"? He had composed moral codes for his own advantage and pretended they were the commands of a divine being, and civilization was little more than the result of this shrewd creature convincing his third cousins to become his servants. By day, she alleged, he wore a mask to hide from the world his dreary indecency, his wearisome stale jokes, his weaknesses, his inconsistencies, his humbug. And at night he ignored the use of passion as a purifying agent, fearful that its brief ecstasies would result in the inevitable periods of emptiness and depression. G.B.S. is surely the model for Florence's description of the three pitiful stages of man's growth. Whereas the three he had outlined for her were the "Idiotically Beautiful . . . the Intelligently Beautiful . . . the Powerfully Beautiful," the plateaus for man (G.B.S.) were the ardent boy attempting to put the world to right in a few weeks, followed by the profound conservative, and last the attempt to strangle the "old Adam that has thickened his blood and made it run bitter in his veins." What, she asked, is this "quintessence of dust"?[10]

It is probably unjust to Shaw to bear him in mind every time Florence denigrates man, but judging from material that she published elsewhere[11] it is certainly Shaw whom she blames for setting before her unreachable ambitions in order to achieve his own ends. Then, in her words, like other, younger enchanted females, confused by life's true values (the spiritual), she had been "cast on the side, worn out and used up." Shaw, in the end, had sympathized with her no more than "a stud groom sympathises with a horse." Speaking then of man as an "Olympian Superman," he "cares for us while we serve his ends, then lets us destroy ourselves or lie as mud in the street."[12] As for the Shavian concept of Superman and what she considered his encouragement of official breeding, she could agree with another *New Age* reader who thought that Shaw spoke like a "dodderer" on the subject. G.B.S.'s antipathy to vivisection, Florence said, compelled him to be a poor representative in any discussion that concerned propagation and the perpetuation of life. What is more, G.B.S. had certainly missed the point that Superman was really Superwoman, and a state of consciousness at that, since it was the female in Eastern and Western religion who had brought forth a savior.[13] Since Florence and Shaw were exempt from the trials of parenthood, one may wonder what regrets they both shared in their barrenness. Perhaps Florence's thoughts on the issue are influenced by Shaw:

> Great spiritual and mental forces are not necessarily accompanied by physical fecundity; then the purpose of each generation has an end of its own, an end which manifests in mental and spiritual energies having a lineage independent of the mortal bodies of mankind. Those atmospheres, which create strange

moods, those enthusiasms which seize whole populations, may
be the force of some barren body concentrated on the tremendous progeny of a mind whose influence will be felt generation
after generation. Some of our greatest men and women have
been childless. They have been the climax of their family, not
the foundation of it.[14]

Had Florence not been childless, however, her feminism would no
doubt have encouraged her to give a female offspring the advice she
offered to other young women. Chastity, for example, could hardly
be called a virtue when temptation could not be measured, and gentle reserve was as useless a characteristic if some women were careless in what they said, but most cautious in their actions. Conversely, many were enormously free in what they did and were
penurious in what they yielded to in conversation. Florence had
heard that some well-brought-up young ladies were practicing free
love, and she hoped that they were aware of the extraordinary differences between the affections of the sexes. The arousal of a man's
passions brought forth little gratification compared to the more
noble alternative of winning his confidence.

> The fact is [that] women can be friends with many men and
> love very few; men can love many women and be friends with
> very few. Until this fact is clearly acknowledged the sexes will
> continue their mutual deception. Women will lament because
> they cannot convince men their love is a great gift, and men will
> regret that women cannot learn that love is a burning torch to
> be put out as quickly as possible, in order that they may set
> about the real work of life.[15]

Florence's most infamous reputation as a feminist occurred as the
result of an article, "The Rites of Astaroth," in which she turned to a
favorite subject, shared with Shaw, that of prostitution. Immensely
sophisticated in her knowledge of Eastern myth and culture, Florence had composed a potpourri of West End whoredom and trained
dancers in the temples of India. What she hoped to accomplish in
her usual confusion of where socialism left off and her "phrase and
a shilling's worth of exoteric Egyptology" began, as Shaw alluded to
her muddling of issues, was the legitimization of prostitution. She
called for the government to substitute trained "dancers" for the
denizens of the gutters of Piccadilly Circus, disease-carrying women
of deservedly ill-repute. Her message was clear: train public opinion
that sexuality is a necessity, that certain men cannot live without it,
that certain women use it for propagation purposes only, that few

women enjoy sexual relations when economic conditions deprive them of marriages of choice, and that the vagaries of nature would best be served in England by comparable British Temples of Joy. Surely this was a better solution than the cold, well-regulated houses of Shaw's Mrs. Warren.[16]

When Florence was assailed for offering a progressive British society two evils from which to choose, she reminded her adversary that his prejudice for the East was an "ignorance of static power that makes us seem like restless children in comparison with the calm sages born of the races we dare to despise. Were not Gautama Buddha, Lao-Tzu, and Confucius nearer to the ideal than Cecil Rhodes and President [Theodore] Roosevelt?"[17]

Another reader in the *New Age* was differently appalled. Surely no decent English woman would agree with Florence to resolve the problem of prostitution by the degradation of any other woman? For her part, the reader agreed with Schopenhauer's advocacy of polygamy. "Better a woman be faithful to the fragment of a man which inexorable Nature doles out as her share than make slaves of some that others may be chaste."[18]

A volley of correspondence concerning "The Rites of Astaroth" continued for some time, with the former assailant persisting that there were only two responsible solutions for prostitution. Socialism, he said, was the panacea for poverty, and compulsory notification against the contaminator, with subsequent criminal proceedings, the sole cure for syphilis. As for Florence's lame excuse that throughout her articles she was addressing herself to those without the Socialist fold, he advised her to turn her two remedies into poetry and to recite them to those without. "The fold and the battle will be half over."

The issue was not lightly dismissed, and a month later a Mr. Alfred W. Southey of 16 Elm Street, Gray's Inn Road, came up with a practical solution, he thought, for a trade union for prostitutes. Moreover, he intended to implement his suggestions by becoming its secretary. Obviously unable to agree, yet not prepared to withdraw from the discussion, Florence sought some advice from Shaw. By this time G.B.S. thought that Florence had probably gone too far and cautiously composed a letter which he believed would "settle" Mr. Southey. Florence would then rephrase his ideas and apply her own signature:

> Dear Sir,
>
> There is no doubt that a union among women would be a great advantage to them and to Society, and that it would be the first step towards rescuing them from the state of outlawry

which makes their condition at present so desperate.

But you must allow me to say that the very condition of such an organization must be that it shall be entirely in the hands of women. If you can induce one of the "clever brainy women" of whom you write to undertake the work, and if you are sufficiently skilled in the history and practice of Trade Unionism, and a sufficiently sensible man to be able to help her with your advice and guidance, then no doubt you can be of service in the matter; but in my opinion you cannot take any more direct part in it. A male secretary would be an improper position at the end. When you consider that the mere existence of a Union would be regarded at first a scandal, you will see how undesirable it would be to make the scandal worse by a feature to which even sympathisers might *justly* take wrong exception.

Shaw also emphasized to Florence that she could not use enough Fabian caution when dealing with "male champions" of the feminist cause. From his own point of view, he questioned the feasibility of putting women into a trade union at all, especially prostitutes who seldom recognized the permanence of their occupation. "They all intend to stop it and get married the next month at the latest." Such a movement anyway, he added, could only be implemented by a "very energetic, muscular, violent woman, with the devotion of a Saint, and the arbitrariness and executive power of a prize-fighter; but such women do not grow on bushes."[19]

Perhaps the most honest response to what was becoming Florence's *bête noire* was from an actual "outcast," a semiliterate ex-servant who had preferred to sell herself "outright" to a man than piecemeal to a woman like Florence Farr who was so busy telling the world what to do that she had little time to observe whether her own maid's life was better than a black beetle incarcerated in a dull, flat kitchen. The harsh regimen instituted by this particular outcast's employer had driven her to prostitution, and now she frankly preferred to be kept by a man in a comfortable house with time to read, to think, to wear what she pleased, and go where she chose. The fact that she despised the man with whom she lived, although she had taught him to "master" his body, didn't take away from the "precious good care" she would exercise to see that no other woman shared him. And that, she said, was a lot more to say for her character than for Florence's society lady who "generally likes some other woman's husband or son because she knows it will annoy some other woman." Then she reminded Florence that if women were as kind to other women as they were to men, the supply of outcasts would not be so great. As for those "Temples of Joy," they were

"Temples of Weakness and Flattery." But what could Florence possibly know about the "burden of bought kisses; there is precious
little joy in them." Really, she added, it was too bad that Florence
Farr enjoyed writing endless articles for useless papers instead of
looking after her own responsibilities. The latter might have been
the making of some man, but the former probably admitted her to
the tables of the great and helped her up the rungs of the ladder of
ambition that she said she despised in others. And to top that, "All
the world knows you and you are well to the front. . . . But really
your lady's time is much too precious to be wasted on anything that
doesn't have bands and banners, speeches and dinners. Besides, all
the self-advertisement and the flattery of the multitude is better than
the making of a man."[20]

Without any doubt, Shaw persuaded Florence to bury this particular document. For an "outcast," it was far too articulate and perhaps
a little too close to the truth for comfort. Shaw thought that the
whole "Rites of Astaroth" controversy had disappeared when a new
affront to Florence's position was questioned by frightened Socialists
in the *Spectator*. Uneasy about sharing her platform, they were obviously unsure whether Shaw was the monster lurking behind her
bad judgment. G.B.S.'s advice was again probably solicited before
she answered that she was her own "mouthpiece"; her articles were
always signed and she had certainly not intended "to express the
policy of any association of people," to wit, Socialists. Since prostitutes were unable to defend themselves, and since it was "insidi-
ous" for men to do so, she believed it necessary for other women to
inform the public of "one of the most important dangers to the
race," and "that," she concluded, "is all."[21] Shaw was undeniably
relieved, especially since he was under attack himself in the *New Age*
for being out of touch with the "present living Socialist movement."

Whereas Shaw had always found it necessary to whip the
younger Florence into being thorough, Florence then considered
G.B.S. to be lacking in thoroughness as a philosopher and "half-
baked" at that. Refusing his advice to withdraw completely from the
subject of prostitution, she hammered away at a last postscript. It
would benefit England, she decided, to create a new race of Amazons who instead of living to spread disease could die in the service
of their country. With utter disregard for the "new women" who
were becoming devotees of ladies' hockey clubs, gymnasiums, danc-
ing schools, archery societies, girl guides, and such, she predicted a
sex war if women's surplus energy could not be harnessed. "The
superiority of the rising generation of women in the matter of size
and stamina points directly to the obvious duty of the War Office.

. . . There seems every reason why this proposal for raising Amazonian forces should be taken seriously. It might bring the necessity home to us if Mr. George Edwardes ordered an opera on the subject, and produced it during the coming season."[22]

When Florence had outlived her usefulness as a journalist for the *New Age,* or to put it another way, when Shaw decided not to prevail upon Orage to keep her feminist tracts on the boards lest they interfere with more important Socialist plans, Florence set about completing her long-gestated book, *Modern Woman: Her Intentions.* Shaw may have persuaded G.K. Chesterton to review it; the most polite comment he could muster, however, was that Florence was in "the habit of dwelling disproportionately on the abnormal and diseased." Still, he considered her a fair philosopher, generally presenting both sides to the point of admitting that the new psychology which she had attempted to defend might turn up after all on the side of the old womanhood.[23]

In unmitigated frustration that she was having such a difficult time in leaving her mark as a feminist, she announced in a letter to the *New Age* that she had joined the Eugenic Education Society and that the committee had given her, with other sympathizers, permission to form a semi-independent committee to forward the movement of the "Economic Independence of Women." But she was still wondering whether she had not really had yet another failure in playing a Shavian role. I have often wondered if some anonymous lines in *The Mint* were not directed at her.

> Strive no more ladies, strive no more
> To prove you're wondrous clever;
> Remember we have Bernard Shaw—
> Sure, that's enough for ever!
> Then sigh not so, but let votes go
> (To us they're not all honey);
> We want you as your own dear selves,
> And like you always sunny.[24]

For Florence Emery, "feminism" became a life-style after Shaw had encouraged her lofty ambitions to become a new, independent woman. And, as the "outcast" so aptly put it, her outspokenness permitted her to enter the sacred intellectual coteries of man that might otherwise have been barred. Once there, however, the restraint she imposed on herself in her relationships so as not to become lost in the old womanhood prevented her from consummating an entirely satisfying life. Whether directed by Shaw or by herself, she showed "restraint from passions as of furnace fires banked under."[25]

Before she died in Ceylon in 1916 still experimenting with female independence among the Tamils, she confessed to being momentarily disenchanted with Shaw for succumbing to Mrs. Pat Campbell's "unwomanly" charms. The renewal of his philandering confirmed her position that laughing at men would be easier than loving them and that, when given the opportunity, women would not have the spunk to secede from the protection of the male.

If her feminism can be encapsulated, one might conclude that her messianism was not so much to improve women's lot as to alter the composition of man. Her wish to refashion man made her more of a Shavian female revolutionary than G.B.S. ever publicly acknowledged.

Notes

1. *The Quintessence of Ibsenism*, p. 32.
2. "The Playhouses," *Illustrated London News* (London, 28 February 1891).
3. *World* (London, 14 December 1892), p. 15.
4. Letter in the Burgunder Collection, Cornell University Library.
5. "G.B.S. and New York," *New Age* (henceforth cited as *NA*) (London, 23 May 1907), p. 57.
6. "Belloc and Chesterton," *NA* (15 February 1908), p. 311.
7. "On Shaw, Wells, Chesterton, and Belloc," *NA* (7 March 1908), p. 370.
8. "Belloc and Chesterton," p. 309.
9. "Our Note Book," *Illustrated London News* (London, 11 June 1910), p. 900.
10. "Man," *NA* (19 September 1907), p. 326.
11. See Johnson, *Florence Farr: Bernard Shaw's New Woman*.
12. "Innocent Enchantress" *NA* (20 June 1907), p. 119.
13. "Superman Consciousness," *NA* (6 June 1907), p. 92.
14. "The Rites of Astaroth," *NA* (5 September 1907), p. 214.
15. "Marie Corelli and the Modern Girl," *NA* (1 August 1907), p. 214.
16. "The Rites of Astaroth."
17. *NA* (19 September 1907), p. 334.
18. Ibid.
19. Letter to Florence Farr, 12 October 1907, in *Collected Letters, 1898-1910* pp. 715-16.
20. G.W. Paget Collection.
21. *The Spectator* (London, 9 November 1907), p. 706.
22. "The Proposed Regiment of Amazons," *NA* (4 March 1909), p. 308.
23. "Our Note Book."
24. *The Mint* (London, 15 August 1908), p. 643.
25. " 'Deirdre' and 'Electra' at the New Theatre," *NA* (10 December 1908), p. 142.

THE GIFT OF IMAGINATION:
AN INTERVIEW WITH
CLARE BOOTHE LUCE

Rodelle Weintraub

Clare Boothe Luce—author, Congresswoman, ambassador, feminist—is best known as playwright of *The Women*. On 19 July 1973 she graciously chatted with me for several hours in her home in Honolulu, discussing Shaw.

I do not remember when I first had the desire to be a writer. I seem to have been born with it. I remember—I was working with other children for the benefit of the Greenwich wartime Red Cross, doing various things, when I got the idea of raising some money by writing and producing a children's play. So I rewrote a fairy story, rounded up some neighborhood children to act in it, designed and made some costumes with them, directed the play, and sold the tickets at the door for the one and only performance. This was in the Old Greenwich School House. According to the press clipping in my scrapbook—my very first press clipping—it made $14.90—the sweetest money I have ever earned.

My young friends and I seemed to read much more than young people do now. We talked about the characters in Dumas and Dickens and Mark Twain the way children today talk about their favorite TV programs. We always went around—at least I always went around—with a book in my pocket. I still have, somewhere, a shelf of those little leather-bound, gold-stamped Everyman volumes of the classics, dog-eared and limp with reading. I had read them all by the time I was sixteen. I remember I used to make notes in the margins—profound remarks, like How true! or How absurd! My first feelings of feminist outrage were aroused by Nietszche's advice to man in "Thus Spake Zarathustra," "to take a whip when thou goest to women."

I began to read Shaw when I was about fourteen—no doubt as a result of my heady success at the School House. In those days most young girls had pictures of their favorite movie heroes in their bedrooms. I had a picture of Shaw on my dresser. I also had one of John Drinkwater, who was very popular in America at that time. Whatever became of Drinkwater?[1] By the time I was seventeen, I had read all of Shaw's plays, and there's no doubt that Shaw fixed in my mind the idea that I wanted to be a playwright. *St. Joan* was my favorite. I think it is Shaw's greatest play. When I became a Catholic, in my forties, I took Joan for my baptismal name.

The Intelligent Woman's Guide to Socialism also had its effect on me. It was, I suppose, my introduction to contemporary thought on political systems. I even thought of myself as a Fabian.

In 1923 I married a New York socialite—George Brokaw. When my first marriage ended in divorce in 1931, I went to work as an associate editor for *Vanity Fair*, and I finally became its managing editor. *Vanity Fair* was edited by Frank Crowninshield and was America's best-known literary and artistic journal. It folded, in 1935, because of the Great Depression. Almost every writer of importance in America and England contributed to *Vanity Fair*. Except G.B.S. Crowninshield was never able to get an article from him. Nor was Edward Steichen ever able to get him to pose for a photograph. But we published many caricatures of him, as I remember.

Most of the plays I have written, seven of which were produced, are satirical comedies. I wrote two during the last days of *Vanity Fair*. The first, called *O Pyramids!*, was about the conflict between an automobile manufacturer and his son, who had become a labor union organizer and was leading a strike against his father's plant. I suppose I fancied that as a Shavian situation—in American terms. The son was the hero, of course. I was all for F.D.R. in the early New Deal days, and New Dealism was certainly the American version of Fabianism.

My first play that made Broadway was *Abide With Me*—which abode with no one. A melodrama without a trace of humor, it was a flop. The reviews would have discouraged anyone less stubborn than I to abandon playwriting forever. My admiration for Shaw increased. The next year, the year I married Harry Luce, I wrote *The Women*. Its success was solid enough to carry it across the ocean. It was produced in London in 1937 or '38. My husband and I went to London to see the production. Rather, I went to see *The Women*, which was produced under my maiden name, Clare Boothe. He, the editor of *TIME, LIFE*, and *FOR-TUNE*, went to see about the offices Time, Inc. was opening in London.

During that London visit, the dream I had had ever since I was fourteen came true: I met Bernard Shaw. I had seen him once when he gave an address at the Metropolitan Opera House in New York. I remember he hadn't wanted to give it and tried to get out of it but couldn't. Everyone was dressed—white tie. Everyone, that is, but Shaw. The talk was a disaster: it had none of the wit of the dialogue of the plays and it insulted the audience. I was terribly disappointed.

Lady Nancy Astor, a long-time American friend of mine, and of Shaw's, arranged for me to call on him. I left Claridge's in a taxi, and all the way to his apartment, on the Thames, I rehearsed the little speech I was going to make to him. The Italians have a word for the kind of speech it was going to be—a *ferverino*. I was going to tell him how much I admired, yea, loved him, and that if I had *not* read and studied his plays, I would not be in London today, with a successful play on the boards, and that I had had the courage to ask to meet him only because I felt I had, perhaps, earned the right to do so, etcetera, etcetera, etcetera.

When I arrived, I was met at the door by his secretary. She could have been the model for Miss Prossy in *Candida*. Black dress, tight lips, hair pulled back in a bun. All efficiency, she led me silently down what seemed an interminable corridor, threw open the door to Shaw's study, said "Miss Boothe," left me standing there and went away. Shaw was sitting at his desk in a swivel chair, his back to me. He didn't move. Had he heard the opening of the door? I stood there, frozen and tongue-tied. I cleared my throat several times. I could get no other sound out. Suddenly he whirled around in his chair, stared at me from under bristling pinkish-white brows for a second, then said, brusquely cheerful, "Well, well, don't stand there. Come here and sit *down*." Still speechless in The Presence, I went and sank in the chair beside his desk. Then he said, "And now, my dear child, tell me, what brings you here?" Not a word of my little *ferverino* did I remember. I just blurted out, "I came because, well, er—ah—if it were not for *you*, Mr. Shaw, I would not be here at all!" He leaned back in his chair, smiling, and said," "Umm . . . Now you must tell me . . . what *was* your dear mother's name?" Then we both laughed. And in no time we began to chat quite amiably. He asked the name of my play and how it was doing. I'm sure he knew, because *The Women* had had a great deal of publicity in the London papers. I explained that if it had not been a success, I would not have had the courage to visit him. When I said my plays had had good reviews, he said, "How I envy you! I have never had good success in the theatre." "What?" I said. "Never," he replied. "It was always the *last* play I wrote that opening night critics admired."

When I told him I had written several screen scripts in Hollywood, he asked me a number of questions about how Hollywood translated plays into movies. He seemed dubious about how well his own plays would screen. He said he had given all the screen rights to some man whose name began with a *P*— yes, Pascal. I said that how faithfully his plays would be presented on the screen would depend on the producers. It was the Zukors, Warners, L.B. Mayers—not the writers—who made the final decisions on the treatment of films. In Hollywood the original author had very little control of the screen script.

In the course of our conversation, I told him that I had read the *Woman's Guide*. We then got into a lively discussion about Socialism. I had gone through my socialist stage that all young people go through, but by that time the rise of Hitler had greatly dampened my enthusiasm for European Socialism. I was a little unhappy that Mr. Shaw did not seem as worried about Hitler as I was.

In the middle of our argument, in walked Mrs. Shaw. She was dowdy and rather domineering, in a very pleasant sort of way. After introductions she asked, "Are we three for luncheon?" Shaw said, "I hope so." I stayed. Every once in a while, during luncheon, Mrs. Shaw would say, "Now you've asked Miss Boothe a question. Do let her answer it."

The next day at Claridge's, I received a postal card from Shaw, written by his very own hand. I read it and propped it up in front of the clock on the mantel piece. When my husband came in, I, very proud, said, "Darling, I got a postal card—a postal card from George Bernard Shaw. Over there. Read it." Very triumphant. He read,

> My dear Clare Boothe,
> In the delirious pleasure of our visit yesterday, I quite forgot to inquire if there was anything I could do to make your stay, and Mr. Boothe's, more pleasant.
> G.B.S.

Harry's face fell. I feel sure that Shaw knew that my husband was Henry Luce. Not only was he very well known; Lady Astor must certainly have told Shaw. I think that that postal card was sheer Shavian impishness—what would be called today a "put-down" of my husband. Or, perhaps, knowing how much more important my husband was than I, he was trying to build me up. Anyway, that was the first and last time in my life I met anyone of importance who didn't know—or pretended not to know—who my husband was.

I never saw Shaw again. But I did hear from him once again. It was in the summer vacation of my second term in Congress (1945). A civic repertory theatre in my Congressional district, Stamford, Connecticut, had announced a production of *Candida* with a group of Broadway stars. About two weeks before the announced opening, the actress who was to play Candida was taken ill, and canceled. The producer and the director came to my home in Greenwich and asked me to play the part. I explained that although I had once been an understudy on Broadway for several child actresses when I was about ten years old, I had never really acted. I was a playwright, which is quite a different thing. But they insisted, and what with one thing or another, I agreed. I thought, first, it would be a lark to play in one of my favorite Shaw plays, and second, that as a professional playwright, I ought perhaps to know how it feels to be on the actor's side of the footlights. But I expect that what decided me was that *Candida* called for a woman of about my own age, and the part was dignified. I thought that my constituents surely wouldn't object to their Congresswoman playing in a Shaw play for the fun of it on her vacation. All of which I tried to make very clear to the local press. Indeed, I went to some lengths to emphasize in the interviews that they asked me for that I had so little opinion of myself as an actress that I would be more than satisfied if, on the opening night, I merely managed to remember my lines.

The play was rehearsed—on my porch—for just one week. I think we had only one on-stage rehearsal. But during that week a few things happened that were to make my first—and only—appearance as a professional actress quite a theatrical event.

Madame Chiang Kai-shek, a close friend of my husband and his sister, was visiting relatives in New York. My sister-in-law asked her to go to the opening, and she accepted. And that got in the papers. The Governor and his wife also decided they wanted to go. And that got in the papers. Pretty soon, a lot of other well-known New Yorkers and Nutmeggers also decided to go, and all that got in the papers. What I didn't know, until the opening night, was that all the New York critics had also decided to come. And then two days before the play opened, someone who asked for tickets at the box office was told, "We couldn't even get tickets for General Eisenhower!" and the rumor got going that General Eisenhower was coming to the opening. The night the play opened, the police had to cordon off the street to hold back the crowds who had come to see Eisenhower.

On the opening night, the news that all the Broadway critics were there, and of the crowds in the streets, threw me into something of a panic. But it put all the pros in the cast very much on their mettle. For one or two of the actors—especially for Marchbanks—it was the greatest audience they had ever had.

We played, of course, in nineteenth-century costumes of the period. In one scene I wore a huge feathered hat on top of a large pompadour wig. The business in this scene called for me to enter wearing the hat and a shawl, carrying a big bag and a parasol. After disposing of the bag, shawl and parasol, I was supposed to stand before a mirror, pluck out the hat pins, lay the huge feathered concoction on a table, and then sit on a sofa, where I was supposed to play a tender scene with Morell—or maybe with Marchbanks? As I went to take off the hat, the heads of the hatpins came off in my hands, and I had to play the whole act wearing that enormous hat. That wasn't all. I learned—the hard way—what professional actors can do to steal scenes from an inexperienced one. Marchbanks and Morell upstaged me from the rise of the curtain on Act I until it fell on Act III. Every scene I wound up either with my back to the audience, or standing, or rather, practically falling out of the dormer window at the back of the stage. Marchbanks was a demon. He played the big "love scene" lying on a rug in front of the fireplace, while I, Candida, sat in a big armchair beside him. Marchbanks had been using a poker as a prop to punctuate an occasional line in his own dialogue. The opening night he used it, literally, to puncture my dialogue, waving it about like a sword when I was speaking my lines. If I had been an experienced actress, I would simply have reached down and taken it away from him and waved it during his lines. But I was using every ounce of concentration I had to remember my own lines. As a matter of fact, I realized my only ambition as an actress—when the curtain fell, I had not missed a line.

The next day was a misery I have still not forgotten. The New York critics devoted as much space to my performance as though I had wanted to outdo Katherine Cornell. And they agreed to a man that I was *not* Katherine Cornell. Further, they agreed that I was not only the worst Candida they had ever seen, but possibly the worst actress. Only Wolcott Gibbs in the *New Yorker* had a kind word to say. He wrote that in view of the fact that I had made it clear I was acting simply as a lark, the treatment the press gave me was, to say the least, ungallant. Then he said that the Broadway critics might have been truthful enough to report that even though Clare Luce may have been the worst Candida ever to tread the boards, she was, nevertheless, the prettiest.

I sent all the clippings to Nancy Astor, with my comments, be-

cause I thought it might amuse her. She must have sent them to
G.B.S., for in time, I got another postal card, this one addressed to
Mrs. Luce. It said only that "the only pertinent criticism was Mr.
Gibbs'."

Some years ago I made notes for a book I never finished, because
my husband died. It was to be called "Portraits of Woman in the
American Theatre." It would have been a very dismal book. American playwrights do not like or understand women—at least not
normal women. None of them has ever managed to create a believable flesh and blood, attractive female character. They have created
stereotypes—mostly dolls, or, as they call them today, "sex
objects"—or women who are neurotics, mental or moral cripples. I
believe many real women haters created women in their plays they
couldn't find in real life. Aristophanes, Euripides, must have hated
women for they wrote magnificent women. I was reminded, while I
was doing this, of how attractive, intelligent and strong Shaw's
women are: Candida, Barbara, Joan, Eliza, and Mrs. Warren. Yes,
Mrs. Warren, not Vivie. No comparable female characters exist in
the American theatre.

I had the feeling that Shaw himself couldn't really cope with
women off-stage. Shaw the man was afraid of them off-stage, I
think, because he knew how strong women are. But because he did
know that, he drew great women characters in his plays. On-stage,
Shaw the playwright could cope with them.

Shaw, it seems to me, was weak as a *political* philosopher. But he
was a great playwright because he understood human nature and
personal conflict. Playwrights should leave politics alone. Politics
interfere with creativity, and involvement with contemporary politics will almost invariably ruin a creative talent. Such small talent as
I had as a playwright was ruined by my involvement in politics. I
had had six plays produced before I became a politician. Nothing
since! Bob Sherwood, Archie MacLeish, and others became involved
like myself in activist politics during World War II, and their dramatic talents suffered greatly afterwards. Shaw will not be remembered for the *Woman's Guide,* or for any of his political writings. He
will be remembered, and played for a long, long time, because he
created dozens of believable characters involved in real-life
emotional—not political—conflicts.

Recently, when my play *The Women* was revived on Broadway, I
was asked by the *New York Times* to write a piece on why there are
so few *women* writing for the stage. Well, I looked at the Broadway
listings that week and asked myself, why are there so few *men*
playwrights? There were ten musicals, of which three were revivals,

and ten were "straight" plays. Three of these were also revivals, including my play which, incidentally, employed most of the actresses on Broadway then. Of the seven remaining plays, two were English imports. Of those five remaining, one was by a woman, Jean Kerr, and two were written by the prolific Neil Simon. He and she were the only *professional* American playwrights on Broadway last winter. The others will probably turn out to be one-shotters.

Why should the blame for poor theatre be laid on women? What we need is more writing for the stage. A playwright is a person who writes plays for the theatre—and writes them, and writes them, and writes them. A professional playwright is prolific. We have almost no professional playwrights left in America. I suppose England had a Shaw because it had had a Shakespeare. America has had no Shakespeares and no Shaws. No Galsworthys, even no Maughams. Perhaps Eugene O'Neill and Thornton Wilder and Tennessee Williams are our only dramatists with a durable body of work. The others are really just one- or two-shotters. For example, Albee, with *Who's Afraid of Virginia Woolf?* or Miller, with *Death of a Salesman.*

Oh. I think I should have said one more thing about Shaw and myself. When he asked me, "Now what was your dear mother's name?" I'm sure that he had intuitively understood that I looked on him as an adored "father figure." You see, after I was six years old, I never saw my own father. And I needed a father-figure. Somehow G.B.S. had become that to me. He had been the giver of a gift to me as a child which is second only to the gift of life—the gift of imagination.

Note

1. John Drinkwater (1882-1937) was once known for his historical play *Abraham Lincoln.* When, after his subsequent *Oliver Cromwell, Mary Stuart* and *Robert E. Lee,* he expressed interest in dramatizing Joan of Arc, Shaw explained his own *Saint Joan* as his attempt to rescue her from Drinkwater.

THE CENTER OF LIFE:
AN INTERVIEW WITH MEGAN TERRY

Rodelle Weintraub

Megan Terry, founder of the Omaha Magic Theatre and feminist playwright, wrote the first rock musical, *Viet Rock*. When she visited The Pennsylvania State University to participate in an experimental course on Women and Creativity in the Arts she consented to be interviewed. I was struck by the many parallels in her statements to those of Shaw [notes throughout for parallels]. Among Terry's works in progress is a play about Don Juan in which the Don, rather than being an iconoclastic male pursued by women, will be played by a woman.

I was born in Seattle, Washington, in 1932, the height of the great depression. We seem to be on the brink of another one; so I'm beginning to feel comfortable again. I really understand how to live on the beach, dig clams, fish and build a house. My mother adored me. I was very lucky. She told me from the minute I was born that I was beautiful and brilliant and she keeps telling me that every time she calls me. And she only phones me when she gets out of touch with me. My mother is Irish and psychic, and the only time she uses "Pa Bell" is if she feels out of touch and then she telephones and says "Are you all right?"

I hated college. It was right after the Korean War that I went to college and it was a vile experience. I hated it so much I took four jobs. It took me seven years to get a BA degree. I had looked forward to college with such hope. I pinned all my hopes on college. What a disappointment! If I hadn't found the French existentialist writers in the library—thank God I learned how to use the library—I would have gone crazy. I hated being a number. I was in a very big institution. I think I waited in line for one week just to register. My teachers didn't know me. They used to run and lock themselves in their offices because there were so many of us trying to talk to them. It wasn't their fault; they were overburdened. I believe in tutorial teaching—a one-to-one relationship. That is what I try to do with the playwrights who come to work with me in our theatre company. I think the theatre can give you a marvelous humanistic education and you can really see the history of emotion in reading the great plays that have been left to us.

I read all of Shaw's plays, his prefaces, everything.

And I acted Clara Eynsford-Hill in *Pygmalion*. I was interested in doing comedy and I thought I was playing first rate, but it was just O.K. And then the director began to speak to me about objectifying subjective works. I didn't know the difference between comedy, tragedy and straight acting. I hadn't resolved a comic attitude. So my director spent many hours speaking to me about objectifying subjective work on a character even though it was a small part. It was in playing that part that I learned the differences in comic attitude—by changing one's attitude toward the character I learned to do a triple thing on the stage. I played the character; I learned to put one eye out into the audience watching me play the character; and I learned to project my personal attitude toward the character I was playing. Once I learned to do that, the audience was delighted with the character and began to respond incredibly toward the way I was playing it, rather than just accepting it or going along with it. It added a lot to the show. The lines worked, everything worked. By the end of the run I was getting a big hand on my exit, which was something new to me. I was just nineteen or so when I played it. I learned how much one's personal attitude toward what one was doing counted on stage. It was a breakthrough for me as an actress at the time.

I had a woman director, a great role model, a woman director who had studied with Stanislavski. Her husband was the leading actor in our company. These people had worked together for twenty years; they were a great ensemble. They are my spiritual parents and I owe them a lot. I am very concerned with passing on the knowledge they gave me. I was radicalized at a very early age. I was brought up in a theatre company, the Seattle Repertory Playhouse, that was so radical—during the McCarthy Era there was a group called the Hollywood Ten—our people were the Seattle Six. At the age of eighteen I was very impressed with the power of the theatre. *They* came all the way from Washington, D.C., to put our people in jail, where Mr. James had a heart attack. One of the things that came out in the trial against one of our directors to prove that they were communists was that they had done a *Lysistrata* in 1936 with an all-Black cast.[1]

After the Seattle Repertory Playhouse was murdered,[2] I tried to pick up the pieces and create my own company with what was left over, and I formed a group called the Cornish Players. I started to do my plays along with Eugene O'Neill's plays at an art school. The concept of the art school was that all the arts should work together and it was begun by a woman named Nelly Cornish and she had teaching there at one time Martha Graham, John Cage, Merce Cunningham. When I went through the attic at that place I found these marvelous pictures of Martha Graham at age twenty-two or twenty-three. I made the mistake, however, of putting on my own shows along with O'Neill. And I started to make money—money started pouring into the school—and people began coming to see the plays. The system of payment at the school was 60–40. Sixty percent to the teacher, forty percent to the school. And that meant sixty percent of the box office. When the administration and the other teachers saw the money pouring into the box office they had a meeting—without me. They wanted a committee which would pick the plays from that day forward. All the other teachers wanted to turn the theatre into a pageant whereby all of the teachers would do a little bit—some kind of a wondrous revue, and they would control the box office. So I resigned and went to New York where I hoped I would find a more hospitable environment for the kinds of plays I was trying to do. But it turned out that the establishment theatre didn't want to hear from me either.

The New York theatre was the theatre of good behavior. What was up there on the stage was theatre of middle-class or upper-class values. Women who were chosen to be in plays had to be five feet six and one-half inches tall with long blond hair and blue eyes—the perfect WASP look. You can see it on any soap opera today. There were no roles unless you looked a certain way, a certain way that the upper structure wanted women to look, and that was it. You know all the stories about women having their noses changed and their bone structure changed. I've met women who've had their legs broken and two inches cut off their legs and reset because they were too tall. My friends were doing stretching exercises because they were too short. People would give a fantastic reading and the director would say "You have a lot of talent, darling, but you're just not the right type." Also, there were no more than two roles in a play for women. It was amazing. There were 20,000 card-carrying members of Actors Equity and only 300 jobs a year. Broadway is even worse now. Most of the plays are British imports with British casts.

America still seems to have an Oedipal complex toward Great Britain and that accent. In many theatre schools they are still trying to teach American voices to change to British or some kind of British accents. It is another kind of mask. Anthony Burgess has a wonderful story about how the British developed their accent. It is only 200 years old. The British used to speak like the Irish do today. Shakespeare's plays were done in what you would think of as an Irish accent. As the British took over the world and colonized more and more people they developed this accent to keep people at arm's length—at a distance. This Oxford accent was consciously developed so that the people who went out to rule the colonies did not get too close to the natives. And that's the way the ruling class runs the rest of us too. There's a whole thing about accent and deportment. What I'm doing in Omaha is not changing my people's voices at all. I *love* all the different ways Americans talk and all I want from my actors is that they be true to themselves, to who they are and to where they come from. I love the variety of sounds.[3] I'm crazy about sounds. I think of speech as music. I think it was John Millington Synge who influenced me more than Shaw about that. It was really through Yeats when he told Synge to go out into the country and listen to the people and then Synge wrote those marvelous plays, *The Tinker's Wedding* and *Playboy of the Western World* and *Deirdre of the Sorrows*. They were huge influences on me when I was a teenager. Such music. Unfortunately Synge died so young. I think we are really singing to each other most of the time and I don't want, in my work, to train all actors to sound alike, or sound like radio announcers or the Royal Shakespeare, as much as I admire certain actors in the Royal Shakespeare Company.

When I went to New York a lot of other people went to New York too—it was late in the fifties or early sixties. The establishment theatre was beginning to suffer the effects of film and TV. Now film is being declared an art form because television is the mass medium—very interesting to see all that has happened in just twenty years. The point is that we had all been trained in theatre and a lot of us who converged there to work in the theatre found that nobody wanted to let us into the theatre. They didn't want to hear from us or allow us to work. They weren't interested in our plays or acting ability. So we got together and created something called the Open Theatre, and just as the culture of the sixties that the young people created was called the alternate culture, we were the alternate theatre or the underground theatre or the radical theatre. And we were followed by the FBI and the CIA and also by Broadway directors who were coming down to take notes and rip off some of our discoveries that they could use commercially. You can see some of our work diluted in musicals like *Company* and *Pippin* and *Hair*. A lot of the work and the opening up of the American theatre came from groups like the Open Theatre. Our production *Viet Rock* was the first rock musical. We made our own theatre and we started a whole movement.

In the sixties, I became quite a bit involved in political theatre— the street theatre. It was very necessary to do it in the sixties to fight the war. I did a lot of it. Constantly. Now we still do it in Omaha and we do it at political conventions and NOW conventions.

I know a lot of people debate whether theatre can be a forum for political change,* a place where people can be educated to new ideas, and say it is not possible because there is no empirical evidence that a play ever changed anyone's mind,† though I have seen it change people's feelings. Besides, the theatre reaches a very small segment of the population. I think one time the Guthrie Theatre made a study, before it opened, of how many people in a given population will go to see live entertainment—and that includes Neil Simon to *Hello Dolly* to community theatre to the most esoteric theatre. They found that only two percent of any people in any city will go to live entertainment. The interesting thing is that these two percent usually are the shakers and movers and their ideas filter down so that even though people say to me "Why are you working in the theatre? It is so old-fashioned. Nobody goes. It

---

* "It [*Widowers' Houses*] is a propagandist play—a didactic play—a play with a purpose; . . . I claim that its value . . . is enhanced by the fact that it deals with a burning social question, and is deliberately intended to induce people to vote the Progressive side at the next County Council election in London." Preface to *Widowers' Houses*.

† "I am convinced that fine art is the subtlest, the most seductive, the most effective instrument of moral propaganda in the world, excepting only the example of personal conduct; and I would waive even that exception in favor of the art of the stage, because it works by exhibiting examples of personal conduct made intelligible and moving to crowds of unobservant unreflecting people to whom real life means nothing." Preface to *Mrs Warren's Profession*.

is a dying . . .''* whatever, I see ten years later the results of my work. I see watered down versions of it on TV. Ideas get disseminated faster than when Shaw was writing, because of television.

I like roles that are funny. Comedy is a healing process. When you laugh you feel better. It churns your guts. The whole body is kinetically involved. O'Casey was a master of mixing comedy and tragedy. Most of my plays are musicals too but people don't realize that. I use farce, every theatrical device that works to make my point.†

I work in three ways. I write personal plays—totally alone about my own *tsouris* [troubles] and whatever is going on in my obsessions. It is possible to write your way to mental health or some degree of mental health. I know maybe some people wouldn't certify me as such but I declare myself sane today. I write history plays like *Approaching Simone* and *Mother Jones/Mollie Bailey Family Circus*. I write plays because I am interested in something and I want to go into a long investigation about it and that all comes out of research and meditation, fasting, deep thought. My next fifteen-year project will be a life of Sappho. Then, as a citizen, I write plays like *Viet Rock* or my latest piece with the Omaha Magic Theatre about women in prison, called *Babes in the Big House*. It's a documentary fantasy musical based on those movies *Caged Women* and *Girl in Cellblock 9* but also on three years of playing prisons all over the United States and Canada and being in touch with people who are truly incarcerated and who write to us and whose stories appear in this play and on the research that has been done by anthropologists and sociologists.

My plays are constructed. That's another interesting thing I discovered. Women must learn—I don't know if they must but it is a good idea to know how—to use tools, to know how to build structures. Many of my plays are based on architectural concepts and the fact that I know how to build a house is some kind of un-

---

* "Weariness of the theatre is the prevailing note of London criticism. Only the ablest critics believe that the theatre is really important." "Author's Apology" to *Our Theatres in the Nineties* (1906).

† "I have given you a series of first-rate music hall entertainments, thinly disguised as plays, but really offering the public a unique string of turns by comics and serio-comics of every popular type. . . . *Make no error V.D. that is the jam that has carried the propaganda pill down* [editor's italics]. Even in Voysey it was the Booth turn, the Clarence turn, the wicked solicitor and the comic old woman that consoled the house for the super drama." Shaw to John Vedrenne, 4 March 1907, in *The Shaw-Barker Letters*, ed. C.B. Purdom (1956).

derpinning for why my plays hang together. A lot of people, especially critics, say that what I write are not plays.* But somehow they
seem to hold an audience; the audience understands even if the critics don't. It is strange that the critics always like the last play.† When
Hot House was done in New York last year (1974) Clive Barnes came

---

*"Oh, please," said the gifted author referred to, "dont call the piece a play.
There was a general agreement that 'John Bull's Other Island' was not a
play, and it has been a success on that understanding. If you put it about
that 'Major Barbara' is a play nobody will come to it. I assure you it is much
less of a play than 'John Bull.' Nor is it tragedy, comedy, farce, or what is
called at the theatre, drama. It is simply a discussion in four very long acts,
and that is what it will be called on the programme. A problem play? Great
heavens! don't speak of it as that. . . . There is no drama, no situations, no
curtains, no feelings, no heart, no dramatic interest." "Drama of the Day,"
an interview drafted by Shaw for the *Daily Telegraph*, 12 October 1905.

†"Is not the play [*John Bull's Other Island*] always spoken of as a masterpiece?
is not Mr. Calvert's Broadbent as famous as Quin's Falstaff? Yes, it is—*now*.
But turn back to the first-night notices, and you will learn that the masterpiece is not a play at all, and that Mr. Calvert only did the best he could
with an impossible part. It was not until Man and Superman followed that
the wonderful qualities of John Bull were contrasted with the emptiness and
dulness of its successor. It was not until Major Barbara came that the extinc-
tion of all the brilliancy that blazed through Man and Superman was announced. And not until The Doctor's Dilemma had been declared my
Waterloo was it mentioned that Major Barbara had been my Austerlitz.
    "Now, I want to make a suggestion to the press. I dont ask them to give
up abusing me, or declaring that my plays are not plays and my characters
not human beings. Not for worlds would I deprive them of the inexhaustible pleasure these paradoxes seem to give them. But I do ask them, for the
sake of the actors and of Vedrenne and Barker's enterprize, to reverse the
order of their attacks and their caresses. In the future, instead of abusing the
new play and praising the one before, let them abuse the one before and
praise the new one. Instead of saying that The Doctor's Dilemma shows a
sad falling-off from the superb achievement of Major Barbara, let them say
that The Doctor's Dilemma is indeed a welcome and delightful change from
the diseased trash which they had to endure last year from this most un-
equal author. That will satisfy their feelings just as much as the other plan,
and will be really helpful to us. It is not the revivals that we want written
up; the revivals can take care of themselves. Praise comes too late to help
plays that have already helped themselves. If the press wishes to befriend
us, let it befriend us in need, instead of throwing stones at us whilst we are
struggling in the waves and pressing lifebelts on us when we have swum to
shore." Complimentary Dinner to Mr. J.E. Vedrenne and Mr. H. Granville
Barker, 1907, Souvenir Brochure, as reprinted in *Platform & Pulpit*, pp. 40-41.
See also Clare Boothe Luce interview, p. 209.

out and said why didn't I write plays like *Simone* [*Approaching Simone*] which was done in 1970. It is so strange. I don't even worry about it anymore. You know, people will say how can you stand it. After you live long enough, you say it doesn't matter. The audience understands even if the critics don't. On the surface the plays may look different, not as traditional and linear as most plays that most people are used to, but actually the plays have very firm architectural foundations. One of my main struggles in building my technique as a playwright is to create plays so other minds could walk around inside my models and take a look at what I am building and see what kind of things they might also want to build or what structures that they might like to build outside of their bodies to show what is going on inside of their head. Some of the reasons for the ways in which the plays are constructed are a result of the process of the way we work, and of the way we think.

I'm so excited about thinking: it's like sex. I get physical pleasure from having ideas. I've just noticed this in the last year and you never get sated from it. I mean the novelty doesn't wear off. You don't come to the end of the joy of having ideas, whereas you know after a few orgasms you can wait a few days, but not with ideas. You can just keep having ideas, ideas, ideas. I don't think enough has been said of the plain old physical pleasure that the human being experiences from learning, discovery, insights.* It is only since I'm past forty that I'm letting myself enjoy ideas. Before I couldn't feel them—or couldn't trust them. It took this long to get the confidence to trust them—to get the mind and the body fused. That is one of the things the feminists keep pointing out: how society alienates the woman's mind from her body and it takes so long to get that back together again—if you do. I tried to write about this fragmentation in a play called *The Common Knowledge*. So part of the reason I write is to set up environments and constructions whereby the actor may discover some of this for herself/himself in working on my work and get into this other area too. I'm interested in ideas, in politics, in religion, in what's happening. I don't have as much time to just sit and think as I would like.

My concern is saving the health of my friends, to keep them writing; we've lost too many people. And my concern is for how the

---

*"To initiate births they had to practice personal contacts which I would rather not describe. Strangest of all, they seem to have experienced in such contacts the ecstasies which are normal with us in our pursuit of knowledge and power, and culminate in our explorations and discoveries." *Farfetched Fables*.

artists and creative people are going to make a living. Times are getting tougher but we're the richest country in the world and this ought to be a fairer system. The other countries of the world have done it. The other capitalistic countries and the Iron Curtain countries—it's about time America woke up and stopped taking this attitude that artists are a bunch of dopers and layabouts. We can't help doing what we do. We are compulsive creators, most of us. And I don't know where it all comes from but it's fascinating. I can't stop writing. Sometimes I wish I could. I'd like to go fishing. But there is an awful lot to do, a lot of people struggled to leave us messages. A lot of people went to the guillotine so we could be sitting here today talking to one another. And I feel responsible toward them and I feel responsible toward you and toward the future. I'm glad more and more writers are coming up because I used to feel terribly responsible that I wasn't going to live long enough to write all the stuff I should write. But now there are going to be so many writers that I could take a few years off, I think.

I work in partnership with actors. In preparing for *Babes* the actors have gone to the prisons and met the people that they are playing in the shows. Our life is our own and our art is our life. We work all the time and we are always trying to develop exercises both for our imagination and our bodies. One thing as you grow older you must learn to keep your body in very good shape if you are going to play the kind of work we do. After twenty-five, you know, the body and brain begin to go downhill and you have to do everything you can to fight gravity and the dying brain cells.

I see the actor as shaman or priest.* Certainly as a colleague too. I think actors are brave and precious beings who open themselves up and keep the human spirit alive, in all of its manifestations; who make great personal sacrifices to get up in front of audiences and work out and work through all sorts of psychological and spiritual problems. I see theatre as a working out in a creative way of our religious impulses and the actor's role in that is a very important one, the same way a priest functions in organized religion.

I think one can explore one's religious impulses in the theatre be-

---

* "The artists of the theatre, led by Sir Henry Irving, were winning their struggle to be considered ladies and gentlemen, qualified for official honors. Now for their gentility and knighthoods I cared very little: what lay at the root of my criticism was their deeper claim to be considered, not merely actors and actresses, but men and women, not hired buffoons and posturers however indulged, but hierophants of a cult as eternal and sacred as any professed religion in the world." "Author's Apology."

cause organized religion has become so rigid.* And religion has become big business. I am extremely interested in exploring pre-
Judeo-Christian concepts right now. What I feel is that the contemporary GOD is male and useless for women,[4] for it makes them into
schizophrenics. I don't see how women can identify with the male
gods that are being crammed down their throats. And if they do
identify with them, they have to split off from their female sides to
do it. From my close observation of my friends, of my mother, their
Catholic guilt has paralyzed their lives. It creates a split and it frag-
ments people, especially women. I've met nuns who call themselves
"Jesus ladies." I think it is really perverted for women to have to
identify with a male god.

I'm interested in the idea of matriarchy and women's religion that
women had created before patriarchy came about and especially
what happened to the Celtic people who had a very strong religion
involved with marvelous sexual rites and healing. When the Chris-
tians came up and took over Ireland all of this was lost. The book
Witches, Midwives and Nurses describes the whole healing knowledge
which was practiced until about 300 years ago. The healing and
birthing, the bringing babies into the world, were the problems of

---

* "It [the theatre] is as important as the Church was in the Middle Ages.
. . . A theatre to me is a place 'where two or three are gathered together.'
The apostolic succession from Eschylus to myself is as serious and as con-
tinuously inspired as that younger institution, the apostolic succession of
the Christian Church.

"Unfortunately this Christian Church, founded gaily with a pun, has
been so largely corrupted by rank Satanism that it has become the Church
where you must not laugh; and so it is giving way to that older and greater
Church to which I belong: the Church where the oftener you laugh the
better, because by laughter only can you destroy evil without malice, and
affirm good fellowship without mawkishness. . . .

"The theatre is really the week-day church; and a good play is essentially
identical with a church service as a combination of artistic ritual, profession
of faith, and sermon. Wherever the theatre is alive, there the church is alive
also: Italy, with its huge, magnificent, empty churches, and slovenly, insincere services, has also its huge, magnificent, empty theatres, with slovenly,
insincere plays. The countries which we call Scandinavian (to the exasperation of all true Norwegians, somehow) produce saints and preachers,
dramatists and actors, who influence all Europe. The fundamental unity of
Church and Theatre—a necessary corollary of the orthodox doctrine of
omnipresence—is actually celebrated on the stage in such dramas as Brand,
and in the Parsifal performance at Bayreuth, which is nothing less than the
Communion presented in theatrical instead of ecclesiastical form." "Author's Apology."

women. And they did it for one another for no money. They did not charge. It was either the barter system or women just took turns helping each other with the birth. But little by little the men decided that there might be some money in it and they began to create the concept of witches. Women who had the power of healing and the power of bringing live babies into the world without pain were branded witches. They started to burn our sisters and great-grandmothers. They burned nine million women—that's an awful lot of women—in order to create a profession that they could begin to charge for. You can see the destruction of matriarchy and the establishment of patriarchy through the group plays and in the Bible too, going back, as far as the big study of that one when He died. One of the history plays I hope to write—I am very interested in writing for television—if they'll let me—is the life of Mary Baker Eddy, the only American woman, the only woman in the past thousand years, to create a worldwide religion and a great international newspaper.

There are so few roles in establishment theatre that are good roles, true roles, written for real women. Among those few good roles are Shaw's Major Barbara and Saint Joan and Candida and Lina Szczepanowska, the parachutist in *Misalliance*. Shaw had some wonderful love affairs with some great actresses, thank God. So he wrote some new parts for women. And he wrote long letters of instruction to them on acting. I think he directed too, didn't he? He was very astute about his lines and his actors. He wrote many directions into the script. I do my own directing, but instead of writing in stage directions, I write in how I arrived at something and show the directors how to get the same thing if they want to.

I think Shaw had wonderful intuition. He really cared about theatre and his mind was so far-reaching. The humor and warmth always come through if you do it right. But to tell the truth, I've only seen one Shaw production that was only halfway good. It was the Guthrie production of *Saint Joan*. Some Shaw, like *Methuselah* and *Farfetched Fables*, I read with such delight and identification. I wish I didn't have so many commitments, because I know I could stage this marvelous material. I would like you to see a terrific Shaw production—maybe next year or so if I could get to it.

I think of the theatre as the center of life. I think the theatre is the brain of the culture, the repository of the real feelings that are going down. I see theatre as a conservative art because it involves human beings and it grows slowly. If you can take a while to gather everything and think about everything and then put it all together and crystallize it, then, I think, theatre is the central art for human beings.

Notes

1. Burton Wesley James and his wife, Florence Bean James, were among six persons who were accused of contempt for refusing to testify before the Canwell Committee (the Washington State Legislature's committee to investigate "un-American activities"). Tried before the King's County Superior Court in 1949, they were found guilty and he was sentenced to thirty days in jail and fined $250. (Mrs. James was given a thirty-day suspended sentence and fined $125.) James appealed the decision to the State Supreme Court which unanimously affirmed the decision. The U.S. Supreme Court refused to hear his appeal although three Justices, Black, Reed and Douglas, dissented. The Court also refused to hear Mrs. James's appeal and the appeal of a third member of the six, Rachmeil Forschmiedt. It was later proven that the Canwell Committee had accepted perjured testimony and that Canwell himself had destroyed documents proving that Melvin Rader, one of the persons being investigated by the committee, had not been at a Communist meeting in New York as one witness claimed. Canwell also pressured the King's County District Attorney to drop criminal perjury charges against that witness. Vern Countryman, *Un-American Activities in the State of Washington* (1951); Melvin Rader, *False Witness* (1969); Cedric Belfrage, *The American Inquisition* (1973).

2. As a result of the Canwell hearings, patronage at the Playhouse fell off drastically, and the Playhouse was forced to accept the University of Washington's offer to purchase it at approximately half of its appraised value. In the words of the University comptroller, this was a "good buy" for the University. Countryman, pp. 151-52.

3. See orchestration of accents in *Captain Brassbound's Conversion*.

4. See *The Adventures of the Black Girl in Her Search for God*. See also Shaw on God as woman in "Fabian Feminist," p. 7.

VI

SHAW ON FEMINIST ISSUES

TORTURE BY FORCIBLE FEEDING
IS ILLEGAL

[*Bernard Shaw*]

The *London Budget* on 23 March 1913 carried a reporter's transcript of a speech Shaw made protesting the forcible feeding of suffragists. The substance of the talk appeared a few weeks later in an unsigned editorial written by him (its authorship validated by editor Clifford Sharp's notes) for the *New Statesman* issue of 12 April 1913 entitled "Forcible Feeding."

Torture By Forcible Feeding Is Illegal

Full Report of Mr. Shaw's Speech, Delivered at the Meeting to Protest Against the Methods of Punishing Suffragists Now in Vogue in English Prisons

Bernard Shaw has scored many triumphs. Few of his successes have been more complete than his speech delivered on Tuesday night at a mass meeting at Kingsway Hall, which was held to protest against the forcible feeding of Suffragists in prison. There were a number of other speakers, including Mr. Forbes-Robertson, the Bishop of Lincoln, and Miss Broadhurst. Bernard Shaw's speech, denouncing forcible feeding as illegal, is a strong document, promising to be historic.

In this speech he was not Bernard Shaw, the dramatist and maker of epigrams, but a citizen protesting against what he considers legalised brutality. The meeting was held under the auspices of the National Political League. The London Budget *takes pleasure in presenting to its readers the following verbatim report of Mr. Shaw's probably epoch-making address:*

I am not a Suffragette speaker. I have become hardened to that reproach. It has been levelled at me for hours together in my own house by such friends of mine as Mr. Laurence Housman. Mr. Forbes-Robertson is, I believe, almost the only one of the gentlemen who supports so eloquently and devotedly the cause of Women's Suffrage, who has not told me I am a dastard and a great many other worse things because I do not come forward on the platform. I have an object in this. I want to point out that our protest against forcible feeding is not only a protest against the forcible feeding of women, because men also are being forcibly fed and it is for that reason I have come here tonight in protest against this practice. I have not come here to speak on behalf of the women. My reason for never having done that since I first declared myself in order that I might clear my own conscience is that after a very careful study of public meetings held on the subject I came to the conclusion that the women were exceedingly well able to take care of themselves. When I saw at those meetings some friends of mine brought forward between petticoats, if I may say so, rough men speaking on behalf of women, I always found they looked so horribly ignominious and did it so very much worse than the women, I made up my mind that my personal vanity would not permit me to come forward.

I say this in order that you may understand that if this were merely a Suffragist meeting I should not be here. I did speak at a meeting on this subject some time ago, and I remember that I addressed some reproaches to the Suffragettes on that occasion. I thought they had not appreciated some previous efforts of mine sufficiently.

HARDIER THAN MEN   The consequence was that next morning the first letter I opened began, "Poor injured darling." I do not resent that sort of treatment because I really do think that we men in our relations with women are really "poor injured darlings." I do not come forward tonight in the sense of a chivalrous man coming to the rescue of the weaker sex. I quite seriously think that those suffering through forcible feeding are for the most part the stronger sex. I quite seriously believe that women are hardier than men.

A woman has to go through experiences in the quite ordinary course of life that I would like to see any man go through. Therefore don't understand me as appealing for special consideration for women. I am not doing so. I don't believe women want to have that done. In fact, I believe the women who are most enthusiastic in the cause are infuriated more by any affectation of magnanimity and protection from my sex than anything else in the world. I myself have the rather original view about woman that she is very much the same sort of person as I am myself. But unfortunately that view is one which does not seem to be very general in official circles.

For instance, I believe that most men do recognize that their own insides are rather complicated machines. When they have to deal with women they apparently believe that what they have to deal with is a sort of sack into which you can put food, that the mouth of this sack is a narrow orifice called the throat, and that once they can poke something into that orifice and squirt food through they have done everything that can be expected in the way of feeding that person.

OVERSHOT OR UNDERSHOT   I want to anticipate the medical gentlemen, and go into anatomical details. On that simple theory the first thing you have got to do to introduce food is to induce the persons to open their mouths. That is not such an easy thing as you might imagine. If a person has got an unbroken set of teeth and is not much overshot or undershot, if those teeth are closed properly it is an extraordinarily difficult thing to open them against the will of the owner of the teeth.

If you have a case of somebody eternally keeping their teeth shut, the first thing that occurs to uneducated or rough people is simply to take an instrument like a chisel and attempt to pry them open. That is an impossible thing to do, because you cannot get the chisel through unless you break the teeth. I want to impress this on you— that for anybody to prise a person's mouth open in that way is to perform an act of extraordinary violence—an act which may be impossible unless you actually break the teeth to begin with.

That, apparently, is the way the thing is done at the present time in prison. Then when you have got the mouth open comes the idea that you have only got to deal with a sort of empty sack.

I can assure you, although I am not a professional man, that it is not so simple as that. There are two ways of getting inside a human being. One is by the larynx or the trachea, the tube which leads to the lungs and which has a remarkable little musical box, by the aid of which I am addressing you—sometimes it is not very musical and along with that is another tube which goes down to the stomach.

THE WRONG TUBE   If you want to thoroughly appreciate how very important it is, you should take the right tube when getting food in. You have only to remember how a short time ago all Europe was greatly shocked by the death of a prominent German politician who unfortunately dropped one of his own teeth—or, rather a tooth purchased from a dentist—into the wrong tube, and the consequence was that the eminent gentleman died.

I hope you all remember that particular instance. There you have got before the eyes of the Government and of Europe a striking illustration of the fact that a slight mistake in the way food may go down may result in the death of the person. These mistakes have been made apparently as forcible feeding is at present conducted. Our wardnesses, perhaps, are not to be complained of for not being educated anatomically, but if they are not educated anatomically they ought not to be set to perform anatomical operations. But pray what are we to say to the medical gentlemen who superintend these operations? It really seems to me they are not properly educated, or else they are in such a temper that they forget their scientific education; at any rate there appears to be no doubt whatever that attempts have been made—and with considerable injury to the person on whom the attempt has been made—to feed persons through the wrong tube.

All that means torture. Mr. Forbes-Robertson said that we could not conceive the condition of mind of the Middle Ages with regard to torture. I agree. But I wish to make it thoroughly understood that I do not mean we are superior to the Middle Ages in that matter. On the contrary, I am absolutely convinced that we have almost entirely lost the peculiar clue which leads men to steer away from torture. The Middle Ages had a good many defects, but they had a religion, and they believed accordingly that certain things did not do and certain things did do. In the Middle Ages they never referred any question directly to their own passions.

MORAL OF SITUATION   They did not write letters to the "Daily Telegraph" half full of lies and half full of suggestions that women should be tortured and the signature at the end is not the signature of the man who wrote the letter. The Middle Ages really always did things—particularly when they did public things and legal things—with some sort of reference as to whether it was the sort of thing God would have done, and even when they did things which shock us it was really because it was part of their conception or thought that God in his hatred of sin might have done that particular thing. I entirely absolve Mr. McKenna [the Home Secretary] and the present Government from any such idea.

The moral of the present situation is that our statesmen have never, it appears to me, tried to refer this question to the larger considerations by which this question should be determined. They have regard to the pettiest considerations as if only their own temper was concerned. They are faced with the heroic temper which produces martyrs, and yet they go back to the fact that they are afraid of having their windows broken, or that somebody will jostle them.

They can take no large view of the matter at all. There is, however, a point which I think they may understand. I contend that this forcible feeding is illegal. I contend that if you are tried in a public court and sentenced to imprisonment you are sentenced to imprisonment, and not to torture, except in so far as imprisonment may be torture, and I think imprisonment on the whole is rather too severe torture to be inflicted on any human being. The public are apt to be careless about these things.

They forget that when a person goes into the hands of a prison governor, that person goes into a place the doors of which are shut. Nobody goes in to see whether the people inside the jail really confine themselves to their warrant.

REFUSING TO EAT   Now supposing I am sent to jail for one month's imprisonment. Suppose I refuse to eat. What is the proper thing to do with me? If the Governor of the prison found himself faced with a new phenomenon, I suppose he would report "I have got in prison here, a prisoner who refuses to eat. I place food before him. I have to report that the prisoner still refuses food, and may possibly die of starvation."

He would logically, I suppose, charge the man with attempted suicide. After that he would be sentenced to a further term of imprisonment, and the Governor having got him back on those terms might then find that he still refused to eat.

Then I presume the Governor would make a report to the Home Secretary, "The prisoner still refuses to eat, and is dying. I, of course, have carried out instructions, and placed food before him. My duty so far is done. However, I let you know."

Suppose the Home Secretary said, "I have certain reasons for not wishing this gentleman to die." I would be rather curious to imagine what those reasons could possibly be, because if this man deserved imprisonment, and public opinion felt that he deserved it, there would be no difficulty in letting him die.

There is no reason, whatever, no obligation on any Government to keep a prisoner alive. But supposing the Home Secretary said, "Well let's try and make this man eat," and after conferring with the Governor, it was suggested to him by the Governor, "Well, we might for instance keep touching him up with a red hot poker."

It is perfectly clear that the Home Secretary would say, "But unfortunately we have not, in law, any power to burn people with red hot pokers. Therefore, we must first induce the Government to bring in a bill to legalise the use of red hot pokers."

Now, if the Government did this and actually brought in, and passed such a bill, I presume the prisoner would have no particular grievance on the score of the use of a red hot poker being illegal.

LEGALISED TORTURE   I content that if the Government wants to break people's teeth with chisels, and force food into the lungs and run the risk of killing them, to inflict what is unquestionably torture on them, their business is to bring in a bill legalising these operations. There is no reason why they should hold back. They have no shame in doing it without the law. Why should they be ashamed to do it with the law?

I think it is a perfectly plain dilemma. If the Government is not prepared to legalise this torture, the only explanation is that not only does their own conscience revolt from this torture, but they do not believe that public opinion would be on their side.

They are not prepared to face the electorate with such a measure as that. Now it seems to me, having brought the matter to that point, that the Government really have discovered that the women have beaten them. It is not merely a question of the women inflicting humiliation on them, and getting the better of them. What the women have proved is that the conscience of the community is on their side. They have proved something more, that the conscience of the very men who are doing this is on their side.

You see uneasiness and shame, and miserable excuses made, which would not impose on an intelligent frog. When I last spoke on this subject you may remember that Mrs. Lee was in Mountjoy Prison, under a sentence of several years for a very serious offence. Well, on that occasion, I challenged the Government to let Mrs. Lee starve. I said that they had no right whatever to forcibly feed her. I argued that the torture was illegal, and I said, "Leave Mrs. Lee's food within her reach and let her starve. It is not your business to compel her to eat."

WANTON SAVAGERY   I am glad to say that on that occasion the entire Press of the country, the anti-Suffragist [press] in particular, jumped at my speech. A very eloquent speech made by Mr. Laurence Housman was not reported at all. Many of these poor reporters had got into such a state of mind that they could not resist saying, "Even Bernard Shaw wants you to starve Mrs. Lee."

No person can pretend that that challenge was not brought to the notice of the Government. Did the Government face the challenge? No: they let Mrs. Lee out straight away. After that, what is there to be said? What is the use of going on with this miserable wanton savagery, when you dare not go through with the sentence? Why don't they get hold of Mrs. Pankhurst and put her in prison, and say that a woman who refuses food is a lunatic and put her in a lunatic asylum?

There is only one objection to what may appear a logical course. It is that they know, and the whole country knows, that Mrs. Pankhurst is not a madwoman. That is the case I want to put before you.

The Government does not dare to take a logical course, which it would take with any person who has the conscience of the community against him. Take Dr. Crippen, for instance.[1] Suppose he had been sentenced to penal servitude and refused food. Do you suppose anybody would have hesitated to say, Let him starve? The conscience of the community was against him and would have been with the Government in allowing him to starve.

CONSCIENCE OF [THE] COMMUNITY   The conscience of the community is not with the Government in this. The whole thing has now become propaganda of spite and rancor. It is a brutality that is degrading our national character. But I don't believe these people's characters [the government personnel carrying out the forcible feeding] are half as much degraded as the characters of the people who are reading the articles [on forcible feeding] now being published in the newspapers. It is degrading the whole moral tone of life to read the horrible ways in which Ministers [of the Government] endeavour to hide the sort of thing that is going on.

Let me offer a challenge to Mr. McKenna. He still occasionally can make out that forcible feeding is rather pleasant. If it is so perfectly easy for him to prove it, why does he not allow us to forcibly feed him? We will do it with his favourite food and he need not resist. We will get skilled surgeons and make it all possible. I don't believe he will want the challenge, but I hope he will accept my other challenge and get rid of the horrible question in the only other way.

There is only one conclusion to come to, and that is the conclusion I came to long ago. On the woman's suffrage question, I have never had particular doubts. I am not usually an orthodox man, because there is a great deal in almost all the major religions in the world which I think it is time to get rid of. But there are many things in the Church liturgy, and other documents, which are very valuable. I have always believed the old simple statement that we are members each of the other. I think that probably [even] at

Westminster most people believe that we are all members one of another, rather than Members of Parliament only.

DUTY TO OTHERS   There is an old sentence which reads, I think, "Inasmuch as ye do it to the least of My brethren, you have done it unto Me." I don't think these gentlemen understand that brethren means sisters as well. I think, also, that men are apt to make little protest on days when people are always talking about duty to others.

I don't care about my duty to others at all. I understand by that "Inasmuch as ye have done it unto the least of these My brethren, ye do it unto Me," that this is the true identification of the least of these—me.

If you take a woman and torture her, you torture me. If you take Mrs. Pankhurst's daughter and torture her, then you are torturing my daughter. If you take Mrs. Pankhurst's mother and torture her, then you are torturing my mother. Let us go further, and say that if you torture my mother, you are torturing me.

These denials of fundamental rights are really a violation of the soul and are an attack on that sacred part of life which is common to all of us, the thing of which you speak when you talk of the Life Everlasting. I say this is not a mystical sense, but the most obvious commonsense, that the denial of any fundamental rights to the person of woman is practically the denial of the Life Everlasting.

Note

1. Dr. H.H. Crippin, notorious Edwardian murderer, whose trial for poisoning his wife was widely publicized.

G.B.S. AND A SUFFRAGIST

An Intimate Interview by Maud Churton Braby

Everything about the tone of this interview, originally published in the *Tribune*, London, 12 March 1906, purportedly by Maud Churton Braby,[1] suggests that it is one of Shaw's inimitable self-interviews, which he often concocted to fend off actual interviews or, on appropriate occasions, to promote an idea or play. These interviews were sometimes offered, in writing, to inquiring interviewees, who thus came away with an interview better written and more witty than anything they had heretofore accomplished, and then possessed, in addition, a marketable manuscript. A number of these are now in public and private collections. Mrs. Braby, who did visit Shaw, was a popular novelist, journalist, and suffragette. Two letters from Shaw to her appear in the *Collected Letters*, Vol. 2, the first dated 1908, two years after the one quoted in this interview.

Mr. George Bernard Shaw at bay is, if possible, even more interesting and amusing than Mr. Shaw in his normal condition of abnormality. The inaccessibility of Mr. Seymour Hicks,[2] the Tsar, Lord Kitchener, and even the Dalai Lama himself is as nought compared with the extreme and superman inaccessibility of "G.B.S." His fortress on the Embankment is practically impregnable; at the moment when all his vast energies were concentrated on electioneering in the Socialist interest one might sit on the doorstep from frosty morn to foggy eve without encountering him.[3]

The dogged patience and unswerving perseverance of your interviewer prevailed, however, in the end; and after a strenuous attack lasting some weeks, the "marked-down victim, the destined prey" (as he would doubtless express it) eventually succumbed, in a moment of fury produced by a demurely presented formal introduction having for its object an interview on the subject of the Suffrage for Women.

"This is the last outrage of all," he wrote. "Can you not understand that you are dealing with a distracted, overworked man, years in arrears with work and business of all kinds. Am I fifty men instead of only ten? Can I put seventy-two hours into the day, instead of only thirty-six? Come to-morrow, either at eleven, when I shall be extremely busy, or at four, when I shall be utterly exhausted. And do not expect any sympathy from me on the suffrage question. You have convinced me that these women must be put down. Yours at bay, G. Bernard Shaw."

Accordingly, on the morning in question, I repaired in triumph and a hansom cab to the Shavian fortress, and found the gates opened, the drawbridge down. Whilst waiting for the marked-down victim to make his appearance I occupied myself in trying to analyse the indescribable charm of Mr. Shaw's sitting-room, but words were entirely inadequate to convey the restful beauty of this unique apartment. Like everything else connected with "G.B.S.," it is unexpected!

"At last!" I said, when the destined prey entered.

"How perfectly fiendish of you to come in the morning," was his genial greeting, spoken, however, in such a manner of subtle cordiality that it conveyed a welcome far more gratifying than anything more conventionally polite would have done.

"The suffrage is nothing to me," he began. "I have no opinion on the subject. I'm not a woman; I've got the suffrage."

"But if, for the sake of argument, you were a woman——?"

"Of course, if I were a woman, I'd simply refuse to speak to any man or do anything for men until I'd got the vote. I'd make my husband's life a burden, and everybody miserable generally. Women should have a revolution—they should shoot, kill, maim, destroy—until they are given a vote."

"And what would you consider the proper qualifications?"

"There's none necessary; the qualification of being human is enough. I would make the conditions exactly the same as for men; it's no use women claiming *more* than men, though probably in the end they'll get more, as they invariably do whenever women agitate for equality with men in any respect."

"For example?"

"Take the Married Women's Property Act! Since that has been law, man is a mere insect, he scarcely has the right to live! Women have the upper hand in every way. Consider their enormous sexual advantage. Why, even in a court of law no man has a chance in the witness-box against a woman. It's quite possible, considering the foolish and sentimental way these things are generally managed, that they will get more political rights than men in the end.

"What sort of Bill would I introduce, did you say? Simply a short Act to have the word 'men' in all the relevant statutes construed as human beings—as mankind—though, as you hear people talking of womankind, I suppose even that would not be understood. It's one of the many drawbacks to our ridiculous language. We have no word which includes men and women. It just shows how little we realize men and women belong to the same species. No one denies that a stallion and a mare are both horses—they wear just the same kind of harness; but a woman is looked upon as an entirely different animal to a man. So everything—costume, coiffer, customs, political rights—everything is arranged as far as possible to accentuate the supposed difference between two human beings practically identical. Of course, it's a great advantage to women to be regarded as a race apart—an advantage which, as usual, they abuse unscrupulously."

At this juncture a change of subject seemed advisable, for I knew that Mr. Shaw's views on the unscrupulousness of women are so extreme that such a form of address as "Infamous, abandoned woman! Devil!" (to quote from *Man and Superman*) is merely, in his opinion, an affectionate remark for a man to make to a woman prior to a declaration of love.

"But if women are to have the suffrage on the same conditions as men," I began, hurriedly, "it would only benefit widows, spinsters, and wives living apart from their husbands. The great majority of married women who are serving the State by bringing up families wouldn't get a vote at all."

"Oh well, if they make marriage a disqualification, of course every self-respecting woman will refuse to marry, and the sex generally will live in a state of concubinage," remarked Mr. Shaw, airily. "That's the only logical result of such unspeakable idiocy as the exclusion of the only woman who knows what womanhood really means."

"Well, having acknowledged woman's right to the suffrage, do you consider they ought to have seats in Parliament?"

"Good heavens! what else do you want votes for? Not to give more votes for men, I hope. The suffrage is useless except as a means of getting women into Parliament. That is the whole point of the reform."

"You think they would be successful as M.P.'s?"

"Certainly! The only decent government is government by a body of men and women; but if only one sex must govern, then I should say, let it be women—put the men out! Such an enormous amount of work done is of the nature of national housekeeping, that obviously women should have a hand in it. I have sat on committees both with women and without them; and emphatically I say that there ought always to be women on public bodies. Decency demands it—simply common decency. Women at once discern evils and omissions which men never think of, especially in matters of public health, sanitation, and the like. In fact, I've found it impossible to get the most necessary things done when only men are set to do them."

This was a triumph for women indeed! I glowed, I beamed, I positively expanded with joy, on hearing such praise for the sex at which every imaginable diatribe has been hurled by men from the pre-historic ages upward; the sex which has been man's scapegoat ever since the time when the first man got out of his first scrape by blaming the only available woman! It seemed hard in such a divine moment of uplifting, when my soul felt ready to conquer worlds, to have to immediately proceed with the prosaic question in hand.

"But," I managed to articulate, still almost speechless with pride, "even though matters of national housekeeping were benefited by having a parliament composed exclusively of women, what would become of things that are obviously not their province, such as the management of the Army?"

"I don't see that armies are exclusively men's province," was the answer. "Nobody could make a worse muddle of Army matters than men have done, anyway. What is the objection to women? There are lots of women in the Army—soldiers' wives 'on the strength,' that's the official phrase. Soldiers have to be clothed and fed and nursed and mended when the enemy knocks them to bits. People imagine that women don't fight; but they do, when they get the chance, as the history of every revolution proves. Besides, what has that to do with it? I don't fight; Parliament is full of civilians who don't fight. Many of them grudge money for fighting just as much as Queen Elizabeth. I grant you she wouldn't buy powder enough to defeat the Armada, which was finished off by a lucky storm when Drake's ammunition was exhausted. But she was much better prepared than our Parliament of men were for the war in South Africa. However, I am not advocating the exclusion of men from Parliament. I only say that if you ever have the chance to choose between a parliament of men and a parliament of women—which you haven't, you never will have—choose the parliament of women. They would prove to be weak precisely where they are supposed to be strong, just as men do; because the ideal man is a woman, and vice versa."

"Then, as women's work is so important, how is it that we're not exactly desperately missed in Parliament?"

"Because the work you could do best there is never done at all now. An enormous number of things remain untouched by legislation because men don't think of them, though women would be down on them instantly. Of course, it's usually pointed out that women are not fit for political power, and ought not to be trusted with a vote because they are politically ignorant, socially prejudiced, narrow-minded, and selfish. True enough, but precisely the same is true of men!"

After the former high praise, this was somewhat of the nature of a cold douche, but I took it smiling. Then from talking of women's work, we got to district visiting, of which, to my surprise, Mr. Shaw spoke quite leniently.

"A great deal of necessary social work—necessary under existing conditions, that is—is done by district visitors. The bad side of it is that the district visitor always tries to corrupt the poor morally by trying to persuade them that poverty and humility are virtuous. They go into a filthy street, and, instead of saying to the inhabitants 'Why do you let such a place exist? Why don't you pull it down, so that a new one will have to be built?' they say that people can be just as happy in a filthy street as anywhere else, if only they'll be pious and obedient. Comfortably-off people who talk like that to the poor ought to be hanged," continued Mr. Shaw in his calmest manner, as if he were stating the most orthodox opinion in the world, "and if the district visitors had any moral sense, they would urge the people in the slums to hang them."

"To return for a minute to politics, tell me whom you consider the most able man in the present Government?"

"My dear lady, my mind doesn't work in superlatives! You might as well ask me who is the prettiest woman in England. Besides, the very idea of parliamentary government utterly excludes such an idea; the whole point of modern democratic government is that the unit of government is not an individual, but a representative committee. If you ask me which Minister could best be spared from the present Cabinet I might have something to say on the matter."

"Oh, please say it!"

"No, no; it would be invidious and certainly unkind"—this in a judicially grave manner.

"But you don't mind that, Mr. Shaw," I pleaded; "You say such dreadful things!"

"I never intentionally say anything unkind; it does not amuse me to hurt people's feelings," Mr. Shaw returned, in his most gentle voice; and, paradoxical as it may sound to call a firebrand gentle, it is nevertheless true that "G.B.S." can sometimes be the perfection of gentleness.

Next we fell to talking about *Man and Superman*, surely the most passionately discussed play of modern times.

"The reason why everybody likes *Man and Superman*," said its author, "is because it's a play entirely about sex. Sex is in itself a very important and attractive subject, and until *Man and Superman*, there had never been a play on this subject before. Oh, you may look astonished, but it's perfectly true. There's not a trace of sex in *Romeo and Juliet*, for instance. That play has never taken in a woman yet, now has it? They just talk valentines and Christmas-cards to each other, that's all—very pretty and very proper, but absolutely devoid of sex. In our ordinary romantic plays it is just the same; someone made up to represent a pretty young lady becomes engaged to someone made up to represent a nice young gentleman; and then all kinds of misunderstandings and adventures occur to separate them until it is time to go home, but there is no sex in that! There isn't a word of sex in *Major Barbara*, though there's a most interesting scene between a man and a woman—quite as effective as the declaration scene that people like so in *Man and Superman*—simply a woman talking to a man about his soul. Indeed it's the most moving scene that's ever been seen on the stage, I think. But *Man and Superman* is about sex and nothing else; and it is the overwhelming novelty of this that has won such a success for it."

I asked if Mr. Shaw was pleased with the presentation of his plays, but he adroitly put me off with a story of how Miss Lillah McCarthy came to be engaged for the part of Ann Whitefield. "Once when I was criticizing the theatres for the *Saturday Review* I went, for my sins, to an amateur performance of *Macbeth* at St. George's Hall. It was—well, the usual amateur performance of *Macbeth*; and the part of Lady Macbeth was played by a wonderful and very young lady, who, as I bluntly declared, couldn't act, couldn't walk, couldn't speak blank verse, couldn't murder Duncan, couldn't help murdering Shakespeare, couldn't do anything an actress ought to do, except give you that sensation which is all any actress need do. I advised her, in print, to spend the next ten years in learning her business, since the stage was clearly her destiny. Having written this, I naturally forgot all about it. One day into this very room there walked a beauteous lady, who said, 'The ten years are up! I've learnt my business, as you told me—now what are you going to do for me?' "

"Quite like Hilda Wangel and Solness," I murmured.

"I was never so astonished in my life," Mr. Shaw went on. "I just looked at her, gasped, and said, 'There you are—Ann Whitefield!' "

"How pleased and Ibsenish she must have felt. But before I go, tell me one thing more: what is your social 'bête-noire'?"

"Good taste!" answered Mr. Shaw, without a moment's reflection.

Notes

1. Maud Churton Braby (1875-1932) was a London novelist and feminist.

2. Seymour Hicks was a well-known London editor-manager who specialized in farces.

3. Shaw's unfortresslike home at 10 Adelphi Terrace.

SIR ALMROTH WRIGHT'S CASE AGAINST WOMAN SUFFRAGE

Bernard Shaw[1]

This book,[2] looked forward to with ecstasy since its author addressed to *The Times* the wildest letter ever published on a subject which might, in view of the antiquity of his view of it, almost be defined as Lovely Woman, could be described as "unexpurgated" only by a particularly innocent and, at bottom, rather chivalrous Irishman. The word is no more than Sir Almroth Wright's apology for not accepting women as angels. The book may be left on the drawing-room table in country house and parsonage without misgiving.

The advocates of Votes for Women, confronted with it, will find themselves in the unhappy position of the journalists in Rudyard Kipling's story. They, it will be remembered, saw the sea serpent. At first they thought they had the chance of their lives; then, overwhelmed by the hugeness of the chance, they dropped their pens and were silent. Their luck was overdone: the real sea serpent was incredible. Sir Almroth Wright is too easy a victim. He offers the Suffragist so many openings that she will, like Achilles surveying Hector, be unable to make up her mind as to which particular spot she will stab. Finally, she will be disarmed by the manifest inhumanity of hitting a defenceless antagonist at all.

Fortunately, it is easy to land Sir Almroth on the flat of his back without doing him any vital harm. He is an intellectual man; and intellect is still so new a toy in evolution that those who possess it are often more interested in their intellectual processes than in their conclusions. Sir Almroth loves to show off his intellectual method, to explain it, to find new names for its stages. If he makes a mistake, he makes it definitely, precisely, and consequently detectably. He does not, as an English writer would, get into a muddle from sheer dread of finding himself out or giving himself away. With admirable honesty and splendid lucidity, he gives himself away on toast done to a turn and buttered with opsonin. He positively guides your finger to the spot at which a flick of your nail will bring down his house of cards in irretrievable ruin.

For example:

> My reasonings have the sanction which attaches to them as based upon premisses arrived at by the method of *diacritical judgment*. . . . When I venture to attempt a generalisation about woman, I endeavour to recall to mind without distinction all the different women I have encountered, and to extricate from my impressions what was common to all—omitting from consideration (except only when I am dealing specifically with these) all plainly abnormal women.

And here is what Sir Almroth extricates as the specifically Feminine, as Woman, Lovely Woman:

> Woman's mind in appraising a statement attends primarily to the mental images which it evokes, and only secondarily—and sometimes not at all—to what is predicated in the statement. It is over-influenced by individual instances; arrives at conclusions on incomplete evidence; has a very imperfect sense of proportion; accepts the congenial as true, and rejects the uncongenial as false; takes the imaginary which is desired for the reality, and treats the undesired reality which is out of sight as nonexistent—building up for itself in this way, when biased by predilections and aversions, a very unreal picture of the external world.

In short, exactly like Man's mind, which is just the fact that Sir Almroth, this time not sufficiently diacritical, thought he was going to disprove. And the criticism is only the echo of that which the most serious woman in Shakespear's human comedy levels at "Man, proud Man, drest in a little brief authority."

There is something staggering in the fact that a writer of Sir Almroth Wright's quality, capable of so penetrating a clinical description of the political disabilities of mankind—penetrating almost to the heights of rhetoric and poetry—should be ludicrously blind to the sex of the patient. Shakespear, speaking of himself and Sir Almroth and me and the rest of us as glassy essences and angry apes, is bitter, but within his rights, and entitled, alas! to the verdict; but what sort of figure would Shakespear have cut had he added:

You must understand, gentlemen, that these remarks are confined strictly to Ann Hathaway, and that I, the Masculine Male Manly Man, am obviously purely intellectual and aniconic in appraising statements; am never over-influenced by individual instances; never arrive at conclusions on incomplete evidence; have an absolutely perfect sense of proportion; cannot be tricked into accepting the congenial as true or denying the uncongenial as false; do not believe in things merely because I wish they were true, or ignore things because I wish they did not exist; but live, godlike, in full consciousness of the external world as it really is, unbiased by predilections and aversions; for such, gentlemen, is the happy effect of the physiological attachments of Man's mind.

Witness it, ye pages of masculine history, ye halfpenny popular men's papers, ye twopenny and sixpenny unpopular men's papers, ye *Church Timeses* and lay *Timeses* and *Spectators* and *Lancets*, ye general elections and by-elections, ye wars and rumors of wars, ye Lords and Commons, ye man-made Cases, expurgated and unexpurgated, for and against Woman Suffrage and all other earthly controversies! Witness it, above all, the reviews which are even now appearing in our most respectable organs applauding all this blazing absurdity, the familiar symptom of ordinary sex-conceit, as a serious contribution to a serious question!

The truth is, it is not a contribution to the question of Woman Suffrage at all; but as a criticism of the political competence of mankind it has its points. It is impossible, in the face of history and contemporary facts, to deny that Man as he exists at present is what Sir Almroth Wright calls Woman, and that even when you give him a liberal education and a scientific profession, and he distinguishes himself in it by exceptional ability, his political and social views are not only womanish in Sir Almroth's most invidious use of the term, but often flatly childish. The case is, indeed, more serious than he thinks; for he is happy in the delusion that we have in the specifically masculine intellect and character a refuge from the follies and errors of the specifically feminine character, whereas there is no evidence that the qualities of intellect and character needed for political organization are any more specifically sexual than digestion or blood circulation or cell structure. Sir Almroth Wright explaining that his mother and his wife are inferior to himself is only the pot calling the kettle black. The utmost that real science can allow him is that there are specifically human qualities of intellect and character; and in conceding this it must not be forgotten that so able and politically experienced a genius as Swift ended by declaring that the evolutionary progress from horse to men was all to the bad. The discovery of evolution has completely knocked on the head the grandfatherly conceit, which Sir Almroth would call grandmotherly, that Man and Brute are essentially and totally different, and that Man differs always in the superior direction.

Perhaps the quaintest thing Sir Almroth sets down is his gibe at the man whom he calls "the complemental male," who "solemnly draws himself up and asks, 'Are you aware, sir, that you are insulting my wife?' " Now it may be conceded that any man who draws himself solemnly up deserves to be let ludicrously down; but he may have a just grievance for all that. Doctors and divines are much given to drawing themselves up solemnly when laymen question their omniscience and infallibility; but this does not prove that the layman is always in the right on the point at issue. As a matter of fact, Sir Almroth Wright does insult everyman's wife and everyman's mother, including his own; and "the unexpurgated case" in his title means simply the frankly insulting case. If a man tells a woman that she is relatively to himself an inferior beast, he insults her. Mr. Sandow can, without insulting me, tell me that he is stronger than I am muscularly; but if he tells me that I am a fool— and this is, in one word, what Sir Almroth Wright calls every woman—he insults me, and can only put himself right by evidence as incontrovertible as that of a spring grip or a set of heavy weights in the muscular instance. Sir Almroth attempts no proof: he simply points to the common experience of the world that we are all fools. Woman will not be satisfied with that: she will ask "Am I a bigger fool than you?" If he answers "No," his case falls to the ground. If "Yes," a flatter insult cannot be conceived.

Lack of space makes it impossible to deal with Sir Almroth's elaboration of his case. So much the better, perhaps; for a great deal of it shews only how incredibly thoughtless and unobservant an exceptionally gifted man can be. In his worst pages the Breadwinner struts unashamed; claiming that his wife does nothing and he everything, because he intercepts her wages and can spend them in drink with impunity. Sir Almroth firmly believes that when the landlord pays the taxes the tenant escapes them; that the supertaxed Nut maintains a State on which the charwoman is an ungrateful parasite; that one of the triumphs of the Male intellect was the discovery that the way to deal with sweating is to Let It Alone (alas for my sex! he is right there only it was hardly a triumph, was it?); that John Stuart Mill was an uxorious gaby who invented the Economic Man; that nobody should have a vote unless they have sufficient physical force to take what they want, and thereby make the vote superfluous; and heaven knows what other worn-out reach-me-downs of the like quality. It is all quite amazing from a man so interesting, so stimulating, so original in his own department.

It is noteworthy that in his criticism of the modern expensive woman and his formulation of the claim for the seclusion of all women on the ground that men are so susceptible that they cannot work when there is a woman within sight, he has been anticipated by Mr. Granville Barker in *The Madras House* and Mr. H.G. Wells in *Marriage;* and that whilst the playwright and the romancer are saturated with the scientific spirit, Sir Almroth Wright is romantic, fact-proof, whimsical, quarrelsome, and jealous to an extent that will certainly provoke Mrs. Fawcett to quiet scorn and Mrs. Pankhurst to withering contempt. My own conviction is that Sir Almroth Wright comes to grief on this subject because he had several brothers and no sisters. He is still afraid of women, still unable to conceive that they belong to his own species, still by turns irritated and attracted by these strange monsters. This theory of his attitude may be erroneous; but at least it is strictly scientific; and the facts are beyond dispute.

The book may do some good, after all. John Stuart Mill certainly was a little uxorious; and it is as well to remind the uxorious that women have all the faults of men, and that Votes for Women will no more achieve the millennium than Votes for Manufacturers did in 1832 or Votes for Working Men in 1867 and 1885. Above all, it may help to effect a reduction to absurdity of Sex Recrimination, that Duel of Sex in which Ibsen and Strindberg were such mighty opposites. It was an inevitable phase; let us hope that it will end over Sir Almroth Wright's book in frank confession and good-humoured laughter.

Notes

1. First published as "Sir Almroth Wright's Polemic" in the *New Statesman,* 18 October 1913, and reprinted as "Sir Almroth Wright's Case against Woman Suffrage"—a penny pamphlet issued by the Irishwomen's Suffrage Federation, Dublin. Reprinted here with the permission of *New Statesman.*

2. *The Unexpurgated Case Against Woman Suffrage.* By Sir Almroth E. Wright, M.D., F.R.S. Constable. 2s. 6d. net. [Shaw's note.] Sir Almroth Wright was Shaw's prototype for Sir Colenso Ridgeon in *The Doctor's Dilemma* (1906), and during the First World War commanding officer of a British Army hospital in France. Despite the tenor of Shaw's review he and Wright were close personal friends.

WHY ALL WOMEN ARE PECULIARLY FITTED TO BE GOOD VOTERS

Bernard Shaw

The *New York American* on 21 April 1907 carried the text of this speech Shaw delivered on why women should be allowed to vote.

I do not wish to be considered in this article as the supporter or representative of any political party. England has a Liberal party; it has a Conservative party; it has a Labor party; it has an Irish party. Unfortunately it has not yet got a Shaw party. If it had, that party would be uncompromisingly on the side of giving the suffrage to women, and I can promise that should they get it the House of Commons will be quite the most amusing Legislature on the face of the globe.

I think I must take my stand as a representative more or less of literature, a profession in which there is no question about the ability of women to stand side by side in all branches of the art with men. I have purposely brought in the subject of literature because I want to explain one literary utterance which I am sure has been greatly misunderstood.

When Mr. Dickinson's bill was about to be discussed in the House of Commons the Times, suddenly feeling that the masculine opposition to that bill was not quite so convincing as it might be, appealed to a very eminent literary woman to come to the rescue of the Times. And the Times has had to do that on several subjects besides women's suffrage, and it has found it quite worth its while to do so. Mrs. Humphry Ward wrote an extremely amusing letter, in which she pointed out that the best arguments for men to use against giving the suffrage to women were the political ignorance of women, their restriction to their own affairs, their narrow outlook on life.

Now, Mrs. Humphry Ward is one of the most able public women in London. Mrs. Humphry Ward has enlarged the whole sphere of her national life by inventing the vacation school, which no man apparently had ever thought of, and which is going to be in the future really the only important part of school life.

She did that by an extremely able piece of public organization, by which she eventually imposed her ideas on the whole of London. Well, Mrs. Humphry Ward quite clearly cannot have meant seriously that women were incapable of public affairs. The question is, What did she mean and what was she doing?

I will tell you. She was getting at my sex. Every single thing that Mrs. Humphry Ward said in that letter about women was equally true of men, and I am bound to say that the letter made such an impression on me that I began seriously to consider whether I had any right to advocate the extension of the suffrage to women, instead of endeavoring to form an active society for the purpose of taking it away from men.

I have decided on the whole not to take that course. If you do not give the suffrage to men or to women I do not exactly see whom you are going to give it to. I quite grant that men and women are very little capable of governing either their own affairs or the affairs of a nation, and if I could find any superior class of beings to entrust the government to I would entrust the government to it. As it is, I think we must put up with what we have got, and that is human nature.

And human nature is human nature. It is not masculine nature or feminine nature. It is human nature. The country is not governed and never will be governed by the mass of its population. What is meant by modern democracy is not the government of the country by the whole people, but the government of the country by the consent of the whole people. You give a man a vote, not because you believe that he is a very politically able person, but because you believe he has intelligence to know when he is uncomfortable.

And, therefore, you may make up your minds that exactly the same arguments that go to give the suffrage for men go to give the suffrage for women.

Now I am sorry to say that the opposition to women's suffrage has brought into existence in England the most entirely disgraceful, the most absolutely contemptible form of conservatism.

I am not now speaking against the conservative party. I am just as much against conservatism as I am against liberalism. Many conservative positions I can respect. But there is a new sort of conservatism coming in which is quite new to me and which is absolutely dastardly beyond anything I can express, because the new sort of conservative does not come forward frankly and say that he opposes such and such a measure of reform, but he says, "I will hear nothing of that measure of reform."

I go further than that. If that sort of conservative had existed in the year 1832 when the great Reform Bill was passed, what would that man have said? Would he have taken the side of the old Tories who believed in the government of England by their country gentlemen, who were with De Quincey when he said boldly: "What nobler class can you have to govern than your country gentlemen?" He would have said: "No, I am an advocate not of this miserable half and half measure which enfranchises the middle class.

"I am in favor of adult suffrage, and until you bring in a bill for adult suffrage, I shall not vote for the reform. I shall stand uncompromisingly against this with my exalted and extreme principles."

And if he had lived in 1887 when a further extension of the franchise was granted, he would have been in exactly the same position. He would have said "Don't give it to the working class. Why should you enfranchise certain members of the working class? Why should you enfranchise two-thirds, when you know one-third would be left out in the cold?

"Let us have down-to-the-bottom adult suffrage or nothing." Now, I am going to tell you what these new Conservatives will say when you offer them adult suffrage. They will say "Adult suffrage! Are the children not to have votes?

"Look at the sufferings of children! Look at the number in industrial employment! Are not children the most important part of the community? Are they not at least as politically intelligent as the majority of grown-up persons in this country?" "Adult suffrage" they will say. "Perish the thought! We will oppose it tooth and nail until you give us humanity suffrage."

And if you took them at their word and offered them humanity suffrage they would complain because you did not give a vote to the cat. Don't be taken in by this trick. No single political measure in England or in any other country can ever be passed that goes right to the logical extremity of the theory which it represents. The thing is entirely impossible and every honest politician knows it.

The man who won't give you an installment does not mean to pay you at all.

I offer this test of the really honest supporter of giving the franchise to women: Ask him or ask her, "If a bill were brought in to-morrow giving the vote only to one woman in the country and that woman a member of the highest and most exclusive class, that woman the queen, would you vote for that bill?"

I would vote for that bill, and anybody who would not vote for that bill, whether it was to give one vote to the Queen or one vote to one washerwoman, will never be a practical politician unless he or she is really not in favor of extending the franchise at all, which I am afraid is the real reason at the bottom of this opposition.

There are a great number of questions, which I have not time to deal with in this article, which absolutely do not exist in England, because women have no direct political existence there at all. There is a whole range of things which have never been mentioned in any newspaper, which are not referred to in any programme which people have not got in their minds, and are not related to politics at all, but which are of vital importance, which would spring into life and spring into the very front of political warfare if only the influence of women began to be felt directly through the vote.

Now, I will give you one single example of that. In England women are not supposed to be directly paid. Married women are not supposed to be directly paid for their labor. The money is given to the man and the man is supposed to hand it on to the woman because she keeps the house for him, bears his children, brings up his children.

Nevertheless she is not paid by the community directly for that, but the money is paid to the man and that fact is recognized, because the man is always given account and yet there is no law in this country to prevent a man, having got his wages and having got the woman's wages—higher wages than women on that express as part of his wages—to prevent him [from] going and drinking [away] all that money and robbing his wife and children.

The man who puts his hand into my pocket and steals five shillings can be punished at once and punished severely. The man who puts his hand into his wife's pocket and steals ten shillings does so absolutely and with impunity. Now, remember, there is another side to this. It is also true that a woman can take wages that belong to her children and drink them if she likes, and she can do that with impunity.

If once you introduce injustice, evil is never left on one side alone. It all comes from the fact that women and men have never been trained by a political constitution to deal honestly with one another.

Now, since the old days of the agitation for women's suffrage, matters have advanced in a very remarkable way, because there is a country called New Zealand, which in many ways I believe to be a country extraordinarily typical of the English middle class, and in New Zealand the suffrage has been given to women. Well, adult suffrage, and I think that I have already dealt pretty sufficiently with that question: but if you suppose we are not quite in a hurry to get adult suffrage—if we can get it for all women—then naturally your mistake.

But if adult suffrage is going to be used to be put in the way of the women's instalment that we are likely to get, then—as I have pointed out, that is not an honest use of it. Does anybody suspect me of being ill-disposed toward adult suffrage if we can get it? I think I heard people say "yes." Some one says I am unfair.

Who am I that I should be fair? Here is a gentleman who says I am unfair. Pray, on which side is the unfairness? On my side, who want to get votes for women or his side, who want to put back the movement for women's suffrage from purely academic causes, merely on the theory of his own mind. Now, I do not know whether this is true that every adult woman in New Zealand has got the vote.

I am very glad if it is so. They are very much better off in that case than every adult man in this country, and yet I presume the gentleman who calls me unfair does not want to take away the vote from men in England because every man does not have the vote.

Now, look at the difference between England and New Zealand. Suppose the very able representative of New Zealand in this country, the agent-general, Mr. William Pember Reeves, were to come up to me and say "Your wife has got no character." Well, now, what should I say to Mr. Reeves? I should say, having regard for the fact that we are both sedentary and peaceful sort of men, "My dear Reeves, you are not yourself when you say that. I am sure you don't really mean it."

And if he said again, "Your wife has no character," I should say to him, "If you say that again I shall get extremely angry." I should say, "Reeves, if you say that again I shall tell your wife." Well, there is no danger of Mr. Reeves doing that to me; but he could come up to me and level this insult at me, "Shaw, your wife has not got a vote."

You will observe when I say that there's a sort of hesitation in your mind. You have not yet realized that that is an insult. You have not realized that the vote is withheld from woman because she is said to be an inferior person, a person who is said to be unworthy of the vote.

I know that many men frankly take up that position. I have a great appreciation of the man who stands up solidly and who says:

"I am a man. I am a broad-chested manly man. I am a lord of creation. I claim my divine right to govern this petticoated thing, this inferior person, with no mind, no knowledge of politics, and of very little use in the world except to make my home comfortable." I can understand that man, and I can enjoy a man who is really a gorgeous idiot.

I like men to be thorough in their absurdity and folly. I even have a sort of liking for the man who comes up to me and says: "After all, you know, think of Michael Angelo and Beethoven. Has any woman ever produced great works of art like them?"

I reply: "My friend, have you ever produced any great works of art?"

I think there is a great deal of sense in the position he takes up. If any government will bring in a bill to-morrow restricting the franchise to persons who have produced great works of art, then I think I shall support that bill. A great many women will have votes under that and the majority of the ladies and gentlemen who are now opposing the franchise for women will be disfranchised by that bill.

Now, the last thing I want to say to you is something which, perhaps, may not have occurred to Englishmen and Englishwomen. They belong to a free country, and what I am going to say to you now is something that would, perhaps, occur only to a man who, like myself, belongs to a country which is not free. The real curse of the nation which is not politically free is that all its deepest spiritual energies, all its political activity, all its philosophic activity—all the very best that it has of human activity, is taken up in the struggle to regain that political liberty which never should be denied to any country or to any nation.

If you want to know why in a country so clever as Ireland you find such a terrible behind-handedness with regard to all those great waves of the human spirit which sweep from time to time over Europe and over the whole world—why things that you are discussing and exciting yourselves about have not yet been heard of in Ireland—I shall tell you the reason.

It is because all the men in Ireland, all the best spirit in Ireland, are together occupied in the struggle to obtain the political freedom of Ireland: and all that energy which might be placed at the service of the world, and might be placed at the service of England, is being taken up with the mere question of political freedom. Now I do not ask you to agree with me on that subject, but I am going to ask you to make an application. Remember that there is in England at present—a very wonderful contingent of women of extraordinary ability, of women who are at present doing first rate work on royal commissions, who in all sorts of social movements have been showing what women can do when they lay their mind to it.

Remember, there is a theory in England that the House of Commons consists of 670 of the cleverest and best men in the country. Well, let me tell you that the House of Commons never will consist of the 670—never as long as it consists exclusively of men— absolutely the best and cleverest people in the country, for some of its best are women.

I will undertake if any government approaches me on the subject and asks me whether, if it empties its benches a little under what they are at present, the seats could be replaced with better women—I will undertake to do it. But the difficulty is that almost all that talent that women have now, instead of being applied to the solution of our social problems—those problems which concern both sexes alike—is wasted in this agitation—an agitation which ought to be utterly unnecessary, because women are struggling to get the franchise.

By giving them the franchise England will set free an immense and beneficial flood of political and social energy which is now being taken up by this question. It will get that question off their minds—a question which in any really intelligent country ought to have been settled a century ago.

Sweep that one difficulty away. Give women, particularly able women, something else to do than going about on platforms clamoring for this right, which should never have been withheld or denied them, and then you will get a united force of both sexes tackling these social problems, without the solution of which we shall be plunged in the ruin that has overtaken other civilizations in history which have towered in the past. You want the help of women in that.

As far as I have been working on these problems in my lifetime, I have always been working with women, on the same objects as women, and I have always found that their help, their assistance and point of view were absolutely indispensable.

I deny that any social problem will ever be satisfactorily solved unless women have their due share in getting it solved.

Let us get this obstacle of the political slavery of women out of the way and then we shall see all set to work on the problems—both sexes together with a will.

THE ROOT OF THE WHITE SLAVE TRAFFIC

Bernard Shaw

Shaw worked out his ideas about the economic causes of prostitution and about society's collective guilt and responsibility in a variety of ways beginning with his publication of the *Quintessence of Ibsenism* and its section on the "Womanly Woman" in 1891. In his earliest plays, the "Unpleasant Plays" *Widowers' Houses* (1892) and *Mrs Warren's Profession* (1894), he developed his thesis dramatically, and in 1912 he published this article in *The Awakener* [I (1), 16 November].

The fundamental condition of the existence of this traffic is that society must be so organized that a large class of women are more highly paid and better treated as prostitutes than they would be as respectable women, and that people who organize the labor of prostitutes make larger profits than those who organize the labor of respectable women. In other words, society must be like English society at the present day, where the heroine of Tom Hood's Bridge of Sighs is much better off than the heroine of his Song of the Shirt, and, as a matter of fact, neither jumps off Waterloo Bridge nor has to work two hours to make 3½d. And until you change this condition of society, and secure to every respectable woman a sufficient wage for a decent life with reasonable hours of labor, you will never get rid of the White Slave traffic.

You may refuse to be convinced of this, and say that we shall soon see whether we cannot get rid of the rascals who live on the profits of prostitution by flogging them soundly under the new Act. Do not deceive yourself: most of those who are living on the profits of prostitution will not be flogged: on the contrary, they are already among the most indignant advocates of flogging. They are ladies and gentlemen, clergymen, bishops, judges, Members of Parliament, highly connected ladies leading society in Cathedral towns, peers and peeresses, and pillars of solid middle-class Puritanism. These people have shares in industrial enterprises which employ women and girls. Thousands of these women and girls get wages which are insufficient to support them, and are treated with less personal respect than any prostitute. If a woman applying for employment complains of the low wage and asks for more she is told that if she will not take it others will. If she asks how she is to live on it she is told that others contrive to live on it. They manage to make it up somehow, she hears. The man is not told that. The somehow is a somehow that applies to women and not to men. The somehow, in short, is on the streets. Of course, she is not told this, because many of the girls and women are quite respectable. They are living with their families, and are saved from the streets by their husbands' or their fathers' wages. But there are always orphans and widows and girls from the country and abroad who have no families and no husbands; and these must submit to the blackest misery that a slum garret and an income of from eightpence to a shilling a day can bring to a lonely, despised, shabby, dirty, underfed woman, or else add to their wages by prostitution. Thus the woman's strength and energy are maintained by what she earns in the street, and used in making dividends for rich shareholders who clamor to have public attention distracted from their complicity by the flogging of a few souteneurs, who are always described as foreigners. But when these souteneurs take a house for their purposes, and offer rents which are high because the neighborhood is a favorable one for the White Slave traffic, do they find any difficulty in getting one? And does anyone ever propose to flog the landlord? Can the Ecclesiastical Commissioners, or any of the rest of our London landlords, show clean hands in this matter? And would a bill for flogging them have much chance of passing through Parliament?

And you, humble reader, who are neither a shareholder nor a landlord, do you thank God that you are guiltless in this matter? Take care. The first man flogged under the Act may turn on you and say, "God shall smite thee, thou whited wall." The wages of prostitution are stitched into your buttonholes and into your blouse, pasted into your matchboxes and your boxes of pins, stuffed into your mattress, mixed with the paint on your walls, and stuck between the joints of your water-pipes. The very glaze on your basin and teacup has in it the lead poison that you offer to the decent woman as the reward of honest labor, whilst the procuress is offering chicken and champagne. Flog other people until you are black in the face and they are red in the back. You will not cheat the Recording Angel into putting down your debts to the wrong account.

And please remark that every additional power you give to the policeman to harry these victims of yours increases the power of the organizer and exploiter of prostitution over the prostitute. When you are robbed and beaten and bullied you call the police: and they protect you. But the policeman himself may bully and beat the prostitute: he may tear her fine clothes to rags and drag her through the mud, and twist her arms almost out of their sockets, and then have her sent to prison on a charge of disorder or solicitation if she annoys him with appeals for protection and if she refuses to share her gains with him. In every police force in the world there are men who do this systematically: for though the policeman may be no worse than the rest of us, you cannot find eighteen thousand angels in London for twenty-four shillings a week to exercise powers which we cut off the head of a king sooner than entrust to him. This is the secret of the terrible power of the White Slave agent over his victim. Why does she cling to him in spite of all she suffers at his hands? Simply because he can always bring her to her knees by threatening to set the police on her. She is far more afraid of the policeman than of the souteneur; for a police magistrate might take her word against a souteneur's; and if she defends herself by main force against his violence he has only his own hands to help him and may get the worst of it; but nobody will take her word against a policeman's; and to assault him is to have to face the whole forces of the State and its prisons as well as the personal vengeance of the officer. The police cell is the only room in which you cannot throw up the window and call for help. That is why, with law and order and police and clergy reigning from the Ural mountains to the island of Achill, women are dragged through Europe by White Slave traffickers more helplessly than they could be through the heart of Africa or the deserts of Arabia. There are plenty of decent, honest policemen, fathers of families, who would like to get the girls off the streets if they could. What do you empower them to offer to the girls? A pious refuge for the fallen. That is, a place which is as likely as not to combine in a single establishment the rapacity of the sweater's don, the cruelty of the prison, and the moral reprobation that makes self-respect impossible. From the frying-pan into the fire is not much of a rescue.

As to the flogging from which all our fools expect so much, it will certainly give a lively stimulus to the White Slave traffic. That traffic makes a good deal of money out of flogging, which is a well-established form of vice. White Slaves make money for themselves and their employers by allowing men to flog them. Whenever a flogging is described in the papers they have a rush of custom. The literature of their trade is full of flogging. Men actually pay women to flog them. In the last epidemic of prostitution in London, when brothels boldly advertized themselves in all directions as massage establishments, the "treatments" always included "Russian Flagellation," which was impudently announced on posters. The new Act will produce another epidemic: and it will also drive the whole business of direct procuration into the hands of women, who are not to be flogged under the Act; though any unemployed laborer whose wife, in desperation at the children's hunger, solicits a man in the street, can be flogged under it. The action of the House of Commons was not sane legislation: it was an explosion of blackguardism, excusable in a bargee whose daughter has been abducted by a White Slaver, but appalling in the rulers of a civilized empire. The subject they were dealing with infected them: and they fell below the level of the men they were legislating to flog.

If a man doubts that this is the real secret and nature of flogging legislation, let him ask himself this question. Why, out of all the many methods by which pain can be inflicted on a criminal, is this particular method chosen? You can hurt a man with an electric brush worse than with any instrument of flagellation. There are intolerable methods of torture actually in use in some American prisons rather than face which I myself would take any flogging that public opinion would stand. Flogging is not more deterrent: on the contrary the same men get flogged for the same offence again and again. Why, then, is flogging chosen? Why do people frantically keep protesting that it is the only punishment that these people fear—that it put down garotting—that its opponents are sentimentalists—any absurd and ten-times-disproved falsehood put forward recklessly in the agonies of a ridiculous longing for this relic of the Cities of the Plain? The answer is obvious. The Act is a final triumph of the vice it pretends to repress.

There is one remedy, and one alone, for the White Slave traffic. Make it impossible, by the enactment of a Minimum Wage law and by proper provision for the unemployed, for any woman to be forced to choose between prostitution and penury, and the White Slaver will have no more power over the daughters of laborers, artisans, and clerks than he (or, under the new Act, she) has over the wives of bishops. I wrote my play, *Mrs Warren's Profession*, nearly thirty years ago to shew this. Queen Victoria's Lord Chamberlain refused to let my play be performed, though he gave his blessing to many a play that brought golden profits to the White Slave traffic. The royal shield still protects the traffic from my exposure. An American newspaper, subsequently convicted of making large sums by White Slave advertisements, got up an agitation against the play in New York, and very nearly succeeded in suppressing it there too. Our whole commercial system, rooted as it is in cheap female labor, instinctively shudders when the truth is told, and tries to shame, or bully, or buy off the truth teller. But the facts are too strong for them: and just as the Flogging Act advertises the White Slave market, the Lord Chamberlain and his American allies advertize me. It remains to be seen which will prevail: my solution or society's dissolution.

VII

BIBLIOGRAPHY

A BIBLIOGRAPHICAL CHECKLIST

Lucile Kelling Henderson

As extensive as this bibliography is, it is by no means complete for "Shaw and Woman." With the early discovery of a wealth of material, the bibliography soon became selective, much as a retrospective exhibit is selective. Some items are admittedly slight but seemed pertinent for reasons I can only hope were not too subjective. Although I had set out to omit all reviews, I found I had to include some because they had an interpretation or a particular viewpoint worth mentioning. To some extent I have tried to indicate the breadth of Shaw's female acquaintances, not solely his friends and enemies. It has been amusing to notice how many "society" women as well as actresses and other professionals were anxious to include him among their "names." I have included only a few of the former, but they are typical, I think.

Works by Shaw

"As Bernard Shaw Sees Woman." *New York Times Magazine,* 19 June 1972, pp. 1-2.
"Aside." *Myself and My Friends,* by Lillah McCarthy. New York: Dutton, 1933; London: Butterworth, 1934. Also includes many letters.
"Bernard Shaw Advises Clara Butt" (letter). *Daily Chronicle* (London), 29 June 1928.
Bernard Shaw and Mrs. Patrick Campbell: Their Correspondence. Edited by Alan Dent. London: Gollancz, 1952; New York: Knopf, 1952.
"Bernard Shaw on American Women." *Cosmopolitan* 40 (December 1905), 247-48. Reprinted in *Independent Shavian* 10 (Winter 1971/72): 1-5.
"Bernard Shaw (who is eighty-three today) Says We Will Have Peace." Interview with E.M. Salzer in the *Daily Express* (London), 26 July 1939, p. 8.

Bodley Head Bernard Shaw. Collected Plays with their Prefaces. 7 vols. London: Max Reinhardt, 1970-74; New York: Dodd, Mead, 1975 (as *Complete Plays with their Prefaces*). Especially, the strong woman in *Captain Brassbound's Conversion;* woman the hunter in *Man and Superman* and *The Village Wooing;* a parody of the "modern" woman in *Too True To Be Good;* the strong-minded, intelligent woman in *Androcles and the Lion, Heartbreak House* and the *Inca of Perusalem;* the "wonderfully zany woman" in *The Music Cure;* and for these and other reasons: *The Apple Cart, Back to Methuselah, Candida, John Bull's Other Island, Major Barbara, The Millionairess, Misalliance, Mrs Warren's Profession, O'Flaherty V.C., Press Cuttings, Pygmalion, Saint Joan, The Simpleton of the Unexpected Isles, Widowers' Houses* and others.

Collected Letters, 1874-1897. Edited by Dan H. Laurence. New York: Dodd, Mead, 1965, London: Reinhardt, 1965.

Collected Letters, 1898-1910. Edited by Dan H. Laurence. New York: Dodd, Mead, 1972.

Dear Liar: A Comedy of Letters, adapted by Jerome Kilty from the Correspondence of Bernard Shaw and Mrs. Patrick Campbell. New York: Dodd, Mead, 1960.

"Duse and Bernhardt." *Saturday Review,* 15 June 1895. Reprinted in *Collected Works,* and in *The English Dramatic Critics,* edited by James Agate. New York: Hill and Wang, 1958, pp. 241-47.

"Ellen Terry." *Pen Portraits and Reviews.* London: Constable, 1949, pp. 165-71. Reprinted from *Neue Freie Presse* (Vienna), 24 December 1905.

Ellen Terry and Bernard Shaw: A Correspondence. Edited by Christopher St. John; Preface by Shaw. London: Constable, 1931; New York: Putnam, 1931; London: Reinhardt & Evans, 1949, 1951.

"Epistle Dedicatory to Arthur Bingham Walkley." Preface to *Man and Superman.* New York: Wm. H. Wise, 1930. (*Plays,* vol. X).

Florence Farr, Bernard Shaw, W.B. Yeats: Letters. Edited by Clifford Bax. Dublin: Cuala, 1941; London: Home & Van Thal, 1946.

"Forcible Feeding." *New Statesman,* 12 April 1913, pp. 8-9.

"Foreword." *My Apprenticeship,* by Beatrice Webb. 2 vols. Harmondsworth, Middlesex: Penguin, 1938.

"Freedom and the State." *The Road to Equality: Ten Unpublished Lectures and Essays, 1884-1918,* by Bernard Shaw. Edited by Louis Crompton. Boston: Beacon Press, 1971, pp. 37-54.

"G.B.S. and A Suffragist." Interview by Maud Churton Braby. *Tribune* (London), 12 March, 1906, p. 3.

"GBS and the Fair Sex" (quotations) with introduction by T.C.F. Lowry. *Ladies Home Journal* 81 (January 1964): 128+.

"G.B.S. on Women" (Quotations). *Vogue* 127 (June 1956): 53.

"G.B. Shaw's Advice to the New York Vice Society." *Edna: The Girl of the Street,* by Alfred Kreymborg. New York: Guido Bruno, 1919.

The Intelligent Woman's Guide to Socialism, Capitalism, Sovietism and Fascism. London: Constable, 1949.

Letters from George Bernard Shaw to Miss Alma Murray (Mrs. Alfred Forman). Edinburgh, Printed for private circulation, 1927.

"Letters to Dame Laurentia McLachlan." *In a Great Tradition,* by the Benedictines of Stanbrook. London: Murray, 1956, pp. 231-78.

"Logic of the Hunger Strike." *Living Age* 307 (2 October 1920): 30-31.

"The Love Letters of Bernard Shaw." *Esquire* 49 (April 1958): 64-65. Reprinted under title: "Letters to Alice Lockett," in *The Armchair Esquire,* edited by Arnold Gingrich and L. Rust Hills. New York: Putnam, 1958, pp. 331-39.

"The Menace of the Leisured Woman." *Time and Tide* 8 (4 February 1927): 106-7. Also in *Platform and Pulpit,* edited by Dan H. Laurence. New York: Hill and Wang, 1961, pp. 168-71.

"Mr. G.B. Shaw on Women's Rights." *Manchester Guardian,* 4 November 1933, p. 16.

"Morality and Birth Control." *Physical Culture,* July 1919. Reprinted in *Independent Shavian* 10 (Spring 1972): 33-36.

More Letters from George Bernard Shaw to Miss Alma Murray (Mrs. Alfred Forman). Edinburgh, Printed for private circulation, 1932.

My Dear Dorothea: A Practical System of Moral Education for Females, Embodied in a Letter to a Young Person of that Sex. London: Phoenix House, 1956; New York: Vanguard, 1956.

"My Mother and Her Relatives." See *Sixteen Self Sketches.*

"The Need for Expert Opinion in Sexual Reform." *Sexual Reform Congress, London . . . 1929.* London: World League for Sexual Reform, 1930, pp. 432-37. Also in *Platform and Pulpit,* edited by Dan H. Laurence. New York: Hill and Wang, 1961, pp. 200-207.

"The Nun and the Dramatist: Dame Laurentia McLachlan and George Bernard Shaw" (with text of their letters; preface), by a Nun of Stanbrook. *Cornhill Magazine* 168 (Summer 1956): 415-58. Also in part in *Atlantic Monthly* 196 (July/August 1956): 27-34, 69-76.

"On Being a Lady in High Comedy." *Shaw on Theatre.* Edited by E.J. West. New York: Hill and Wang, 1959, p. 80. See also Dukes, Ashley.

"The Play and Its Author." *Souvenir Program* for Brieux, *La Femme Seule.* London: The Women's Theatre, 1913, pp. 10-12.

The R.A.D.A. Graduates' Keepsake & Counsellor. A gift from the Council. 2d ed. London: Printed for private circulation by the Royal Academy of Dramatic Art, 1948.

"Redistribution of Income." *The Road to Equality: Ten Unpublished Lectures and Essays, 1884-1918, by Bernard Shaw.* Edited by Louis Crompton. Boston: Beacon Press, 1971, pp. 195-278.

"The Rights of Women Now." *News Chronicle* (London), 17 November 1943.

"The Root of the White Slave Traffic." *Awakener* 1, no. 1 (16 November 1912): 7-8.

"Saint Joan." *Listener* 15 (3 June 1931): 921-22, 947.

Shaw: An Autobiography, 1856-1898, selected from his writings by Stanley Weintraub. New York: Weybright & Talley, 1969; London: Max Reinhardt, 1970. pp. 163-71, *et passim.* Also *Shaw: An Autobiography, 1898-1950.* New York: Weybright & Talley, 1970; London: Max Reinhardt, 1971, pp. 46-48, 131-34, *et passim.*

"Shaw versus Roosevelt on Birth Control" (letters). *World Today* 46 (September 1925): 845-50.

"Shaw's Letters to Ellen Terry." *The Literary Repository* (Catalogue of J. Stevens Cox, Beaminster, England), No. 2 (1954). Two new letters.

"Sir Almroth Wright's Polemics." *New Statesman,* 18 October 1913, pp. 45-47.

Sixteen Self Sketches. London: Constable, 1949; New York: Dodd, Mead, 1949.

Speech at the Annual General Meeting of the Association of Post Office Women Clerks, 1 July 1907. *Association Notes,* July 1907.

"Think, Odette, Think!" *Lilliput Annual* 6 (January-June 1940): 340. Retort to Odette Keun, q.v.

To a Young Actress: The Letters of Bernard Shaw to Molly Tompkins . . . 1921-1949. Edited by Peter Tompkins. New York: Potter, 1960.

"To Frank Harris on Sex in Biography." See *Sixteen Self Sketches.*

"The Unmentionable Case for Women's Suffrage." *Englishwoman* 1 (March 1909): 112-21. Reprinted in Lloyd Hubenka, ed., *Practical Politics.* Lincoln: University of Nebraska Press, 1976.

"What is Mr. Asquith up to Now?" *Independent Suffragette* No. 3 (October 1916): 10-11.

"Why Not Personify God as a Woman?" A Journalistic Transcription of Shaw's Lecture, "Some Necessary Repairs to Religion," in Essex Hall, London, on 29 November 1906. Printed in the *New York Times.* Reprinted in *Independent Shavian* 10 (Fall 1971): 1-2.

"Woman—Man in Petticoats." *Platform and Pulpit.* Edited by Dan H. Laurence. New York: Hill and Wang, 1961, pp. 173-78. Originally published in *New York Times Magazine,* 19 June 1927; reprinted in the *Cecil Houses (Inc.) Report 1927/8.*

"Woman Since 1860." *Time and Tide* 1 (8 October 1920): 442-44.

"The Womanly Woman," *The Quintessence of Ibsenism.* London: Constable, 1913, pp. 36-45, *et passim,* esp. "What Is the New Element in the Norwegian School?" pp. 139-40.

Women as Councillors. London: The Fabian Society, 1907? (Fabian Tract No. 93).

"Women in Politics." *Leader* (London), 25 November 1944.

Works about Shaw

Aldrich, Richard Stoddard. *Gertrude Lawrence as Mrs. A.* New York: Greystone, 1954, pp. 249-55.

Bandel, Betty. "G.B.S. and the Opposite Sex" (review). *Shaw Review* 8 (May 1965): 77-80.

Barker, Felix. *The Oliviers.* Philadelphia: Lippincott, 1953.

Barnard, Eunice Fuller. "G.B.S. The Father of the Flapper." *New Republic* 47 (28 July 1926): 272-73.

Barnicoat, Constance A. "Mr. Bernard Shaw's Counterfeit Presentment of Women." *Fortnightly Review* 85 (March 1906): 516-27.

Barzun, Jacques. "Love and the Playwright." *New Republic* 127 (3 November 1952): 17-18.

Batson, Eric J. "Mr. Bernard Shaw and Ladies" (review). *Shavian* 2, no. 4 (June 1961): 23-27.

Belmont, Eleanor Robson. *The Fabric of Memory*. New York: Farrar, Strauss & Cudahy, 1957.

Bennett, Patrick. "Shaw's *Man and Superman* Mating Pattern." M.A. thesis, Hardin-Simmons University, May 1969.

Bermel, Albert. *Contradictory Characters: An Interpretation of the Modern Theatre*. New York: Dutton, 1973.

"Bernard Shaw as Seen by Mary Lawton." *Theatre* 19 (May 1914): 234-36.

"Bernard Shaw Bossed by Wife" (A Talk between George Bernard Shaw and Adolphe Menjou), *One Day*. Philadelphia: *The Evening Bulletin*, 1929, pp. 136-40. (*The Evening Bulletin* for 4 June 1928, ɹ   lished in book form. Interview taken from *London Daily Mail*.)

Besant, Lloyd. "Shaw's Women Characters." Ph.D. dissertation, University of Wisconsin. 1964.

Besdine, Matthew. "The Jocasta Complex, Mothering and Genius." Part II, *Psychoanalytic Review* 4, no. 4 (Winter 1968-69): 574-600.

Block, Toni. "Shaw's Women." *Modern Drama* 2 (September 1959): 133-38.

Briden, E.F. "James's Miss Churm: Another of Eliza's Prototypes?" *Shaw Review* 19, no. 1 (January 1976): 17-21.

Bright, Mary Chevalita Dunne. *A Leaf from the Yellow Book: The Correspondence of George Egerton*. Edited by Terence de Vere White. London: Richards Press, 1958, pp. 64-67, 101-2, 144-47.

Brooke, Sylvia. *Queen of the Head Hunters*. New York: Morrow, 1972.

Brown, John Mason. "Joey and Stella: Letters of GBS and Mrs Pat." *Saturday Review* 35 (6 December 1952): 20-22+.

———. "Paper Love and Mr. Shaw." *Saturday Review of Literature* 8 (3 October 1931): 161-62.

Bryden, Ronald. "Pygmalion." *Plays and Players* 21, no. 9 (June 1974): 30-31.

Burgunder, Bernard F. "Shaw and Ethel Barrymore." *Cornell Library Journal* No. 9 (August 1969): 58-64.

Campbell, Beatrice Stella. *My Life and Some Letters*. New York: Dodd, Mead, 1922.

Chappelow, Allan. *Shaw—"The Chucker Out:" A Biographical Exposition and Critique*. London: G. Allen, 1969, pp. 61-102, *et passim*.

———. *Shaw the Villager and Human Being . . . .* Foreword by Sybil Thorndike. London: Skilton, 1961; New York: Macmillan, 1962.

Churchill, Jennie Jerome. *The Reminiscences of Lady Randolph Churchill*. New York: Century, 1908, pp. 381-82.

Clarke, Austin. *A Penny in the Clouds*. London: Routledge, 1968.

Cohen, Harriet. *A Bundle of Times*. London: Faber, 1969.

Cohn, Erna. *Eltern und Kinder . . . .* Leipzig: Helm & Thornton, 1927.

Colbourne, Maurice. *The Real Bernard Shaw*. London: Dent, 1949.

Cole, Margaret. *Beatrice Webb*. London, New York: Longmans, 1945.

Collis, Maurice. *Nancy Astor*. New York: Dutton, 1960.

Cornell, Katharine. *I Wanted to Be an Actress.* New York: Random House, 1939.

Craig, Edward Gordon. *Ellen Terry and Her Secret Self.* London: Low, 1931.

Crane, Gladys Margaret. "The Characterization of the Comic Women Characters of George Bernard Shaw." Ph.D. dissertation, University of Indiana, 1968.

———. "Shaw's *Misalliance:* The Comic Journey from Rebellious Daughter to Conventional Womanhood." *Educational Theatre Journal* 25, no. 4 (December 1973): 480-89.

Cummins, Geraldine. *Dr. E. OE. Somerville: A Biography . . . .* Preface by Lennox Robinson. London: Dakers, 1952.

Dalrymple, Jean. "An Interview with Mr. Shaw." *Theatre Arts* 32, no. 3 (April-May 1948): 34-35.

De Pue, Elva. "Bernard Shaw and His Buried Treasure." *Seven Arts* 2 (July 1917): 344-55.

Du Cann, C.G.L. *The Loves of George Bernard Shaw.* New York: Funk, 1963; London: Barker, 1963.

Duffin, Henry Charles. *The Quintessence of Bernard Shaw.* London: G. Allen, 1920, pp. 62-128, *et passim.*

Dukes, Ashley. "*A Doll's House* and the Open Door, with two letters from George Bernard Shaw." *Theatre Arts Monthly* 12 (January 1928): 21-38.

Dukore, Bernard F. " 'The Middleaged Bully and the Girl of Eighteen': The Ending They *Didn't* Film." *Shaw Review* 14 (September 1971): 102-6.

Dunbar, Janet. *Flora Robson.* London: Harrap, 1960, pp. 60-61, 244-50.

———. *Mrs. G.B.S.: A Portrait.* New York: Harper, 1963; London: Harrap, 1963.

Farmer, Henry George. *Bernard Shaw's Sister and Her Friends: A New Angle on GBS.* Leiden: Brill, 1959.

Farr, Florence, "G.B.S. and New York." *The New Age,* n.s. 1, no. 4 (23 May 1907): 57. Reprinted in *Independent Shavian* 9 (Spring 1971): 37-38.

FitzGerald, Desmond. *Memoirs 1913-1916.* London: Routledge, 1968.

Fowler, Lois Josephs. "Sirens and Seeresses: Women in Literature and the High School Curriculum." *English Journal* 62, no. 8 (November 1973).

"G.B.S. as Woman's Guide." *Literary Digest* 98 (7 July 1928), 18-19.

Gad, Lily. *Bernard Shaw, profet og gogler.* Copenhagen: S. Hasselback, 1920.

Gallichan, Catherine G.H. *The Truth about Women.* London: E. Nash, 1913.

Gassner, John. "The Puritan in Hell." *Theatre Arts* 36 (April 1952): 67-70. Reprinted in *Shaw Society Bulletin,* No. 49 (December 1952): 7-14.

Gatch, Katharine Haynes. "The Last Plays of Bernard Shaw," in *English Stage Comedy.* Edited by W.K. Wimsatt. New York: Columbia University Press, 1955, pp. 126-47.

Gerrard, Thomas J. "Marriage and George Bernard Shaw." *Catholic World* 94 (January 1912): 467-82.

Gilmartin, Andrina. "Mr. Shaw's Many Mothers." *Shaw Review* 8 (September 1965): 93-103.

Glenavy, Lady Beatrice. *Today We Will Only Gossip.* London: Constable, 1964.

Grecco, Stephen. "Vivie Warren's Profession: A New Look at *Mrs Warren's Profession.*" *Shaw Review* 10 (September 1967): 93-99.

Gregory, Isabella August. *Lady Gregory's Journals, 1916-1930.* Edited by Lennox Robinson. London: Putnam, 1946; New York: Macmillan, 1947, pp. 199-216.

Hanley, Tullah Innes. *The Strange Triangle of G.B.S.* Boston: Bruce Humphries, 1956.

Hardwicke, Sir Cedric. "GBS and Mrs. Pat: A Long Love Affair." *New York Herald Tribune Book Review,* 9 November 1952.

Harris, Frank. *Bernard Shaw: An Unauthorized Biography Based on Firsthand Information.* New York: Simon and Schuster, 1931; London: Gollancz, 1931.

Hastings, Michael. *Tussy and Me.* London: Weidenfeld & Nicholson, 1970.

Heilbrun, Carolyn G. *Toward a Recognition of Androgyny.* New York: Alfred A. Knopf, 1973.

Helburn, Theresa. *A Wayward Quest.* Boston: Little, 1960.

Henderson, Archibald. "G.B.S. on Women." *Encore* 10, no. 23 (July 1946): 118.

Higgs, Calvin T., Jr. "Shaw's Use of Vergil's *Aeneid* in *Arms and the Man.*" *Shaw Review* 19, no. 1 (January 1976): 2-16.

Hopkinson, Henry Thomas. "Flirtation with Stella." *Books of the Month* (London) 67, no. 11 (November/December 1952): 38-40.

Huneker, James. "Bernard Shaw and Women." *Harper's Bazaar* 39 (June 1905): 535-38.

Johnson, Josephine. *Florence Farr: Bernard Shaw's "New Woman."* Totowa, N.J.: Rowman and Littlefield, 1975.

Johnston, Sir William Hamilton. *Mrs Warren's Daughter: A Story of the Woman's Movement.* New York: Macmillan, 1920.

Kester, Dolores Ann. "Shaw and the Victorian 'Problem' Genre: The Woman Side." (Wisconsin 1973) *Dissertation Abstracts International* 34 (November 1973), 2566-A.

Keun, Odette. "G.B. Shaw and the Amazon." *Lilliput Annual* 6 (January-June 1940): 335-39.

Khanna, Savitri. "Shaw's Image of Woman." *Shavian* 4 (Summer 1973).

Kornbluth, Martin L. "Two Fallen Women: Paula Tanqueray and Kitty Warren." *Shavian* 1, no. 14 (February 1959): 14-15.

Langhorne, Elizabeth. *Nancy Astor and Her Friends.* New York: Praeger, 1974.

Leary, Daniel, and Foster, Richard. "Adam and Eve: Evolving Archetypes in *Back to Methuselah.*" *Shaw Review* 4, no. 2 (May 1961): 12-24.

Le Mesurier, Lillian. *The Socialist Woman's Guide to Intelligence: A Reply to Mr. Shaw.* London: Benn, 1929.

Lengnick, Paul. *Ehe und Familie.* Saalfeld: Gunther, 1931.

Lillie, Beatrice. *Every Other Inch a Lady.* Garden City, N.Y.: Doubleday, 1972, pp. 241-46.

Long, Helen. "The Creative Evolution of Shaw's Womanly Woman." Unpublished master's essay, University of Vermont, 1962.

Lorichs, Sonja. *The Unwomanly Woman in Bernard Shaw's Drama and Her Social and Political Background.* Uppsala, Sweden: University of Uppsala Studies in English, 1973.

———. "The Unwomanly Woman." *Shavian* 4 (Summer 1973).

MacCarthy, Desmond. "What Is Sauce for the Goose—G.B. Shaw on Woman's Emancipation." *New Statesman and Nation* 27 (15 April 1944): 255.

McCarthy, Mary. *Sights and Spectacles, 1937-1958.* London: Heinemann, 1959, pp. 37-42, 149-60, 193-96.

McKenna, Siobhan. "An Imaginary Conversation with George Bernard Shaw." *Esquire* 48 (December 1957): 194-95.

———. "Shaw and the Actor." *Theatre Arts* 41 (March 1957): 29-30, 89.

Mason, Michael. "*Caesar and Cleopatra:* A Shavian Exercise in Both Hero Worship and Belittlement." *Humanities Association Review* 25, no. 1 (Winter 1974): 1-10.

———. "*Captain Brassbound's Conversion:* A Coat of Many Colors." *Signum* 1, no. 2 (May 1974): 23-29.

Mattus, Martha Elizabeth. "The 'Fallen Woman' in the fin de siecle English Drama: 1884-1914." (Cornell, 1974) *Dissertation Abstracts International* 35 (January 1975), 4738-A.

"Miss Pola Negri Fascinated by Mr. Bernard Shaw." *Daily Mail* (London), 1 December 1928.

"Mrs. G.B.S.: The Power Behind the Dome." *Literary Digest* 115 (22 April 1933): 31-33.

"Mrs Shaw's Profession." *Time* 42 (27 September 1942): 38.

Molnar, Joseph. "Shaw's Four Kinds of Women." *Theatre Arts* 36 (December 1952): 18-21, 92.

———. "Shaw's Living Woman." *Shaw Society Bulletin,* No. 49 (June 1953): 7-11. (Adapted from "Shaw's Four Kinds of Women.")

Moore, Doris. *E. Nesbit: A Biography.* Rev. & augm. ed. Philadelphia: Chilton, 1966.

Moore, Nina. *Bernard Shaw et la France.* Paris: Champion, 1933.

Murphy, Daniel J. "The Lady Gregory Letters to G.B. Shaw." *Modern Drama* 10 (February 1968): 331-45.

Musulin, Stella. "Der Freidenker und die Nonnes." *Wort und Wahrheit* 13 (1958): 398-400.

Nathan, George Jean. "Shaw as a Lover." *American Mercury* 13 (February 1928): 246-48.

Nethercot, Arthur H. "Bernard Shaw, Ladies and Gentlemen." *Modern Drama* 2 (September 1959): 84-98.

———. *The First Five Lives of Annie Besant.* Chicago: University of Chicago Press, 1960.

———. "G.B.S. and Annie Besant." *Shaw Bulletin* 1, no. 9 (September 1955): 1-4.

———. *Men and Supermen: The Shavian Portrait Gallery.* 2d ed. corrected. New York: Benjamin Blom, 1966, pp. 77-126.

———. "Truth about Candida." *PMLA* 64 (September 1949): 639-47.

Offenberg, Maria. "Die Aebtissin Laurentia und G.B. Shaw." *Die Christliche Frau* 47 (1958): 71-75.

Patch, Blanche. *Thirty Years with G.B.S.* New York: Dodd, Mead, 1951; London: Gollancz, 1951.

Pogson, Rex. *Miss Horniman and the Gaiety Theatre, Manchester.* London: Rockliff, 1952.

Pollock, Ellen. "The Lightness in Shaw." *Modern Drama* 2 (September 1959): 130-32.

Reuben, Elaine. "The Social Dramatist: A Study of Shaw's English Family Plays." Ph.D. dissertation, Stanford University, 1970.

Rhondda, Lady. "Shaw's Women." *Time and Tide* 11 (7 March-11 April 1930): 300-301, 331-34, 364-66, 395-96, 436-38, 468-70.

Richter, Helene. "Die Quintessenz des Shawismus." *Englische Studien* 46 (1913): 367-469.

Riding, George A. "The 'Candida' Secret." *Spectator* 185 (17 November 1950): 506.

Roberts, R. Ellis. "The Inhibitions of Bernard Shaw." *Bookman* (London) 79 (October 1930): 4-7.

Ross, Betty. *Heads and Tales.* London: Rich & Cowan, 1934, pp. 257-77.

Rossett, B.C. *Shaw of Dublin.* University Park: Pennsylvania State University Press, 1964.

Rypins, Stanley. "Influential Women in Bernard Shaw's Life." *PMLA* 76 (March 1961): 156.

St. John, Christopher Marie. *Ethel Smythe: A Biography.* London: Longmans, 1959, pp. 184-87, 278-79.

Schlauch, Margaret. "Symbolic Figures and the Symbolic Technique of George Bernard Shaw." *Science and Society* 21 (Summer 1957): 210-21.

Shields, Jean Louise. "Shaw's Women Characters: An Analysis and a Survey of Influences from Life." Ph.D. dissertation, University of Indiana, 1958.

Sime, Georgina, and Nicholson, Frank. *Brave Spirits.* Privately printed, n.d.

Smith, J. Percy. *The Unrepentant Pilgrim: A Study of the Development of Bernard Shaw.* Boston: Houghton, 1966.

Stavrou, C.N. "The Love Songs of J. Swift, G. Bernard Shaw and J.A.A. Joyce." *Midwest Quarterly* 62 (Winter 1965): 135-62.

Stone, Susan C. "Biblical Myth Shavianized." *Modern Drama* 18, no. 2 (June 1975): 153-63.

Sykes, Christopher. *Nancy: The Life of Lady Astor.* New York: Harper, 1972.

Tanner, Juanita, pseud. *The Intelligent Man's Guide to Marriage and Celibacy.* Indianapolis: Bobbs, 1929.

Terry, Dame Ellen. *Ellen Terry's Memoirs.* New York: Putnam, 1932. Published in 1908 under title: *The Story of My Life.*

Thorndike, Russell. *Sybil Thorndike.* London: Rockliff, 1950.

Thorndike, Dame Sybil, and Jefford, Barbara. "From *The Cenci* to *Saint Joan.*" *Shavian* 1, no. 16 (October 1959): 24-26.

Tissi, Silvio. *Al Microscopio Psicanalitico . . . Shaw.* Milan: U. Hoepli, 1946.

Tompkins, Peter. *Shaw and Molly Tompkins.* New York: Potter, 1962.

Torn, Jesse. "A Figleaf in Her Bonnet: A Scene and a Preface." *Shaw Review* 5 (May 1962): 61-68.

Tsuzuki, Chuschichi. *The Life of Eleanor Marx, 1855-1898: A Socialist Tragedy.* London and New York: Oxford, 1967.

Vanbrugh, Dame Irene. *To Tell My Story.* London and New York: Hutchinson, 1948.

Wasserman, Marlie P. "Vivie Warren: A Psychological Study." *Shaw Review* 15 (May 1972): 71-75.

Watson, Barbara Bellow, "Introduction," *An Unsocial Socialist,* by Bernard Shaw. The Norton Library. New York: Norton, 1972.

———. "Sainthood for Millionaires: Major Barbara." *Modern Drama* 2 (December 1968): 227-44.

———. *A Shavian Guide to the Intelligent Woman.* London: Chatto, 1964; New York: Norton, 1964.

Weales, Gerald. "Mr. Shaw's Own Eliza." *Reporter* 24 (19 January 1961): 65.

Webb, Beatrice. *Diaries, 1912-1924.* Edited by Margaret Cole. London and New York: Longmans, 1954.

———. *Diaries, 1924-1932.* Edited by Margaret Cole. London and New York: Longmans, 1956.

Webster, Margaret. *Same Only Different: Five Generations of a Great Theatre Family.* New York: Knopf, 1969.

Weintraub, Stanley. "Bernard Shaw's Other Saint Joan." *South Atlantic Quarterly* 64 (Spring 1965): 194-205.

———. *Journey to Heartbreak: The Crucible Years, 1914-1918.* New York: Weybright and Talley, 1971.

———. *Saint Joan: Fifty Years After 1923/24-1973/74.* Edited with an Introduction by Stanley Weintraub. Baton Rouge: Louisiana State University Press, 1973.

Weissman, Philip. "Shaw's Childhood and *Pygmalion.*" *Creativity in the Theatre: A Psychoanalytic Study.* New York: Basic Books, 1965.

West, E.J. "G.B.S. and the Rival Queens—Duse and Bernhardt." *Quarterly Journal of Speech* 43 (December 1957): 365-73.

West, Rebecca. "Contesting Mr. Shaw's Will; An Analysis of G.B.S.'s Final Word on Women and Socialism." *Bookman* (New York) 67 (July 1928): 513-20.

"The Whole Duty of Woman," by "Ambrosia." Reprinted from *World,* 30 May 1905, *Independent Shavian* 8 (Fall 1969): 14.

"Women Wooers." *Current Literature* 39 (July 1905): 81-82.

Young, Stark. "Ellen Terry and Bernard Shaw." *New Republic* 68 (4 November 1931): 327-29.

Zeller, Herman. *Die Frauengestalten in Bernard Shaw's Dramatischen Werken.* Tübingen: A. Brecht, 1936.

Film

Shaw and Women. A BBC-TV Production (U.S. Distributor: Peter M. Robeck and Company, Inc., 230 Park Avenue, New York, N.Y. 10017). 16 mm. black and white, 45 min.

CONTRIBUTORS

ELSIE ADAMS
Associate Professor of English, San Diego State University; author of
Bernard Shaw and the Aesthetes and other writings on Shaw

GLADYS M. CRANE
Associate Professor of Theatre, University of Wyoming, Laramie

ANDRINA GILMARTIN
Author of a novel as well as short fiction published in *McCall's, Good
Housekeeping, Women's Home Companion, Ladies' Home Journal*; re-
ceived her M.A. at Wayne State University

GERMAINE GREER
Lecturer in English, Warwick University (England); author of *The
Female Eunuch*

NORBERT GREINER
Wissenschaftlicher Angesteller, Department of English, University
of Trier (West Germany) has a book on Shaw forthcoming

LUCILE KELLING HENDERSON
Professor and Dean Emeritus, School of Library Science, University
of North Carolina, Chapel Hill, and widow of Shavian biographer
Archibald Henderson

JOSEPHINE JOHNSON
Professor of Speech and Head, Department of Communications,
University of Miami, Coral Gables; author of *Florence Farr: Bernard
Shaw's 'New Woman'*

DOLORES KESTER
A recent graduate of the University of Oklahoma Law Center; holds
her doctorate in English from the University of Wisconsin

SONJA LORICHS
Teacher, lecturer and journalist, Uppsala, Sweden; author of *The
Unwomanly Woman in Bernard Shaw's Drama and Her Social and Political
Background*

JANIE CAVES McCAULEY
Department of English, Miami University, Oxford, Ohio

RHODA B. NATHAN
Assistant Professor of English, Hofstra University

LISË PEDERSEN
Associate Professor of English, Department of Languages, McNeese State University, Lake Charles, Louisiana

SUSAN C. STONE
Assistant Professor, Department of English, University of Calgary (Canada); author of articles on Shaw published in *The Shaw Review*, *Modern Drama, English Studies in Canada*

TIMOTHY G. VESONDER
Assistant Professor of English, The Pennsylvania State University, Shenango Valley

SALLY PETERS VOGT
Assistant Professor of English, Yale University

MARLIE PARKER WASSERMAN
Editor, University of Chicago Press

BARBARA BELLOW WATSON
Professor of English and Director of Women's Studies, City College of the City University of New York; author of *A Shavian Guide to the Intelligent Woman* and other writings on Shaw

MICHAEL WEIMER
Has taught literature at Yale and at the University of Oregon and is currently an active participant in the Folger Institute for Renaissance and Eighteenth Century Studies

RODELLE WEINTRAUB
Assistant Professor, Department of English, The Pennsylvania State University; assistant editor, *The Shaw Review*, co-author of *Lawrence of Arabia: The literary impulse*

STANLEY WEINTRAUB
Research Professor of English and Director, Institute for the Arts and Humanistic Studies, The Pennsylvania State University; editor, *The Shaw Review* and *Shaw: An Autobiography*; author of *Journey to Heartbreak* and other writings on Shaw

CREDITS

"Shakespeare's *The Taming of the Shrew* vs. Shaw's *Pygmalion:* Male Chauvinism vs. Women's Lib?" revised from an article originally published in *The Shaw Review*

"Kipling on Women: A New Source for Shaw," revised from an article originally published in *The Shaw Review*

"The Shavian Sphinx," revised from an article originally published in *The Shaw Review*

"Mill, Marx and Bebel: Early Influences on Shaw's Characterization of Women," revised from an article originally published in *The Shaw Review*

"The New Woman and the New Comedy," copyright *The Shaw Review*, The Pennsylvania State University Press, University Park

"Mr. Shaw's Many Mothers," revised and enlarged from an article originally published in *The Shaw Review*

"Feminism and Female Stereotypes in Shaw," copyright *The Shaw Review*, The Pennsylvania State University Press, University Park

"A Whore in Every Home," originally appeared in the program of The National Theatre's production of *Mrs Warren's Profession*, premiere 30 December 1970

"Vivie Warren: A Psychological Study," revised from an article originally published in *The Shaw Review*

"The Root of White Slavery," originally published in *The Awakener* 1 (1), 16 November 1912

"Why All Women Are Peculiarly Fitted to Be Good Voters," text of this speech was published in *The New York American*, 21 April 1907

"Torture by Forcible Feeding Is Illegal," text of this speech was published in *The London Budget*, 23 March 1913

"G.B.S. and a Suffragist," originally published in the *Tribune*, London, 12 March 1906.

"A Bibliographical Checklist," enlarged from bibliography originally published in *The Shaw Review*

"The Gift of Imagination: An Interview with Clare Boothe Luce," revised from an interview originally published in *The Shaw Review*

"Sir Almroth Wright's Polemic," was originally published in the 18 October 1913 *New Statesman* and is reprinted with the permission of the *New Statesman*